CHALLENGING CONFINEMENT

Challenging Confinement

*Mass Incarceration and the Fight
for Equality in Women's Prisons*

Bonnie L. Ernst

NEW YORK UNIVERSITY PRESS

New York

NEW YORK UNIVERSITY PRESS
New York
www.nyupress.org

© 2023 by New York University
All rights reserved

Please contact the Library of Congress for Cataloging-in-Publication data.
ISBN: 9781479825561 (hardback)
ISBN: 9781479825592 (library ebook)
ISBN: 9781479825585 (consumer ebook)

This book is printed on acid-free paper, and its binding materials are chosen for strength and durability. We strive to use environmentally responsible suppliers and materials to the greatest extent possible in publishing our books.

Manufactured in the United States of America

10 9 8 7 6 5 4 3 2 1

Also available as an ebook

For my mother, Betsy Ernst, and sister, Megan Ernst,
and in memory of my grandmother, Mary Reynolds

CONTENTS

Introduction

Women's Movements and Mass Incarceration

On May 19, 1977, a racially diverse group of incarcerated women in the Detroit House of Correction filed a class action lawsuit alleging that the prison's widespread gender-based discrimination had violated their constitutional rights. In their complaint, they claimed, "Treatment programs for women are unequal to those provided for men in both quality and quantity," and the state was "perpetuating the idea that the role of women in society emanates from their 'natural' abilities as wife and mother, and their 'natural' inabilities as thinker and worker."[1] The incarcerated women sought remedies from the federal court for the violence, neglect, and inequality that they endured in Michigan's only prison for women.

Many incarcerated women requested to proceed anonymously because they feared retaliation and harassment from Michigan Department of Correction (MDOC) employees. One woman asked the court to list her as "Mary L. Doe" because "on several occasions after making complaints about the inadequate medical attention given to inmates my needed medication was withheld as a form of punishment."[2] Another woman asked to be called "Jane Doe" because employees spread rumors about her among the incarcerated population after she complained about the conditions of confinement. The subsequent harassment made her fear for her life. She described how the prison blocked mail and telephone calls from her lawyers and family.[3]

Mary Glover, a twenty-two-year-old white woman, became the class representative. Glover was one of seven children born into a middle-class family in Flint. She was intellectually curious and had been training for her nursing degree, but her criminal ordeal earned her a life sentence. Like other incarcerated women, Glover's confinement changed her life abruptly and disrupted her educational and professional goals.

Referring to her arrival at the Michigan prison, she said, "When I first came here, I couldn't believe it. There was nothing, absolutely nothing. Women sit for hours and hours and hours, with nothing to do all day."[4]

Lynda Gates, Jimmie Ann Brown, Jacalyn Settles, and Mannette Gant also volunteered to be named plaintiffs. Gates, a Black mother to a young son, had been a factory worker when she began a three-year sentence. The dire environment in prison made Gates willing to fight to improve conditions for women. Jimmie Ann Brown, a white mother of a young daughter, had been working as a clerk behind a meat counter before she was incarcerated. Brown had attended Lansing Community College and aspired to be an English teacher and a writer. In prison, her job was sweeping the floors. Brown contended that education and job training would help women succeed once they left prison. Glover added, "I want to walk out of here with a master's degree or a PhD. The men can walk out of Jackson fully educated. My husband is doing the same amount of time and he's going to college full time, working on his degree."[5] Many of the incarcerated women filing the lawsuit had been breadwinners, students, and dependable parents before their legal troubles.[6] Settles, a Black woman, was sent to prison for seven and a half years, and she spent most of her time in her cell.[7] The diverse group of class representatives sought to cement key principles of liberal feminism and social justice in the prison. They had navigated racism and sexism in their homes, schools, and workplaces, and confronted these issues again in Michigan's criminal legal institutions.

These incarcerated women initiated the nation's first major legal fight for gender equality in prison. Filed in federal court, *Glover v. Johnson*, 478 F. Supp. 1075 (E.D. Mich. 1979), grew out of the women's own understandings of feminism and civil rights. Through correspondence with boyfriends, husbands, and male family members in prison in the 1970s, women learned that men were given access to high school and college courses, vocational training, and the courts. In contrast, the women's prison offered a single home economics course. The final exam asked women to cook a meal for four people. At the same time more women were being thrown into prison, more women were also graduating from law schools. A new generation of lawyers who had been shaped by civil rights lawyering perceived the gender discrimination as violating incarcerated women's constitutional rights.

Michigan and other states started to incarcerate more women of color in the 1970s than in previous decades and at disproportionate rates compared to white women.[8] Juanita Thomas was one such Black woman. Thomas had been living in Lansing, Michigan, with her children and had been a member of the cleaning staff at Michigan State University when she was sentenced to life without parole for murdering her abusive boyfriend, whom she said she had killed in self-defense. She went to prison in 1980 amid renewed challenges by feminist groups about the rights of women to defend themselves from physical and sexual assault.

Stacy Barker, a Black woman from Detroit, was sent to prison for life in 1987 after she defended herself from an attempted rape at an assisted living community, where she worked as a home aide. Barker became an activist in prison and launched several lawsuits that sought to end sexual abuse of incarcerated women. The legal ordeals of Thomas and Barker galvanized antiviolence movements of the late twentieth century while also highlighting the racial disparities in prisons for women.

Sharleen Wabindato, an enrolled member of the Little River Band of Ottawa Indians, has spent most of her life confined in prison after her abusive boyfriend killed a man in Muskegon, Michigan, in 1977. A few hours before the murder, her boyfriend had beaten and drugged the twenty-one-year-old Wabindato. Fearing for her life, Wabindato participated in the robbery that went awry. Like Thomas and Barker, Wabindato was convicted of first-degree murder, and the judge imposed a mandatory sentence of life without parole. She has petitioned for clemency with the support of the American Civil Liberties Union (ACLU) of Michigan and the Michigan Women's Justice and Clemency Project, a group of feminist activists working to secure freedom for incarcerated women, many of whom survived intimate partner violence. Now in her sixties, Wabindato is still confined in Michigan's only women's prison. That prison—Huron Valley—houses much of the history that follows.[9]

The convergence of activism among different strands of women's movements and social-justice campaigns in the late twentieth century forged new pathways for reform and resistance to incarceration. The story of how incarcerated women tried to build on the gains of the women's movements, I argue, tells us much about social-justice movements and challenges to mass imprisonment. Charlene Snow, a white attorney in Detroit, worked for decades on the *Glover* lawsuit. At the time

Snow wrote, "The influence of the women's movement cannot stop at the prison door."[10] Launched in Detroit, the prisoners' rights movement for women ignited prolonged legal battles for equality, bodily integrity, and personal security that started in the 1970s and concluded in the early 2000s. A racially diverse coalition of incarcerated women, attorneys, activists, and academics fought for equitable and humane terms of punishment. Their successes and shortcomings fill this book.

Michigan offers a valuable location in which to study the prisoners' rights movement for women in the United States. When incarcerated women made plans to reform Michigan prisons, mass incarceration was first becoming visible and revealed trends that played out in different ways across the country. While still a small subset, women were the fastest-growing group within the incarcerated population in the final third of the twentieth century.[11] In 1979, 12,995 women were incarcerated in the United States. By 1989, the female prison population had grown to 40,612, an increase of 212 percent. In comparison, the male prison population had increased from 301,462 to 671,752, a 122 percent increase.[12] As their numbers increased, incarcerated women in Michigan grew adept at organizing and challenging mass incarceration in federal courts. They also organized with activists and artists to petition for clemency, document torture, and curtail physical and sexual violence.

Historians have demonstrated how deindustrialization and suburbanization laid the groundwork for mass incarceration. That history necessarily runs through Michigan, which makes the state a significant site to examine the country's soaring prison population. Thomas Sugrue's history of Detroit, *The Origins of the Urban Crisis*, illustrates how white supremacy supplied the logic for the criminalization of Black communities and the deindustrialization that accelerated after World War II.[13] Andrew Highsmith has analyzed how projects of demolition and renewal in Michigan exacerbated urban poverty and inequality.[14] Also, in 1974, Michigan created barriers to racial integration of its schools, allowing white suburban school districts to maintain segregated student populations and shielding them from litigation, an approach upheld by the Supreme Court in *Milliken v. Bradley*, 418 U.S. 717 (1974). *Milliken* effectively permitted white communities to turn their backs on the pursuit of equality outlined in *Brown v. Board of Education*, 347 U.S. 483 (1954). With the rise of neoliberalism and mass incarceration, urban areas like Detroit transformed into spaces where "punishing the poor" became routine in policy and practice.[15] Heather Ann Thompson has noted that by the early 2000s, there were fewer Detroiters holding union jobs in auto plants than those under correctional supervision.[16] In 2009, the Pew Center on the States found that, out of the thirty-five states the organization studied, prisoners in Michigan served the longest average sentences.[17] The state committed to segregation and depletion of resources in cities, and removal of industry fueled brutal policing, the war on drugs, and criminalization of people of color and women.

Scholarship on mass incarceration has emphasized causal factors and the political and social fallout from this late-twentieth-century phenomenon. Academics have investigated how federal and state governments from both parties worked, intentionally or unintentionally, to build the demand, capacity, and incentives for mass incarceration.[18] The prevailing literature advances the argument that, beginning in the 1960s, those in power embraced a "punitive turn" in American politics, culture, and society that fueled aggressive policing, vengeful criminal trials, and overcrowded prisons.[19] With emphasis on the rhetoric of political elites, national legislation, and structural causal factors, scholars have illustrated how mass imprisonment intensified racial, economic, and political inequalities.[20] *Challenging Confinement* complements scholarship on mass imprisonment by shifting the focus to incarcerated people and their allies who resisted and contested the new prison regime. This book joins a growing group of scholars examining how people challenged confinement in America's criminal legal system.[21]

Challenging Confinement investigates how incarcerated people, activists, attorneys, and families supported the prisoners' rights movement for women. The book focuses on women's efforts to reform and resist incarceration in Michigan as they mobilized around gender equality, gendered harm, and race from the Progressive Era to the era of mass incarceration. Tracing how women's movements inspired new approaches to challenging and critiquing the prison reveals that incarcerated women and activists formed coalitions focused on radically different conceptions of confinement when increasingly harsh prisons became acceptable in the Midwest and across the country.

Challenging Confinement engages with historical scholarship that has bound together women's history and carceral history to refocus studies of punishment, race, gender, and civil rights. For example, Emily Thuma's book, *All Our Trials*, sheds new light on how feminist activists amplified critical perspectives on police, prisons, and the state. Thuma defines anticarceral feminism as an overlooked strand of late-twentieth-century women's movements in which diverse coalitions developed an "antiviolence politics that was defined by a critique of state violence; an understanding of race, gender, class, and sexuality as mutually constructed systems of power and meaning; and a practice of coalitions-based organizing."[22] Incarcerated women and activists in Michigan critiqued state violence embedded in prison by deploying social-justice and human-rights frameworks. They worked within criminal legal institutions and sought parity with men's programming, clemency, decarceration, and alternatives to Michigan's prison regime.

Historians have also produced scholarship on race, gender, and punishment that prioritizes Black women. Focusing on New York and concluding in the time period when my book begins, *Talk with You like a Woman*, by Cheryl Hicks, investigates how Black women, mostly southern migrants, navigated tension among personal aspirations, realities of urban life, and contact with reformers, welfare agencies, and criminal legal institutions.[23] Works by Kali Gross, Sarah Haley, and Talitha LeFlouria offer insights regarding Black women's critical position within the state during this period of carceral expansion.[24] Danielle McGuire's book, *At the Dark End of the Street*, expands historical knowledge of the civil rights movement by centering Black women and their activism to prevent rape and preserve bodily integrity.[25] These works inform my study in that I apply similar questions and themes to the history of mass incarceration of women.

Challenging Confinement begins with an investigation of how community leaders and incarcerated people built pathways for protest and reform, but ultimately did not address the persistent shortcomings of Michigan's prisons for women. The first chapter situates early prison reform within the history of the women's movement of the 1920s, the Great Migration, and state building in Detroit. In the twenties, Michigan was in the middle of a frenzy of institution building, and the state's economy was booming thanks to the automobile industry. Mostly white women who were members of social clubs and philanthropic associations seized the moment and campaigned for a new women's prison.

Their efforts produced the Detroit House of Correction Division for Women, which used "maternal justice," or an ideology of punishment based on women's place in society, as window dressing for racialized punishment and exploitative labor practices.[26] Incarcerated women challenged their confinement by participating in labor strikes in which they demanded prison reform.

The second chapter shows how the feminist movements of the 1970s served as a catalyst for the fight for gender equality in prisons. In prison, women learned that they were denied opportunities for higher education, work, and access to the courts because of their sex. In the wake of national legislation, like the Civil Rights Act of 1964 and the Voting Rights Act of 1965, attorneys understood gender-based discrimination as a violation of the prisoners' constitutional rights. This chapter traces the origins of the first major prisoners' rights lawsuit brought by women, *Glover v. Johnson*, and documents how different strands of women's movements influenced critique and action in Michigan's only prison for women. The chapter reveals how gender parity, a standard that was first established in *Glover*, was too vulnerable a standard to deliver lasting change in women's prisons.

The third chapter discusses the rise of the anti–domestic violence movement in Michigan and the nation. This chapter focuses on the legal ordeal of Juanita Thomas. An all-white jury convicted Thomas of first-degree murder, despite her claims that she acted in self-defense. She received the mandatory minimum sentence of life without parole. The chapter argues that defense campaigns for women like Thomas brought together coalitions of anti–death penalty attorneys, incarcerated women, and feminist activists. Their work illustrates the competing power of the feminist movements and the carceral state in the 1970s and 1980s.

The fourth chapter explores official responses to the prisoners' rights movement and tracks how the state of Michigan ushered in a new punitive political ethos by enforcing harsh mandatory minimum sentences and building more prisons. In the 1970s, two major United States Supreme Court cases ignited debates regarding the death penalty. In *Furman v. Georgia*, 408 U.S. 238 (1972), the Supreme Court ordered a moratorium on the death penalty until states could rewrite their statutes to adhere to constitutional standards. In *Gregg v. Georgia*, 428 U.S. 153 (1976), the Supreme Court reinstated the death penalty. Michigan was the first state in the country to abolish the death penalty, in 1847, but in the wake of urban unrest in Detroit, state politicians debated whether executions should be revived. Michigan ultimately rejected the death penalty, but the state legislated punishments of life without the possibility of parole for violent and nonviolent crimes. These shifts increased what sociologist Heather Schoenfeld calls "carceral capacity," or the state's ability to confine more people by the end of the twentieth century.[27] The chapter examines the harsh-sentencing and prison-construction boom that characterized the 1980s and 1990s, as well as MDOC director Johnson's efforts to counter these trends. Although Johnson attempted to respond to complaints raised by the prisoners' rights movement with innovative ideas about incarceration, other forces won out in this period, with deleterious results for incarcerated individuals throughout the United States, including women in Michigan.

The fifth chapter focuses on what I call "equality born of retrenchment," which describes the sterile, bureaucratic, and violent environment of the women's prisons during the later years of the prisoners' rights movement. At this point in time, incarcerated women shifted their discourse from civil rights to human rights for women—a change that illustrates the extremely violent conditions they endured in prison. Women documented sanitation crises, medical problems, and rampant physical and sexual assaults in prison. However, President Bill Clinton signed the Prison Litigation Reform Act in 1996, which, among other provisions, erected barriers for prisoners filing class action lawsuits in federal courts against state prison systems. In this chapter, I explore how incarcerated women pursued legal advocacy while navigating political hostility toward people convicted of crimes. Incarcerated women filed major lawsuits in courts, documented complaints with the internal grievance system, and attracted investigations by the Justice Department and international human rights organizations. In the 1970s, the prisoners' rights movement articulated far-reaching plans to reform prisons. Three decades later, faced with political retrenchment and legal hurdles, incarcerated women scaled back strategies for overhauling prisons and pursued campaigns to secure rights to dignity, privacy, and security. The state responded with hostility to feminist ideals and ultimately circumscribed critiques of the prison made by incarcerated women, attorneys, and activists.

The epilogue shows how formerly incarcerated women continue to advance social justice in a variety of ways. I follow the stories of Juanita Thomas, Mary Glover, Stacy Barker, and Sharleen Wabindato to consider how women's movements and prison activism have shaped prison abolition and decarceration work in Michigan.

By the end of the twentieth century, Americans had started reflecting on the legacy of mass incarceration. In 1998, Juanita Thomas gained her freedom after filing a state postconviction petition with the assistance of well-known anti–death penalty attorney Andrea Lyon. Thomas had spent over eighteen years in prison, missing precious moments as her children grew up. Governor Engler commuted Mary Glover's sentence in 2002. The parole board had denied her application for release nine times. Reflecting on her time in prison, she remained proud of her work for incarcerated people and gathered strength from the reentry community. Stacy Barker gained her freedom in 2009. However, many of the women who signed on to *Glover* and participated in prison activism are still in prison. Sharleen Wabindato remains in Michigan's only women's prison, and the state has repeatedly opposed her petitions for release. The stories of incarcerated women and their legal victories and losses illustrate the struggles of the prisoners' rights and women's movements with the carceral state.

This history demonstrates how incarcerated women challenged confinement in Michigan. A sense of collective purpose propelled the diverse coalition to conceive of a legal system that might be humane and just. Although many of their goals fell short, the prisoner's rights movement for women sheds new light on how we consider the expansive and interconnected fights for gender equality, racial justice, and decarceration.

1

"We Are Dealing with Women"

Race, Gender, and Prison Reform in the Detroit House of
Correction, 1926–1957

In the fall of 1924, Gertrude Russian, a Black woman, moved with her
husband from Arkansas to Detroit. Born in 1892, Russian was among
tens of thousands of southern migrants moving to Detroit as part of
the Great Migration in the first half of the twentieth century, when
Black people fled the Jim Crow South seeking a reprieve from racialized violence and economic oppression. Russian had only a third-grade
education because of segregated schools in Arkansas whereas Michigan
had statutes that prohibited discrimination in public spaces and segregation in schools. Michigan also allowed interracial marriage. Those
laws should have facilitated racial equality, but white people built upon
a dizzying array of informal discriminatory practices. Housing segregation, restricted access to capital, and violence over perceived threats to
white supremacy obstructed opportunities for Black people in Michigan. Black men could find factory jobs with automobile companies, but
they were usually relegated to the least desirable production tasks and
almost never performed skilled labor, which was reserved for native-
born white workers.[1] Black women were barred from manufacturing
jobs in the 1920s, and the informal but strictly enforced politics of col-
orism dictated where they found work: department stores and hotels
hired only Black women with lighter skin, while women with darker
skin found work as domestic servants in white homes. They began shifts
before dawn and left after sunset to start long commutes home. Wages
in Detroit were higher than what women earned in the South, but the
work was physically exhausting. Gertrude Russian may have hoped for
a job as a store clerk, hotel staff member, or domestic worker.[2]

Racism and violence escalated as Detroit's Black population grew.
In 1910, Detroit had a Black population of 5,741. By 1920, 40,838 Black

people lived in Detroit. Five years later, the Black population reached 81,831.[3] White hostility toward the Black residents came in different forms. One automobile plant installed separate toilets for Black and white workers. City government offices received requests to hire more Black people and rejected them all.[4] The Ku Klux Klan's (KKK) membership skyrocketed in cities and towns in the Midwest. The hate group cultivated a strong base in Chicago, with fifty thousand members, and the Detroit chapter counted thirty-five thousand members in the 1920s.[5] Many Black Detroiters believed that white policemen who had grown up in the South and patrolled Black neighborhoods infused their work with their own version of racial animosity. In the 1920s, only fourteen Black men worked in the three-thousand-person-strong Detroit Police Department.[6]

Criminal legal practices and gender politics reconfigured racialized discrimination in Detroit, leading to dangerous and fatal encounters for Black residents. This chapter examines how carceral practices in the early twentieth century created gendered and racialized punishment for women. Police targeted Black women for extralegal violence with impunity as Michigan expanded its carceral regime.

Just before midnight on November 25, 1925, the night before Thanksgiving, three white police officers dressed in plain clothes arrested Gertrude Russian for streetwalking, or prostitution. The police report and subsequent newspaper coverage offered sparse details. Russian may have been simply walking alone at night. The officers threw her into a Ford police car. One policeman sat next to her in the car while the other two investigated an incident across the street. Witnesses told the *Detroit Independent*, a Black newspaper, "The officer remaining got into a heated dispute with his arrested victim and was seen in the act of striking her with his blackjack." She carried a knife, presumably for self-protection, and stabbed the officer. In the police report, the officers wrote that he shot her in the neck, "killing her instantly." However, the *Detroit Independent* ran a different story: "The woman made desperate by the blows pulled out her knife and began slashing the officer across the stomach; the officer fired, the bullet making a gunshot wound in the leg." Witnesses heard the officer yell, "She cut me," and Russian respond, "He shot me!" Russian may have been hoping bystanders or, against the odds, the other officers would intervene and pull the policeman off her. Instead, the two policemen returned to the car and drove down the street a few yards with Russian still trapped inside. Witnesses heard two shots fired in the vehicle. The police threw Russian out of the car and drove away. She died on the street.[7]

Russian's killing reflects Sarah Haley's conclusion that criminal legal cases of Black women "represented a cultural battleground in a contest over gendered and racial constructions of humanity."[8] Black newspapers in Detroit reported one version of her death while police countered with a self-protective version. The conflicting accounts illustrate the dangers Black women faced during police encounters. The police officers' public disregard for Russian's life underscored the brutality of state violence and punitive policing of women, especially women of color, in northern cities in the mid-twentieth century.

Episodes of women being punished or killed during criminal legal encounters inspired new strategies for activism and penal reform among women's clubs in Detroit in the early twentieth century. Thousands of Black and white women joined these clubs, which remained largely segregated. They advanced a range of issues, including education, public health, civil rights, and social services for women.[9] The clubs also assisted women migrating to cities by focusing on their social welfare, moral education, home life, and economic opportunities, and Victoria Wolcott has charted how Black women in Detroit advanced social and racial equality in the interwar years through activism and community engagement.[10] Extending these conclusions to carceral practices shows how Black women were vulnerable to police violence and how Black women's organizations countered penal expansion with strategies intended to divert women from criminal legal contact in Detroit. At the same time, white women's groups fought for new women's prisons that advanced a racialized narrative of white female prisoners as deserving of rehabilitation and justice.

This chapter begins with analysis of how penal power expanded and targeted women in Detroit. It then examines the social and political dynamics that shaped clubwomen's campaigns for reform and the limits of their work. Although their demands for a women's prison were successful, what was meant to be a feminine carceral space distinct from the conditions of the Detroit jail turned into a farm and factory. Exploitative labor, racial discrimination, and gendered rules were dressed up in the rhetoric of rehabilitation. The chapter then describes how incarcerated women confronted the failing reforms with protests that brought carceral industries to a halt. The tactics of the labor movement permeated social and political life in Michigan, and incarcerated women deployed these tools when protesting for better conditions, culminating in the labor strikes of 1957, which rattled public officials and created a crisis of rehabilitation.

State Expansion, Penal Power, and Incarcerated Women

The history of Detroit's penal regime for women underscores how ideas of gender, race, and class influenced prison reform in the first half of the twentieth century. Responding to a series of scandals in the Detroit House of Correction Women's Division, the only prison for women in the state, clubwomen threw their support behind constructing a new women's facility. Wealthy women had shaped penal reform in New England, where reformers advocated for separate prisons that catered to the needs of women. These reformers, as historian Estelle Freedman has shown, rallied around "maternal justice," or individual rehabilitation that promoted "salvation through maternal love." Because of their roles as mothers, upper- and middle-class, often white women claimed a unique perspective on reform. They emphasized that women's reproductive and nurturing capacities made them well suited for prison reform work, and this ideology dominated women's prisons until the 1960s.[11] The history of Detroit's women's prison highlights how clubwomen, incarcerated women, and city officials contested the rehabilitative ideal.

The Women's Division of the Detroit House of Correction was the product of an institution-building explosion in Detroit in the late nineteenth century, but by 1910, the prison sat in a dangerous state of disrepair.[12] The Twentieth Century Club, a white, middle-class women's organization, launched a study of the fifty-year-old prison, and their findings convinced civic leaders to build a new facility. By 1920, the prison conditions deteriorated to such an extent that the mayor of Detroit assembled a reform board, chaired by Dr. Mary Stevens, a white physician with experience advocating for prison reform. Stevens served as the superintendent and lived in the prison during a gap in leadership. She turned down her husband's offer to live in the prison with her because she wanted "to show the world that a woman could handle an emergency in any job given her as well as a man could." After her six-week residency, she moved home and rustled up support from women's clubs to build a new women's prison.[13] The campaign relied on prevailing conceptions of gender, race, and class to expand punishment for women.

When planning criminal legal reforms, clubwomen leveraged their experience fighting for new roles in public life. In 1917, a Wayne County circuit judge relented to clubwomen's calls for a female advocate for women entering divorce proceedings or custody matters involving children born to unmarried parents. They established a Women's Division in the Detroit Police Department in 1920, led by Eleonore Hutzel, a white woman. They also supported the hiring of Josephine Davis, the first female police officer in Detroit. Davis contended that a Women's Division would prevent crime and assist female defendants in court. She argued that policewomen could connect with young people and, in particular, educate girls regarding city life, making subtle connections to policing sex and morality.[14] In 1921, fourteen policewomen joined the Detroit Police Department (DPD). New female recruits needed a college degree and a background in social work, ensuring that mostly white women were eligible. Grayce Murphy was the first Black woman hired by the Women's Division, where she worked from 1921 to 1923. The Women's Division hired Gracie Hagerman, a Black woman, in 1924, and she retired in 1949.[15] Hutzel's Women's Division valued the emotional labor policewomen were expected to conduct but did little to decrease the gendered and racialized harms many women of color experienced at the hands of the police.

The disproportionate contact Black women had with criminal legal institutions underscored the prevalent racism in the Jazz Age. Issues of public health, crime, employment, and education were compounded by structural racism. Those problems grew worse as Detroit's population increased precipitously throughout the 1920s. The city's population began that decade with 993,675 people, of whom 40,838 were Black. In 1930, the population increased to 1,568,662 and the Black population nearly tripled at 120,066 people.[16] The resulting racial tension gave rise to a KKK-backed third-party candidate in the November 1925 mayoral race, Charles Bowles, although he lost to incumbent John Smith.

The election was held amid a major criminal trial that shed light on race relations, housing segregation, and Black people's right to self-defense. Ossian Sweet, a Black doctor, had moved into a white neighborhood just east of the Black Bottom neighborhood. Sweet bought his home in May 1925 and moved his family in early September. An angry white mob, by some counts of four hundred to eight hundred people, congregated outside of the house on the second night Sweet took residence. As the evening wore on, white people threw rocks and bottles that landed on the roof and crashed through windows. Sweet's family and friends were armed, knowing that they might have to defend themselves. Sweet had sent his daughter, Iva, only a toddler, to stay with her grandmother. As the violence escalated, someone inside the house fired shots into the crowd that injured one person and killed Leon Breiner, a white man who had joined the mob.[17]

Police were patrolling the house, ostensibly to protect the Sweet family, and they promptly stormed the house and arrested everyone inside, including Sweet's wife, Gladys, the only woman present. The Wayne County prosecutor charged all ten people with first-degree murder. The National Association for the Advancement of Colored People (NAACP) rallied to Sweet's defense and hired Clarence Darrow to represent the defendants. Darrow had just completed the "trial of a century" defending John Scopes, a Tennessee teacher who taught the theory of evolution to his students in the small town of Dayton, Tennessee.[18] Darrow's representation of Sweet ensured that the case received national attention. In his closing arguments Darrow concluded, "My clients are here charged with murder, but they are really here because they are black."[19] The jury deadlocked. The prosecutor initiated a new trial of Henry Sweet, the alleged shooter, and an all-white jury acquitted him in 1926. The trials illustrated the dangers of segregation and racist policies that constrained Black life in northern cities.

The harms of the criminal legal contact that the state foisted on the Sweet family extended beyond the trials. Gladys Sweet, Ossian's wife, was incarcerated in the Wayne County Jail, where she likely contracted tuberculosis and passed it along to their young daughter, Iva. Gladys and Iva relocated after the first trial to Arizona, where doctors believed warm, dry air would soothe their lungs. Tragically, two-year-old Iva succumbed to the disease and passed away. Gladys Sweet, only twenty-seven years old, passed away shortly after Iva. The young mother's incarceration and death underscored the unsanitary and dangerous conditions prevalent in jails and prisons. Ossian Sweet returned alone to his brick bungalow on Garland Street. He took his own life in 1960. Sweet and his family and friends avoided incarceration in Michigan prisons, but the harms of the criminal prosecutions shattered their lives.[20]

On the heels of the trials, Detroit mayor John Smith tasked an interracial committee to survey race relations during the summer of 1926. Their findings shed light on how police disciplined Black women. The committee concluded that Black people in Detroit lacked adequate housing, education, and job opportunities, and suffered from discriminatory and unfair treatment in the criminal legal system. The report pulled some punches when it noted, "There is evidence that in many cases Negroes are treated with undue severity, not to say brutality, by the police."[21] A vice squad within the DPD arrested Black women suspected of prostitution in large numbers after the American Social Hygiene Association described Detroit as the "blackest hole of crime and vice in the United States."[22] By the 1930s, Black women made up 75 percent of women incarcerated for prostitution convictions in Michigan.[23] Policewoman Hutzel, the leading female officer in the department, argued that too few job opportunities for Black women explained the racial imbalance of arrests and convictions.[24] Her argument may have been perceived by some people as a plea for more jobs for Black women, but it also legitimated the disproportionate contact Black women had with police by failing to question the racial bias in the arrests and harassment of Black women.

The high rates of arrest for Black sex workers, which sometimes included women wrongly profiled as sex workers, complemented trends around the country and illustrate the severe racial bias in policing of women in Michigan. As Black community leaders protested, vice squads targeted their neighborhoods. As the secretary of the YWCA explained to the mayor's interracial committee, young Black women arriving in Detroit who could not be housed in one of their thirty-six rooms usually had no other option but to find housing in the vice districts.[25] The vice districts overlapped significantly with Black neighborhoods and fueled higher arrest rates of Black people in Detroit.[26] Simon Balto has examined the way Chicago police and politicians intentionally confined vice districts to Black and "other undesirable neighborhoods," which meant that vice policing in Chicago was racially biased from its inception, and similar patterns emerged in Detroit.[27] Police targeted people of color at disproportionate rates to white people, illustrating the pernicious racism that shaped Michigan's growing carceral regime.

Instances of police brutality made clear how police devalued Black life in Detroit. In 1925, Detroit police shot over a dozen Black people, some of whom were killed. One of these was Lillie Smith, a Black woman, who was born in Charleston, South Carolina, in 1900. The circumstances of Smith's death were reported in conflicting narratives that pitched one story to white readers and another to Black readers. The official police report stated that patrolman Fred Williams heard gunshots and tried to stop a truck driven by Smith's husband in which Lillie Smith was a passenger. Williams wrote that he ordered the truck to stop and the driver refused so he shot at the truck, striking twenty-five-year-old Lillie Smith in the neck. His report did not reveal that Smith was in the final weeks of her pregnancy. As the *Detroit Independent Report*, a Black newspaper, described the incident, "Fred Williams, a policeman, deliberately murdered Mrs. Lillie Smith, expectant mother."[28] Both the newspaper and police report confirmed that Smith was taken to the Detroit Receiving Hospital, where she died. The police report omitted key details of Smith's physical condition in the hospital. The gunshot wound had shattered her jaw. She survived for a week, gave birth to her baby, and passed away from the injuries. The *Detroit Independent Report* lamented, "Mrs. Smith . . . died a double death, by giving birth to an infant who still lives."[29] The meaning of "double death" is unclear from the story. The paper might have used the term to express the weight and senselessness of Smith's killing. In any case, the erasure of Smith's pregnancy in the police report and the oversimplified description of her injury exemplify the DPD's disregard for the lives of Black women in the 1920s.

Williams, the officer who killed Smith, was charged with manslaughter, and the conflicting narratives emerged at trial. Williams stated that he fired at the truck because James Smith was driving over the speed limit.[30] The *Lansing State Journal* reported that police had ordered Williams to fire at the truck. Williams was acquitted.[31] The police report and white papers prioritized Williams's version of events whereas Black newspapers elevated Smith's story, which challenged the police report and white newspapers. Infusing Smith's story with humane details that ran counter to the blunt police reports contested a carceral regime that increasingly drew boundaries around Black life.

Clubwomen and Prison Reform

Women's clubs created another avenue for police accountability and penal reform. Prominent women's associations, like the Detroit Federation of Women's Clubs (DFWC), concentrated some of their considerable wealth and social standing to pursue prison reform.[32] Over one hundred women's clubs joined the DFWC, and it counted fifteen thousand women as members in the 1920s and 1930s. The DFWC's goals and strategies were diverse. After women secured the vote, the organization's leadership encouraged political participation and improvements in civic life. Edith Alvord, a leading member of the DFWC, drew connections between mothers being good citizens and modeling civic engagement for their children.[33] The DFWC was a mostly white women's organization although the Detroit Study Club and the Entre Nous Club, two Black women's clubs, were members of the federation.[34]

Improving perceptions of and resources for Black women was one of several goals that brought Black women together in clubs and associations. Black women's clubs viewed racialized lies in newspapers as particularly harmful. Mary Church Terrell was the first president of the National Association of Colored Women (NACW), established in 1896. The NACW maintained different chapters around the country that focused on education initiatives, voting rights, social welfare, and racial discrimination. In her speeches Terrell emphasized the importance of a healthy home, and the motto of the NACW was "lifting as we climb." Speaking in Chicago in 1899 Terrell argued, "In no way could we live up to such a sentiment better than by coming into closer touch with the masses of our women."[35] Drawing membership largely from educated, middle- and upper-class Black women, the NACW increased access to education for children, improved labor conditions in the industrial North, and campaigned for decent childcare for Black, working-poor women. Through their broad mission, the NACW confronted assumptions that connected Black women to criminality, immorality, and deviant sexual behavior.

The NACW's critique of convict leasing expressed an expansive vision of equality and justice for Black people. Convict leasing was a practice in which states leased men and women to private industries, farms, and homes after a swift conviction—often based on trumped-up charges. Convict leasing repurposed the tools of racism and social control deployed during slavery to expand the criminal legal system in the South after the Civil War.[36] Historian Sarah Haley has analyzed how the NACW framed convict leasing as "an obstacle in the progress of black women." The NACW convinced thousands of clubwomen around the country that subjecting one Black woman to the horrors of convict leasing expanded the penal tools "of white supremacist *patriarchal* terror."[37] Responding to different campaigns to abolish convict leasing led by the NACW and the Women's Christian Temperance Union (WCTU), Georgia established a segregated incarceration system that refused to acknowledge Black womanhood.[38] Georgia ended convict leasing in 1908 and replaced it with mixed-sex chain gangs, a punishment reserved only for Black women. White women went to the all-female division of the Milledgeville state farm prison.

A decade later, the incarceration of white suffragists brought public attention to the conditions of incarceration for women. In 1913, the National Women's Party (NWP), a more militant organization of white suffragists, separated from the National American Woman Suffrage Association led by Elizabeth Cady Stanton. Under the leadership of Alice Paul and Lucy Burns, the NWP organized protests and marches around the country and focused on passing an amendment to the US Constitution that would extend the right to vote to women. They regularly picketed outside the White House in Washington, DC. In June 1917, police arrested women picketing. In jail, they started a hunger strike on November 5, 1917, to protest the abysmal prison conditions and the warden's refusal to allow them to purchase their own food, a privilege extended to other prisoners. After a week, prison officials force fed Alice Paul and Rose Winslow. The women described to the press the torturous procedure while the prison denied that the women were forcibly fed.[39] A media frenzy criticized the jail's treatment of the suffragists. On November 10, 1917, the jail transferred many of the incarcerated women to the Occoquan Workhouse, a prison in Virginia. On November 15 Superintendent Raymond Wittaker ordered forty guards to beat over thirty of the women in what became known as the "Night of Terror." Guards viciously dragged, strangled, kicked, and hit the women. Guards restrained Lucy Burns by fastening her hands to a cell bar above her head while they beat her. They left her in that position overnight.[40] The brutal treatment of the suffragists illustrated the men's perceived threat of women voting and having their own political voice.

In the spring of 1919, a carefully selected group of twenty-six white NWP members toured the country by train on the "Democracy Limited Prison Special," where they raised awareness of the violent prison conditions and campaigned for the right to vote. The slogan of their tour was "from prison to people." They performed a theatrical interpretation of their incarceration, gave speeches stressing the urgent need to grant women the vote, and criticized the Wilson administration's reluctance to support the suffrage movement. The NWP's "Prison Special" departed from Washington, DC, and traveled south before reaching California. It returned east via Chicago and Detroit, and its last stop was in New York. The tour raised awareness of jail conditions and shocked audience members with the poor treatment of educated, white women.[41] It encouraged many women's clubs to scrutinize incarceration of women in their own states. Congress passed the Nineteenth Amendment on June 4, 1919. Tennessee was the thirty-sixth state, the last necessary, to ratify the amendment on August 18, 1920. That fall, more than eight million women voted in the presidential election that put Warren G. Harding in the White House. After securing the right to vote, women's clubs in Michigan joined the national prison-reform movement and campaigned for a new women's prison in the 1920s. The mostly white clubwomen's call for prison reform advanced ideologies of gender, race, and class that had consequences for incarcerated women that endured well into the twentieth century.

Maternal Justice and the Eugenics Movement

Lareta Coleman Lee's incarceration created a crisis for the Women's Division in the Detroit House of Correction. Lee was a white, twenty-two-year-old mother accused of armed robbery of the Meir Jewelry Store in 1922. In court, her tone and actions defied acceptable female behavior. Scholars have shown how women facing criminal charges received lenient outcomes when they acted according to gendered norms, but at trial and in interviews, Lee did not behave submissively or express regret.[42] One newspaper described how "not a tear glistened in her great expressive eyes. Her voice lacked emotion, pitched in an ordinary, conversational tone. She talked freely, unhesitatingly, often answering questions which she knew, she would not and could not be asked if she were not a convict."[43] Observers interpreted her demeanor as a signal of her criminal nature. At trial, jurors found Lee guilty and the court sentenced her to serve eight to twenty years in prison.[44]

White clubwomen seized the moment to push for reform. They petitioned for her release. Constructing a maternal and sometimes condescending narrative of Lee, they emphasized how she became a young mother with few resources who pursued desperate means to support herself and her child. Lee had been an orphan as a young girl and became pregnant at seventeen. She married the child's father but was estranged from him at the time of her trial. The state sent Lee to the decrepit and overcrowded Detroit House of Correction where thirty women, Lee included, slept on wet mattresses on the cement floor. Diseases spread quickly, and Lee became gravely ill.[45]

For white clubwomen, Lee's story underscored urgent reasons for a new prison. Clubwomen were convinced that Lee needed "maternal justice," which emphasized familial relationships among incarcerated women and matrons and prioritized curriculums that instructed prisoners in homemaking skills.[46] A newspaper revised earlier assumptions of Lee's deviance and considered, "It may be that the lack of a mother's guiding hand, or perhaps pleasures and clothes had something to do with the slip that Lareta made, or fell perhaps before the insistent urging of male companions and aided in the contemplated robbery."[47] The newspaper's speculations encouraged readers to understand Lee as a typical woman of moderate means who desired social and economic advancement. She became relatable to middle-class white readers: she wanted to wear nice clothes, appear feminine, and learn how to be a good mother. The article suggested that her fate would have been different had she received loving, maternal guidance.

Clubwomen provided the maternal care that they claimed Lee lacked. In 1926, the prison transferred Lee to a hospital where clubwomen comforted her and ferried visitors to her room to pray for her recovery. Clubwomen described Lee as a devoted mother and a kind prisoner. They brought Lee's nine-year-old son, who lived with his father, to the hospital. Her son told the press he did not recognize her. Lee confessed that if she could return to good health, "I would never try to get my son back. I love him more than anything else on earth but I suppose it would spoil his happiness if I, a convicted criminal tried to claim him."[48] Through such statements, the clubwomen helped Lee demonstrate her transformation from a hardened criminal to a selfless mother. Michigan governor Alex J. Groesbeck pardoned Lee while she lay in her hospital bed, but she died four days later.[49] The clubwomen used the momentum from Lee's case to pressure city officials to build a new women's prison.

In their rhetoric, state officials connected prison construction to national trends of modernization, eugenics, and social purity, which sometimes confronted and complemented maternal justice. The eugenics movement advanced the notion that criminality and low intelligence were biologically determined. Eugenicists pushed for harsh immigration policies and forced sterilization laws that preyed on vulnerable communities and individuals, such as women accused of crimes. The eugenics movement amplified the widely held false belief that such women were especially deviant and especially likely to have deviant children. Therefore, as criminologist Lucia Zedner has shown, reformatories for women exiled them from "social circulation for as many of their child-bearing years as possible."[50] Eugenicists aspired to prevent so-called undesirable women from having children, and prison sentences and institutionalization in state hospitals became a means to that end.[51]

One of the most infamous legal cases in American history was the product of the eugenics movement. The United States Supreme Court upheld sterilization of people with intellectual disabilities in *Buck v. Bell*, 274 U.S. 200 (1927). Carrie Buck was a poor white woman who had grown up in the foster care system. She was committed to a Virginia mental institution because doctors labeled her "feeble-minded" although she had no physical or intellectual disabilities. A state law permitted forced sterilization of people committed to mental institutions, but required a hearing before the operation. Justice Holmes, writing for the court, notoriously penned, "Three generations of imbeciles are enough."[52] The Supreme Court held that forced sterilization laws did not violate the Constitution and supported the laws as a tool to prevent the country from "being swamped with incompetence."[53] Such statutes targeted poor women and women of color who were vulnerable to state violence. Forced sterilizations in mental hospitals and prisons were not uncommon in the 1920s. When the eugenics movement was at its height, thirty-two states upheld sterilization laws. California performed twenty thousand nonconsensual sterilizations on people who had been categorized by medical and state officials as insane or feeble-minded. It is estimated that sixty thousand people were victims of forced sterilizations in the United States in the twentieth century.[54]

Within this context, white clubwomen in Detroit successfully campaigned to remove incarcerated women from the Detroit House of Correction. The media coverage described how the club members' "insistent and uncompromising demands" eventually convinced city commissioners and state legislators to construct a women's prison.[55] In 1928, female prisoners moved to the newly constructed prison farm in the rural town of Plymouth, approximately thirty miles west of Detroit.[56]

The Built Environment, Discipline, and Labor in the Women's Prison

The social hierarchy and built environment of the new prison implemented maternal justice. Katherine H. Campbell became the superintendent of the Women's Division on September 1, 1928.[57] A member of the Twentieth Century Club, Campbell had helped investigate the State Training School for Girls in Adrian, Michigan, where there had been accusations of cruel treatment of children in 1919.[58] Campbell managed a staff of forty-seven matrons and seven other employees, including secretaries, a visiting psychiatrist, a nurse, and a social service worker.[59] Campbell had traveled the country learning about prisons, and she had insisted on the cottage plan.[60] Each cottage at the Detroit House of Correction held a dining room, kitchen, living room, and "play yard." There were six cottages for white women and two cottages for Black women. Incarcerated women were "taught how to prepare a meal and serve it" and "everything pertaining to domestic science."[61] The prison had a hospital, an administrative building with a kitchen and dining room for employees, a factory building, an industrial laundry room, and lodging for matrons. Conveying middle- and upper-class aspirations for incarcerated women, the housing resembled the architecture of women's colleges where female students were housed in "cottages" rather than dormitories. As one report described it, "In the design all the traditional ideas of prison construction were thrown overboard and a plant has been erected which, in exterior, resembles more an educational institution than what is conventionally thought of as a prison."[62]

Similarly, university housing for women reinforced societal pressures to remain focused on their obligations as housewives and mothers. In the 1910s, the University of Michigan built the Martha Cook Building for college coeds. The funders indicated that the architecture should communicate the dual role of coeds as both students and women who "civilize" the impulses of male undergraduates.[63] Art historian Carla Yanni argues, "The Martha Cook Building was intended as a quasi-domestic retreat within the setting of a masculinist campus: it was a quiet haven amid a bustle of a midwestern city, but it was not a beacon of egalitarianism."[64] Designers of the Detroit House of Correction applied a similar architectural philosophy to the prison. The women's prison was a place of discipline that was disguised by gentle aesthetics produced in its architecture and rhetoric.[65]

Within the new prison, Black women received treatment that rarely befell white women. An incident in 1930 illustrates the racially charged disciplinary practices. Campbell called for two male guards stationed in the Men's Division to, in her words, "handle a colored inmate" named Belle Smith on December 29. The men forcibly removed Smith from her room and placed her in solitary confinement. Campbell did not document the details of Smith's transfer. Superintendent Denniston asked Campbell for more information when he wrote, "I have received no report from you relative to this matter. It would seem that if this was serious enough to call men from the Men's Division, there should be some kind of a report in this office."[66] Campbell defended her unusual decision to call for male guards to restrain and confine Smith. No male guards worked in the women's buildings. In a memo, Campbell focused on Smith's transgressions on December 29 and again on January 15, 1931. Smith's privileges were not restored until February 12. Denniston expressed some concern that male guards physically overpowered Smith in her room; however, he devoted a similar amount of ink to express his concerns that Campbell may have been too quick to restore Smith's privileges. He noted, "Unless these inmates are made to feel that the taking of privileges means something, we had better stop taking privileges from them."[67] Denniston requested no further explanation, suggesting that he was satisfied with Campbell's response while also communicating that discipline of women should not be capricious.

The growing population of incarcerated women revealed the impact of racialized policing and sentencing of women of color. Heather Ann Thompson has demonstrated how Detroit, like other northern cities, became a destination for Black migrants after World War II, and brutal fights for equality played out in political arenas and the labor movement.[68] Applying her insights to Detroit's women's prison shows how fights for better wages, improved working conditions, and sanitary living quarters incorporated strategies of the labor movement and gave voice to an increasingly Black population of incarcerated women.

Incarcerated Labor Strikes

Prison leaders expected incarcerated women to work. Labor exploitation in prison factories and agriculture ensured that the prison was economically self-sufficient. By the mid-twentieth century, incarcerated women asserted their roles as workers and incorporated labor-movement tactics to protest prison conditions. The laundry room held contracts with city agencies, making it one of the busiest prison industries. Incarcerated women laundered uniforms and linens for the DPD, the Detroit Fire Department, the Department of Street Railways, the Municipal Lighting, the Redford Branch of the Receiving Hospital, and the Detroit House of Correction. Women also worked in the prison's canning factory, bake shop, and kitchen. Incarcerated people cultivated produce and managed livestock consumed by prisoners and city employees. Prisoners canned fruits and vegetables and shipped them to welfare agencies in surrounding towns. The prison only assigned women with clean health records to jobs in the canning factory, dining room, kitchen, and bake shop. The most demanding and least desirable jobs were in the poultry department. Incarcerated women raised chickens, collected eggs, and slaughtered birds. The physical rigor of the bloody routine along with the shoddy conditions caused many injuries. However, most incarcerated female workers were stationed behind one of forty industrial sewing machines adjacent to the canning facility, where they stitched prison linens and uniforms for various city agencies.[69]

The prison controlled incarcerated workers through harsh conditions and social isolation. In early October 1929, incarcerated women attended a meeting in the administration building and listened as prison staff rolled out new rules. Incarcerated workers could no longer take smoking breaks during their shifts. Rose Muller, a white incarcerated worker in the canning factory, stood up from her station and announced that prisoners would take "a rest anyway." The supervising matron ordered Muller to return to her station. Muller refused. The matron described in her report that Muller "went back to her position in an indifferent way but not to work. She peeled one beet, cut it up in a manner as much as to say she would do as she pleased during the 15 minutes. . . . During this time, she did not do any work except this one beet." Muller told Campbell that the women had decided that "if they could not have their smokes, they would not work during that period and . . . [Muller] was the only one who had the nerve to stand by their decision."[70]

The ramifications of prison protests rippled beyond the workplace, spilled into living quarters, and elicited a sharp rebuke from the matrons. When Campbell discovered that Muller had been planning a labor strike, she told Muller that "the girls were not running the Canning Factory or any part of the Institution and that she would have to take her punishment for assuming the position she did." Campbell stripped Muller of all her privileges. As a result, Muller was confined to her cottage, where she was given half-portion meals of coffee and bread for three days. On the fourth day, Campbell sent Muller back to work. Satisfied, Campbell reported, "I feel that she had sufficient punishment for the offense and that this is a good lesson to the other girls." At the same time, Campbell may have doubted whether Muller would stay in line as she compiled a record for the warden's office that would help preserve her authority.[71]

Incarcerated workers in the laundry room endured gruesome safety hazards, and Campbell tried unsuccessfully to get the prison to correct dangerous conditions in 1931. Broken steam pipes in the laundry room made the floor extremely hot and caused blisters to grow on the women's feet. Campbell detailed how some of the officers and prisoners had broken sores that bled through their socks and shoes. Campbell added, "Unless the situation is given immediate attention, we will be unable to work in this department."[72] The physical demands revealed the limits of the rehabilitative ideal clubwomen had imagined for the women's prison.

Harsh labor conditions were exacerbated by overcrowding, and women of color were incarcerated at disproportionate rates to the state population of women. In 1935, the Women's Division held 462 white women, 507 Black women, and sixteen indigenous women even though in 1940, 9.2 percent of Detroit's population was Black, up from 7.7 percent in 1930.[73] In 1940, 270 white women, 229 Black women, and ten indigenous women were incarcerated. The prison supported two choirs segregated by race: "one composed of white girls and one of negro girls, who sing on alternating Sundays at the church services."[74] The term "girls" to describe the women advanced the ideology of maternal justice that relegated incarcerated women to being wards of the state and undeserving of the privileges and respect of adulthood.

What Khalil Gibran Muhammad calls "the condemnation of blackness," or the conflation of Blackness with criminality, was becoming increasingly apparent in Michigan's women's prison.[75] In 1945, the prison held 406 white women, 230 Black women, and thirty-eight indigenous women. By 1950, the annual report recorded 374 white women, 353 Black women, and twenty-five indigenous women in prison.[76] In 1955, there were 368 white women incarcerated compared to 455 Black women and seventeen indigenous women.[77] In comparison, approximately 7 percent of the state's population was Black and 0.1 percent of the state's population was indigenous in 1950.[78] The disproportionate representation of Black and indigenous women in prison compared to the state population reveals the harsh treatment they received as they moved through the criminal legal system.

By the 1950s, the prison population had outgrown the cottages, and the Detroit House of Correction faced a housing crisis. In 1956, the *Detroit News* documented severe overcrowding. A photograph captured women sitting on cots lined up and down a hallway, and the caption asked, "Who will stop this?" Eighty incarcerated women slept on these makeshift beds in 1956, and many women had been living in the hallways for the previous three years.[79] The lack of privacy and personal property in such an environment must have been unrelenting.

Tension among prison administrators, city officials, incarcerated women, and the MDOC made progress in tackling overcrowding and safe working conditions impossible. No one agreed on the best path forward. On May 1, Superintendent Paul Brown resigned, accusing the commission, an advisory committee that was composed primarily of clubwomen, of interfering in the prison's operations. Brown's abrupt departure renewed public scrutiny of the clubwomen managing the Women's Division and the problem of overcrowding. Brown stated that the clubwomen were unqualified to advise him and his staff on prison management, but this accusation punted his responsibility for the decrepit conditions. Mrs. James P. McEvoy, a fifty-seven-year-old white volunteer, served as the chairwoman of the women's prison steering committee, and when journalists grilled her on her lack of experience working with prisoners, she deflected, "You must bear in mind that the superintendent and his assistant are responsible for the operation of the prison."[80]

Even with the negative press, the city made no concerted effort to improve the Women's Division. Incarcerated women were already frustrated by working conditions, sanitation problems, overcrowding, and arbitrary rules. The controversy over the transition created an opportunity for incarcerated women to make their concerns public; Brown's abrupt departure created an opening for incarcerated women to demand better treatment. They wanted decent housing and working conditions, but McEvoy refused to meet with prisoners. Incarcerated women prepared for a strike in the laundry room, the most profitable prison industry. On Friday, May 10, 1957, 190 incarcerated laundry workers showed up for their shifts. They sat at their stations and refused to work. A self-appointed committee of twelve incarcerated women made their demands. The prison chaplain tried to negotiate, but the women refused to talk to him and asked for a delegation of journalists to meet with them in the laundry room, signaling their desire to publicly expose the prison conditions. The prison acquiesced, and women presented their demands, which were handwritten on scraps of brown paper bags. They focused on overcrowding, medical care, nutrition, safety, and arbitrary rules.[81]

In response, the prison quickly mobilized the police power of the state. One hundred Northville policemen parked their patrol cars outside the gates and waited for further instruction. Detroit mayor Louis C. Miriani caught wind of the uprising and was shocked by the formidable

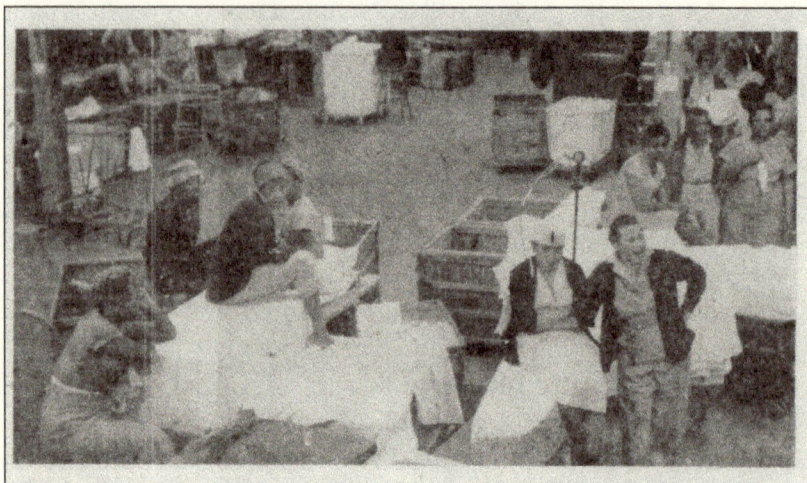

Figure 1.1. Incarcerated laundry workers launch a strike in the Women's Division of the Detroit House of Correction. "Free Press Settles Women's Jail Strike," *Detroit Free Press*, May 11, 1957.

police presence. Miriani told the press, "You could have knocked me down with a feather. . . . We are dealing with women. [The police are] swinging bats and clubs." He added, "But the girls must realize they are prisoners and not in a boarding school."[82] Miriani's comparison of the incarcerated workers to adolescent students aligned with both the built environment and the power structure in the prison. The protest, however, was also a move that identified the incarcerated women as laborers. The women negotiated with three commissioners, but they failed to reach a resolution. Reporters printed the women's complaints in the next day's paper:

1) Cessation of placing State prisoners in the hall to sleep months before their parole date.
2) Better medical care. The prisoners said they have to buy their own dentures and glasses.
3) Better quality food. It was charged that since the departure of former Supt. Paul Brown, both the quality and quantity have fallen off.
4) Better ventilation in the cottages and laundry room, where it was said temperatures often rise to 100 degrees.

5) Better recreation facilities. The women said the only recreation is a weekly movie for a privileged few.

6) Education and rehabilitation facilities. The strikers said the only education offered is a typewriting class once a week.

7) Alleviation of overcrowded conditions.

8) Later lockup time in the cottages in the summer. The prisoners want a 10 p.m. lockup instead of 8 p.m.

9) An increase in daily pay from 35 to 50 cents. The strikers say they must buy their own personal effects from the commissary and are bitter because more than 50 items have been taken off the commissary list.

10) Abolishment of the inmate police system and the punishment rooms.[83]

The list focused on the physical space, rehabilitation programs, and basic needs. The incarcerated women requested better food and ventilation systems in the laundry and sewing rooms. They wanted to abolish the "inmate police system," which facilitated abuse and illustrated staffing shortages. They survived on "scanty fare," which usually consisted of "dry toast and black coffee for breakfast, a luncheon and a small bowl of bread and milk at night." Women described regular sightings of "cockroaches and rats as big as kittens." Prisoner Dolores Topps stated, "We don't know what's gonna happen over this, but we're telling the truth and we're hoping. We're scared, but we are telling the truth." Close to half of the four hundred incarcerated women at the Detroit House of Correction participated in the strike.[84]

Journalists granted incarcerated women publicity but undermined the women's complaints with gendered rhetoric. Reporters sexualized incarcerated women and deployed clichés of "bad girls" who deserved punishment. One article described thirty-eight-year-old Sina Wisner, the spokesperson for the strike, as "a buxom blond Flint burglar." The emphasis on women's physical appearance and criminal convictions exposed the sexism that hindered the way the complaints of the incarcerated landed with the public. After meeting with the incarcerated women, commissioners told the press, "All of the items of complaints will be refused."[85]

A competing narrative of the strike focused on class and racialized confrontations between upper-class white clubwomen and incarcerated women, most of whom were poor and women of color. The *Detroit Free*

Figure 1.2. Sina Wisner and other incarcerated women present their demands to a group of reporters inside the Detroit House of Correction. The photograph was published on the front page of the *Detroit Free Press* on May 11, 1957.

Press expressed sympathy for the white clubwomen who were "caught in the middle of a sitdown strike at the Detroit House of Correction."[86] McEvoy acknowledged that the clubwomen moved "slowly but tactfully" because it was the first time any of the four volunteer commissioners had negotiated in a labor strike, implying that the women did not come from working-class backgrounds and were unfamiliar with protest strategies. The press credited McEvoy with resolving the strike, but did so in gendered terms: "The ladylike, 15-hour strike ended peacefully without any violence or general outbreak."[87] The coverage confirmed that the prisoners and commissioners acted according to acceptable female behavior.

Incarcerated women deployed protest strategies that working-class communities in southeastern Michigan had developed. Detroit was the birthplace of United Auto Workers (UAW), one of the most powerful labor unions in the country. Labor strikes forced large corporations to improve economic stability and job security for thousands of wage workers. For example, for two months in the winter of 1936–1937, thousands of workers at General Motors factories in Flint halted production with what came to be known as the "Great Flint Sit-Down Strike." Workers won collective bargaining rights.[88]

After the 1957 strike, the city of Detroit invited, reluctantly, an outside investigation to survey the climate of the Detroit House of Correction. A committee from the American Correctional Association, an organization that accredited prisons across the country, found the institution riddled with "confusion, frustration and disorganization."[89] Their report concluded, "The major problems found at the Detroit House of Correction, of which there are many, have been developing for a number of years."[90] They also urged the MDOC to manage the prison as city prisoners made up less than 1 percent of the incarcerated women's population. The committee recommended more clothing, improved nutrition, and personal hygiene items for women. The report outlined disciplinary recommendations that followed due process and training for matrons. It suggested updating the women's sewing room and cannery and transferring laundry to the men's institution. The report concluded that laundry would generate more revenue with incarcerated male workers.[91]

State legislators largely ignored the report. Republican state senator Elmer R. Porter, the chairman of the state Senate Appropriations Committee, stated, "I want no part of the Detroit House of Correction if Detroit wants to give it to us. If Detroit can't find funds to operate it, where would the State get the money." Meanwhile, mayor of Detroit Albert Cobo was eager to turn the prison into someone else's problem. "We've been trying to turn the place over to the State for years but nothing ever happened."[92] In the late 1930s, states across the country established centralized agencies to manage prisons,[93] and the MDOC was established in 1937 to manage and standardize men's prisons, but incarcerated women fell outside of the agency's responsibilities. Cobo suggested that the committee members had exaggerated the problems. He boasted, "Before we're through I'm going to investigate every division and every nook and cranny there. I'm going to eat some of the food."[94] Through such statements, he frantically undermined the conclusions of the 1957 report.

After the rounds of protests, the state wanted nothing to do with a women's prison. Prison leaders argued that the laundry operated at a profit and saved the city money, making it essential.[95] Prison administrators aligned exploitative labor practices with the rehabilitative model:

> We have a large number of women who have led a kind of life in which a steady work routine was unknown, in which no habits of industry could be developed. Many of these women have prostituted and have never held a job. For them the institutional laundry provides excellent training in industrial routine, in addition to teaching various skills required in a commercial laundry. It must be remembered that our women working in the laundry are placed there because they need the laundry, not because the laundry needs them. Basically the operation is utilized for its therapeutic value in our rehabilitation program.[96]

This description of the rehabilitative aspects of prison industries failed to mention the economic profits the laundry bestowed on the prison. In any case, prison administrators gradually removed prison industries from the Women's Division,[97] thereby reducing women's work-training opportunities. By the 1970s, work-training programs were sporadic and the prison offered only occasional classes.

Limits of Reform

The police brutality against Black women and clubwomen's fights for prison reform illustrate how ideas about gender, race, and rehabilitation bolstered incarceration of women in Michigan. The police killings of Gertrude Russian and Lillie Smith, two Black women, were largely ignored while the death of Lareta Lee, a white incarcerated woman, fueled action. Clubwomen fought for the construction of a new prison that was guided by the ideals of maternal justice and rehabilitation. The construction of women's prisons, in Michigan and across the country, also reflected renewed national anxiety about the expanding role of women in public institutions and the growing Black population in northern cities like Detroit. Clubwomen designed a new prison that they hoped would serve as a vehicle for social improvement, but their efforts to support incarcerated women were compromised by over-crowding, political fights, gender stereotypes, and racial discrimination.

Frustrated and fed up, incarcerated women engaged in labor pro-tests that exposed ongoing problems with prisons. By the 1950s, the labor movement, liberalism, and democratization had reshaped the way many Americans thought about workers' rights, women, and public in-stitutions. In the annual report of 1960, Superintendent Albert Shapiro explained, "Since September of 1957, there has been a gradual reorganiza-tion of manpower and operation at the Detroit House of Correction. The change has been away from the policy of emphasizing incarceration as punishment to one of treatment toward rehabilitation."[98] By reframing prison industries in therapeutic terms, the prison reasserted its power over the incarcerated workforce and the fruits of their labor.

The labor strikes captured public attention and spurred women's prison activism. Women leveraged their position as laborers, garnered media attention, and negotiated with administrators. The protests of the mid-twentieth century fell flat because civic leaders, prison manag-ers, and politicians refused to remedy prisoners' grievances. This fueled resentment among incarcerated people that would erupt again in the 1970s. Americans watched as prison uprisings from New York to Cali-fornia inspired a new consciousness among incarcerated people, who demanded equality and freedom from oppressive punishment prac-tices. In Michigan, incarcerated women fused the momentum of the women's liberation movement with that of the prisoners' rights move-ment in their attempts to alleviate the harms of incarceration and create opportunities for themselves behind bars. The contested origins of the Women's Division of the Detroit House of Correction created pathways for incarcerated women to challenge their confinement.

2

From Mass Action to Class Action

Origins of the Prisoners' Rights Movement for Women

In 1976, the Detroit House of Correction received a woman whose name would become synonymous with the fight for gender equality in American prisons. Just twenty-one years old, Mary Glover faced three concurrent life sentences, and her new home was bleak.[1] She recalled, "On arrival at the prison, I could not believe my eyes. The 180-bed institution was completely uninhabitable. The building had been condemned and the housing 'cottages' were filthy. I was processed as a new commitment and taken to the hospital dining room for lunch. It was crawling with cockroaches and mice. . . . They fed me black, burned hot dogs and beans. It was hot and muggy. Flies were everywhere. I was sick and in shock."[2] The mattress in her cell reeked of urine. In the winter, incarcerated women tried to stay warm despite sporadic heat. They suffered through sweltering temperatures in the summer.[3] Like prisoners across the country, incarcerated women in Michigan navigated dilapidated and overcrowded buildings. They lacked access to education, vocational training, and legal services, which made them vulnerable to arbitrary and cruel punishment. In contrast, incarcerated men could enroll in college courses and get job training in factories and farms. These discrepancies fueled discontent and inspired activism in Michigan's only women's prison.

In the late 1960s and early 1970s, uprisings in New York and California drew global attention to racism and prison conditions. Informed by the Nation of Islam, the Black Panther Party, and other political movements, incarcerated people garnered national media attention that showcased racialized violence.[4] Historian Heather Ann Thompson has detailed one of the most well-known prison protests, the Attica prison uprising of 1971, which inspired a new generation of activists devoted to acknowledging civil and human rights of incarcerated people.[5]

Scholars of the prisoners' rights movement have focused on states either in the Northeast or in the Sunbelt, and they depict prison organizing as normatively masculine. If women appear at all in these accounts, they do so as girlfriends, wives, mothers, and female activists pursuing reform in men's prisons.[6] In Michigan, however, incarcerated women engaged in an activism all their own. This chapter examines how incarcerated women carved new pathways for reform based on their interpretation of the women's movement, infusing prison reform with critiques of gender-based discrimination. I argue that the prisoners' rights movement for women created avenues for incarcerated people, attorneys, and activists to interrogate the purpose of imprisonment through the lenses of gender, race, and class. The movement sparked a new sense of political consciousness among incarcerated women, whose aims aligned with the broad goals of liberal feminism, which sought gender equality through legal and institutional reform. The movement was also influenced by radical feminism, which, as historian Alice Echols has shown, challenged male supremacy and raised political consciousness among women, especially white women in cities. Although both forms of feminism were reluctant to incorporate differences of race, class, and sexual orientation, they influenced feminist jurisprudence in prison litigation of the 1970s.[7] By giving testimony and participating in litigation, incarcerated women launched critiques of the prison, discussed male privilege in society, and imagined different opportunities for themselves.

This chapter traces the way women's movements and feminist jurisprudence influenced prison activism in Michigan. It shows how conceptions of gender equality, as articulated by incarcerated women through testimony, grievance reports, and a federal class-action lawsuit, gained traction in courts and prisons. Examining the multiple ways in which incarcerated women fought for gender equality expands upon other studies of grassroots challenges to mass incarceration and reveals how incarcerated women claimed space despite punitive policies.[8] Incarcerated women asserted their right to equal opportunity by grounding their legal claims in the Fourteenth Amendment. They compelled the federal courts to prohibit gender-based discrimination in state prisons with the lawsuit *Glover v. Johnson*, 478 F. Supp. 1075 (E.D. Mich. 1979), which was the country's first major case addressing gender inequality in prisons. The litigation inspired incarcerated women to launch similar cases in other states.[9] The impact of mass incarceration by the 1980s ultimately curtailed progress toward gender equality in prison; however, its dominance should not diminish the significance of the coalition's work to radically alter the conditions of confinement. As this chapter will show, the *Glover* decision was particularly fragile because the MDOC interpreted gender equality as race neutral and gender neutral, allowing the state to disassemble rehabilitative programs for men and women. This history sheds light on the expansive quality of women's movements and the contingency of mass incarceration.

The origins of the prisoners' rights movement for women reveals a more nuanced connection between feminism and punishment than has previously been recognized. Scholars have exposed the hollow aspects of narratives that credit white, middle-class women with being the main activists and beneficiaries of the women's movement of the 1970s. Serena Mayeri asserts, "Historians have uncovered . . . tremendous diversity of background, thought, and activism, a multiplicity of movements within a movement obscured by an exclusive focus on mainstream, predominantly white organizations and advocacy."[10] An interracial coalition of incarcerated women confronted the political force of mass incarceration. They attempted to dismantle stereotypes of women in prison by organizing around their understandings of gender, race, and power. Examining how incarcerated women fought for equal rights underscores how feminism shaped the prisoners' rights movement in Michigan and the nation.[11]

Discipline through Gendered Programs

The significant gap in opportunities for incarcerated men and women offended core principles of the civil rights and women's movements. Michigan had gradually increased the prison population and constructed more facilities for men. Male prisoners gained a wider set of job-training programs and industry experience. College courses spread across a number of maximum-security prisons. There were also low-security work camps, and prison farms scattered across the state. For example, men incarcerated in Jackson made license plates, shoes, highway signs, and metal office furniture. The prison also maintained a textile plant that manufactured clothing and flags.[12] In contrast, the state sent all incarcerated women to the Detroit House of Correction, where they found few opportunities to further their education or develop job skills.[13]

Many incarcerated women discovered the gender gap in training and education through their communication with boyfriends and husbands who were also incarcerated. For example, Mary Glover's husband told her about how the State Prison of Southern Michigan in Jackson had educational and vocational training programs, a law library, and sufficient heat. In comparison, the incarcerated women lived in unsanitary cottages and showered over a thick sheet of ice in the winter. The prison's law library's collection was out of date by decades. The most recent decisions from the state courts, the *Michigan Reports*, were from 1923 and covered in mold.[14]

Glover interpreted the discrepancies in the treatment of male and female prisoners as a signal that the women's prison had yet to acknowledge the rights and needs of incarcerated women. She reflected on her first few years in prison in a three-part essay series published in the *Michigan Daily*, the student newspaper at the University of Michigan, where she argued that prisons should be radically different institutions that emphasized job training and education. She described how, in 1976, "I was locked into a crumbling, graffiti-littered room and placed in 'quarantine' with nothing but the clothes on my back." When guards released her to the main prison campus, she confronted what she called "the biggest disappointment of all": no vocational or educational programs. Glover had nearly completed her training to become a registered nurse when she was sentenced to three concurrent life sentences. She lacked only the final exam.[15] Being so close to a professional goal and facing a long prison sentence, she was eager to continue her education. She wrote, "I wanted an education and to better myself as a woman while incarcerated, but survival took precedence."[16] Incarcerated women held prison jobs cleaning toilets, mopping floors, washing dishes, and picking up the kitchen. The prison offered only an infrequent smattering of high school and college-level courses. For example, another woman serving a life sentence took classes every chance she got, but after eight years, she still could not cobble together enough credits for a two-year associate's degree.[17] Education was limited to "womanly arts," such as decorating, cooking, and sewing—a curriculum that had been stagnant since the 1920s.[18]

Imprisoned women faced onerous sex-based expectations that reconstructed patriarchal power. Kathy Engle was twenty-one years old when she was first incarcerated. Engle was a white woman and the stepdaughter of a Detroit police officer. She had worked as a "bunny" at the Detroit Playboy Club and turned to prostitution to support her drug addiction. The *Detroit Free Press* equated Engle's physical appearance with her declining social status from a club worker who had been the object of male desire to a lowly, disheveled prisoner in 1970.[19] The writer reveled in her decline: "Kathy used to be a sexy, blond bunny at the Detroit Playboy Club. She doesn't look sexy anymore. She's overweight. She wears a knee-length powder blue prison uniform with a white sweater, black knee socks and tan tie shoes."[20] Such descriptions, common

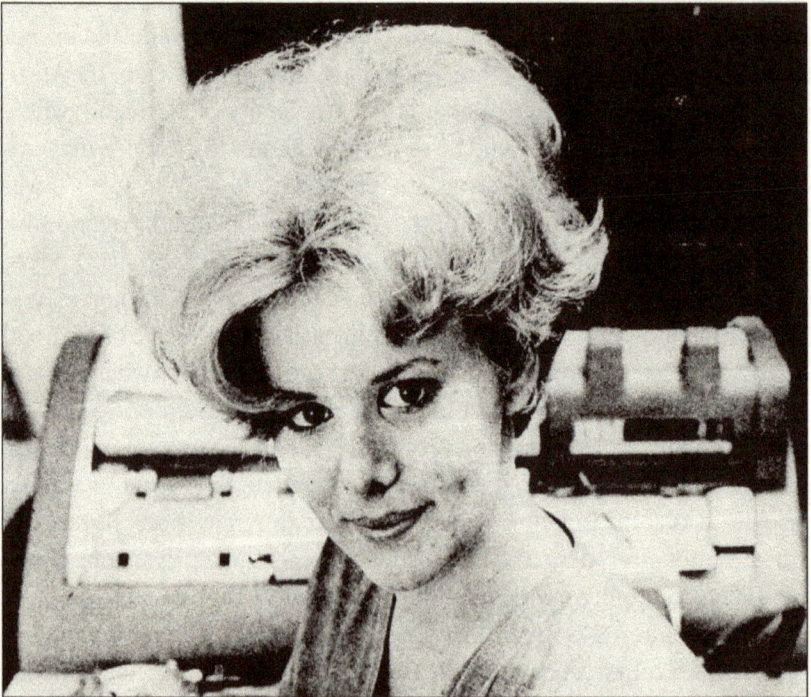

Figure 2.1. Kathy Engle incarcerated in the Detroit House of Correction. This portrait was taken in front of an IBM punch card machine, one of the few and sporadic job-training programs for women in 1970. Tom Ricke, "The Tragedy of Kathy: A Detroit Girl's Fast Short Trip from Second Avenue to DeHoCo," *Detroit Free Press*, February 1, 1970. © Photograph by Ira Rosenberg—USA TODAY NETWORK.

among journalists, revealed how women were disregarded if they did not conform to unreasonable beauty standards. For example, referencing women's weight was common in criminal legal newspaper coverage and implied that women on trial or in prison lacked self-discipline. In fact, it was nearly impossible to find healthy food in prison, and many women feared that the meals were contaminated. Violet Allen, a white incarcerated woman, had seen mouse droppings in the food. She tried to eat only out of vending machines when she had money in her account.[21]

The prison also policed the morality of incarcerated women. A married woman needed permission from her husband to meet with a man during visitation hours, but male prisoners were under no such restrictions. Engle was separated from her husband while incarcerated, but she had to receive her husband's permission to have a man attend visitation hours.[22] By the 1970s, incarcerated women complained that the facility was woefully out of date.

"We Can't Run a New Institution with Old Rules and Regulations That Are No Good": Documenting Problems in the Detroit House of Correction Women's Division

Prison uprisings pushed Americans to reevaluate state prisons.[23] In 1971, thirteen hundred male prisoners took control of Attica, a large prison in upstate New York. The nation was captivated. For five days, prisoners made demands, and showed the world the racism they endured. The rebellion ended in the state's violent takeover of the prison in which the state of New York killed over forty people.[24] It is difficult to overstate the impact this uprising had on correctional departments and incarcerated people in America. In an opinion piece for the *New York Times*, writer Tom Wicker, who also observed firsthand the conditions in Attica, argued, "Attica—like most prisons—is not a 'correctional facility' at all; the phrase is a gruesome euphemism. No 'correctional officer' there has any real training in correcting or teaching or counseling men; rather, they are armed guards set to herd animals."[25] In the following months, journalists, activists, and public-interest lawyers echoed similar critiques of the prison, questioning its dismal outcomes and purpose. In 1972, the ACLU established the National Prison Project, an initiative focused on constitutional and human rights for incarcerated people.[26] The uprising infused the prisoners' rights movement with new energy, and incarcerated people made pressing demands for medical care, education, job training, grievance procedures, and access to the courts.[27]

After Attica, states across the country grew nervous that their own prisons were fertile ground for similar rebellions.[28] In 1973, the Michigan state legislature formed a special committee to take inventory of its prison. The committee took testimony from incarcerated people and employees at Michigan's ten prisons. They were dismayed to find no successful models of rehabilitation, the state's explicit goal of incarceration.[29] Referring to the Women's Division, the committee concluded, "In all of the institutions, we found deplorable conditions, but in none of the men's institutions could conditions compare with those that were revealed to us at the Detroit House of Correction."[30] Disagreements between the state and Detroit over who should fix the Women's Division continued until the Michigan Department of Corrections (MDOC) opened a new prison for women in 1977.

Incarcerated women seized opportunities to shape reform according to new interpretations of gender equality. In their testimony to the special committee, incarcerated women impressed upon the state legislators how terrible confinement was at the Women's Division at the Detroit House of Correction.[31] Kathy Engle, the subject of the *Detroit Free Press* article, served as a spokesperson for her housing unit when the special committee visited. She stated, "In order to start doing anything out here, I feel like we need a new administration as far as women's division. . . . We can't run a new institution with old rules and regulations that are no good."[32] Engle's use of the first-person plural communicated her understanding of the prison as a collective enterprise, with prisoners and prison staff sharing responsibility for a well-run prison.

Women's testimony documented how the prison failed to provide meaningful grievance procedures, making incarcerated women vulnerable to arbitrary punishment with no due process. If a matron accused a woman of any kind of disciplinary infraction, she was "in effect, deemed 'guilty,' and could be stripped of all clothing and personal possessions and locked in a room with only a bed, a chamber pot and a Bible."[33] This practice was called "reflection," a euphemism for solitary confinement and a relic of nineteenth-century punishment practices. Engle explained, "We have reflection for women. They're put behind a gate in a room. They have maybe fifteen minutes to take a bath, wash clothes, if they're let out to take a bath. I've seen them go four days without taking baths. They're complaining about this. They won't go in the rooms now because they aren't allowed to take baths. Then they get more time."[34] A woman could remain in a cell with no plumbing for days while waiting for a hearing.[35] The special committee expressed concern about these complaints and perhaps worried that a growing sense of injustice could inspire a lawsuit or uprising. "We saw little evidence of administrative due process in disciplinary proceedings," the visiting legislators concluded.[36]

In the 1960s, the United States Supreme Court brought sweeping changes to procedural protections for the criminally accused, which shaped the way incarcerated people could contest prison rules and conditions.[37] In *Cooper v. Pate*, the Supreme Court held that prisons must recognize constitutional rights of prisoners. Thomas X. Cooper was a Black prisoner at Stateville prison in Illinois. Cooper tried to register as a member of the Nation of Islam (NOI), but the prison had labeled the NOI a hate group. In a *pro se* petition filed while he was in solitary confinement, Cooper claimed that the prison had violated his right to religious freedom by denying NOI materials and meetings with spiritual advisors. The Supreme Court affirmed that prisoners maintained civil rights, and the case established a precedent for subsequent legal victories.[38] In *Wolff v. McDonnell*, a 1974 Supreme Court decision, Justice White wrote, "A prisoner is not wholly stripped of constitutional protections when he is imprisoned for a crime."[39] The legal victories signaled a departure from the "hands-off" approach federal courts had taken with prison litigation in the first half of the twentieth century and paved the way for more cases challenging prison conditions.[40]

The decisions galvanized attorneys and incarcerated people to fight for the expansion of constitutional rights in prisons and the curtailment of arbitrary disciplinary practices. For example, Michigan prisoners knew the disciplinary procedures to be subjective and unreliable in the 1970s. Prisoner Ann Johnson testified, "Here, everything you do you get locked up for. Even if you don't go to reflection, they have what they call lock-ins. Any infraction you commit, they're going to lock you up in some way."[41] Women grounded their complaints in the language of due process rights and equality while navigating growing hostility. Women interpreted the arbitrary use of solitary confinement as an additional form of punishment. The prison did not provide any opportunity for incarcerated people to document or contest how they were being punished, which permitted guards to arbitrarily impose additional sanctions against the women.

Both prisoners and, when pressed, guards failed to articulate the purpose of incarceration beyond incapacitation. Engle gave testimony to the special committee that described how the lack of job programs created a hopeless environment in which incarcerated women felt restless with no structure. On her first trip to prison in 1970, Engle had participated in a work-pass program with the League of Catholic Women.[42] By 1973, Engle discovered that the program had been discontinued. She complained, "We have nothing to do. Unless you have some type of skills out here that you come into the Detroit House of Corrections with, you have nothing."[43] Prison employees agreed with the incarcerated women's characterization of the problems. When the special committee asked matrons to describe rehabilitative programs, Matron Boyce responded, "I don't really know of any . . . I can't really say that there's anything that they really have." When asked what purpose the Women's Division served, Boyce replied, "I don't see where it serves any useful purpose. Not any, I really don't."[44] The testimony documents how the organizing principle of rehabilitation in prison had been subsumed by punishment, retribution, and neglect.

Scholars agree that the final third of the twentieth century was marked by a "punitive turn," which describes America's embrace of punitive politics that supported mass imprisonment: higher incarceration rates, longer sentences, and an emphasis on punishment rather than rehabilitation of incarcerated people.[45] However, that shift was gradual. The special committee in Michigan supported rehabilitation, at least in theory. The transcripts of the hearings document their surprise and dismay that no rehabilitative programs existed for the incarcerated women.

The particular plight of imprisoned women came into sharp relief during the hearings, especially as a result of the testimony by women themselves. Women described how the prison remained committed to gender stereotypes at a time when other state institutions were creating more opportunities for women. Gwendolyn Wilson, an African American woman, described her belief that equal treatment would improve prison culture.[46] Ollie Fulghan, a woman serving a life sentence for second-degree murder of a police officer during a routine traffic stop in 1969, served as a cottage representative.[47] She implored state officials to implement an industrial job-training program and wages equitable to those earned by incarcerated men. Fulghan stated, "If women have some actual training leading to a regular standard-wage-paying job, I feel the majority will accept such responsibilities with regards to carrying over into their institutional behavior."[48] Together, the testimonies presented a cohesive argument focused on equality and education.

In the final report the committee members stated their commitment to reform; however, they did not advocate for programs beyond training for jobs in the service industry. The report captured the urgent need for job training, but it focused on traditional service and administrative jobs. The committee proposed that the prison "foster programs providing marketable skills for such jobs as waitresses, clerical help, beauticians, nurse's aides and counselors."[49] Despite a range of manufacturing jobs in Michigan, politicians confined women's potential to the service industry, traditionally a field that employed mostly women. Ultimately, the committee's desire for prison reform confronted state legislators' inclinations, which ran in the opposite direction. The final recommendations were met with political opposition, and problems in the prison grew.

Instead of expanding community-based programs, the MDOC made plans to bring the Women's Division into its bureaucratic fold and build a new prison.[50] The shift exacerbated longstanding problems and ultimately increased the state's ability to incarcerate more people, expanding what Heather Schoenfeld calls "carceral capacity."[51] The MDOC hired Martha Wheeler as the new superintendent of the Women's Division. Wheeler was a white woman who had graduated from law school and spent most of her career working in prisons in Ohio. She saw herself as a trailblazer in the male-dominated field of corrections but viewed imprisoned women according to conventional gender norms. She generalized, "Our women residents have pretty traditional views of themselves."[52] Tension between Wheeler and incarcerated women festered while Wheeler insisted that most women aspired to be homemakers, wives, or mothers.[53] Her assumption revealed race and class biases in that many women of color and poor women were heads of households who did not have the opportunity to be supported in the role of homemaker.

Wheeler's approach to prison reform had the unintended consequence of raising political consciousness among incarcerated women. Barbara Zwald, a white incarcerated woman, and Charmaine Cornish, a Black incarcerated woman, explained the misapprehensions of their new superintendent in a letter to the *Detroit Free Press*: "Ms. Wheeler is grossly mistaken when she says the women here prefer to continue in the traditional roles of housewives, homemakers and mothers. The majority of the women here are heads of households. Where is the money coming from to run these households and support these children? From welfare? A gradual or fast return to crime?"[54] They added, "Perhaps Ms. Wheeler should have retired and made room for someone younger and more progressive who can relate to today's women and their problems."[55] Incarcerated women did not appreciate being misunderstood and poorly served. Their letter highlighted the stakes of education and job training, while expressing their frustration that women's and civil rights movements had not informed penal policies.[56] Before prison, most incarcerated women had obtained a ninth-grade education while managing homes without financial support from a partner. Incarcerated women's expectations for programs aligned with the official stance of the MDOC, which supported rehabilitation. In a 1976 report, MDOC officials wrote, "Rehabilitation is viewed by the department as a process of internalizing values, social attitudes and the skills necessary for social integration."[57] In practice, however, women received few opportunities to advance their education or develop skills that would help them succeed once they left prison. They contended that prison programs for women were infused with sexist values and attitudes that relegated women to inferior positions in society. Zwald and Cornish's critique advanced feminist ideology by applying egalitarian values to prison programs.

The Prisoners' Rights Movement for Women

In the 1970s, incarcerated women relied on the goodwill of volunteers to provide educational programs, and the volunteer groups became an important site for advancing grassroots feminism and feminist jurisprudence in prison. A local chapter of the American Association of University Women ran a program called Lifeliners that offered meetings for women serving life sentences. The volunteers attempted to fill a large programming gap and operated in a period when prisons were more open and accessible to visitors than they are today. The volunteers brought dinners, facilitated individual counseling, and collected clothing and hygiene items for women. They coordinated family visits and solicited Christmas gifts for prisoners and their children. They continued "lobbying for enlightenment and improvement in the Corrections System."[58] Glover found solace in Lifeliners. At the meetings, women could voice complaints and discuss visions for new prison programs. The meetings facilitated solidarity among women by forging connections among incarcerated mothers, children, and a community of female volunteers, many of whom were mothers themselves.

At the behest of Lifeliners, volunteer attorneys began offering legal courses. In 1976, a small group of attorneys and law students offered a class on civil and criminal procedure for the women serving life sentences. Public-interest lawyers from the Detroit area held meetings that were steeped in principles of participatory democracy. Glover was impressed by how the attorneys "listened to our problems, complaints, our struggles to survive, which were only too obvious as the table discussion was frequently interrupted by plaster falling on us from the decaying ceiling."[59]

The group of attorneys and law students raised funds for a new women's law library. They received a grant of several thousand dollars from the "Buck Dinner." The event, steeped in Michigan's deer-hunting traditions, with a cartoon buck as a mascot, was an annual fundraiser for social-justice causes and progressive lawyers in Detroit. The dinner started in 1929 when Maurice Sugar, a labor lawyer who was born in the Upper Peninsula and an avid hunter and sportsman, "bagged a buck." He and his wife, Jane, invited a dozen friends, who held common leftist political beliefs and supported the emerging labor movement in Michigan, to their home to enjoy the feast. The venison dinner became an annual tradition among leftist lawyers in Detroit and served as a fundraiser for an array of social-justice issues. The proceeds went to civil rights organizations, the labor movement, and feminist groups in Michigan. The dinner also donated grants to the local chapters of the National Lawyers Guild, the ACLU, and the Maurice and Jane Sugar Law Center for Economic and Social Justice. During the 1950s, the FBI tracked many Buck Dinner attendees for alleged communist sympathies. Some participants even had friends drive them to and from the dinner so that their cars would not be tied to the event. During the civil rights era, donations from the Buck Dinner were distributed to Congress of Racial Equality (CORE), the NAACP, the Martin Luther King Vote Campaign, the Southern Conference Education Fund, and the Tallahassee Bus Appeal.[60]

In the 1970s, the Buck Dinner supplied grants to improve prisoners' rights and prison conditions in Michigan. Ernest "Ernie" Goodman became a regular organizer of the Buck Dinner. Goodman was an attorney in Detroit who focused on labor and civil rights. He represented the incarcerated men who participated in the Attica rebellion in one of the key trials following the uprising and won an acquittal in 1975. Goodman had served as the president of the National Lawyers Guild, a national organization that advocated for civil rights and leftist issues and a key organization that supplied legal representation in prisoners' rights cases.[61] One of the Buck Dinner grants supported a new law library for incarcerated women.

The Michigan Department of Corrections (MDOC) had been implementing gradual reforms for vocational training, education, and access to the courts. For example, in 1979, the Corrections Commission, a steering committee for the MDOC, had expanded community residential programs for men. The committee largely denied allegations of severe overcrowding, inadequate medical care, and abuse. "However," they acknowledged, "the women's population presents a very tenuous situation on a day-to-day basis."[62] The language in this memorandum to Perry Johnson, the director of the MDOC, also suggested that the women's prison was fertile ground for unrest.

In August 1977, almost three years after legislation for a new women's prison had passed, the MDOC opened Huron Valley Correctional Facility in Ypsilanti, the first state-run correctional facility for women.[63] Huron Valley promised improved prison conditions, but the facility was overcrowded from the beginning. The prison was designed to hold 240 women, but in its first two years, it consistently held over 400 women. By the end of 1979, the prison population reached 611 women. Desperate for space, prison officials moved a portion of the population into mobile trailers scattered around the prison grounds. Another slapdash remedy involved rotating sixty women in and out of the Kalamazoo County Jail every few weeks. The conditions at Kalamazoo were much worse than those at Huron Valley. The *Detroit Free Press* explained, "The spillover goes to Kalamazoo County Jail, a far more stringent environment than Huron Valley, reminiscent of the old Dehoco situation."[64] At Kalamazoo, women lived in jail cells designed for male detainees. There was a single toilet in the middle of each cell. Women had no privacy, and guards could see when they were menstruating.[65] The unpredictable transfers disrupted routines that the women relied on, especially those serving long sentences.

Glover and many incarcerated women interpreted transfers to the Kalamazoo jail as an additional form of punishment. By spring of 1977, Glover had acquired a reputation as an agitator. She was educated, articulate, and popular among different groups of prisoners. Guards shackled Glover to a loud, drug-addicted woman for the transfer. Glover interpreted this transfer as retaliation orchestrated by Warden Gloria Richardson. She was the last prisoner hauled on the bus, giving the woman chained to her time to stew. For hours, the woman yelled at the bus driver, prison guards, and fellow prisoners. The experience rattled Glover.[66]

Court records confirm that many incarcerated women concluded that a transfer to Kalamazoo Jail was a punitive measure. Georgia Manzie, an incarcerated woman, submitted an affidavit confirming Glover's suspicions. In August 1977, Richardson called the women in Manzie's housing unit to a meeting where Richardson unveiled the plan to transfer prisoners to Kalamazoo to alleviate overcrowding. Manzie recalled how Richardson warned the women, "But you (Units 1 and 8) could be sent if you don't behave, like get several write-ups (misconduct reports) or attempt to escape." Manzie had interpreted a transfer to the jail as a "means of punitive detention."[67] Prisoners navigated capricious disciplinary policies in the jail and Huron Valley.

In 1976, a coalition of incarcerated women, law students, and attorneys crystallized to sue the prison. The group laid plans for litigation that they hoped would force the MDOC to acknowledge their rights to due process and equal opportunity. Attorney Judith Magid had been working with Michigan Legal Services in the men's prison at Jackson, and she convinced her friend Charlene Snow, a young attorney in Detroit who specialized in employment law, to join the case. Bringing Snow on the case strengthened the women's argument for equal access to job training. Attorneys convinced incarcerated women that they would have a decent shot at reforming the prison by using the courts to remedy gender-based inequality.[68]

In the 1970s, the United States Supreme Court gradually dismantled laws that preserved discrimination based on sex. In *Reed v. Reed*, 404 U.S. 71 (1971), the court held that a classification based on gender had to be "reasonable, not arbitrary, and must rest upon some ground of difference having a fair and substantial relation to the object of the legislation, so that all persons similarly circumscribed shall be treated alike."[69] In 1973, the court held that laws that maintained the male-breadwinner-and-female-dependent income structures were unconstitutional.[70] In 1976, the court struck down an Oklahoma law that insisted on different drinking ages for women and men.[71] In a trial brief, the Michigan attorneys cited Supreme Court cases that examined gender-based discrimination. They stated, "It must be emphasized that the Defendants have not offered any legitimate or compelling reason, having a fair and substantial relation to the object of incarceration, which supports this inequality of treatment and opportunities based on gender."[72] The *Glover* lawsuit contributed to the legal landscape of gender equality.

Deciding who would be named in the lawsuit was a delicate matter because of the considerable risks of retaliation. Launching a lawsuit against the MDOC director, Perry Johnson, carried significant safety risks for incarcerated people. In the initial complaint, several women petitioned to proceed as "Jane Doe." They described how they had filed grievances against the prison and endured subsequent harassment. Women described barriers to medical care and abrupt removals from prison jobs. Others had their lives threatened because of vicious rumors guards had spread about them.[73] Furthermore, Magid worried that journalists would unearth sordid details from the women's crimes that could overshadow arguments for equal treatment.[74]

Other women stepped forward to put their names on the lawsuit. Years later, Mary Glover recalled how she thought the prison could not do anything worse than what they had already done to her. She was angry about the unequal treatment of incarcerated women and wanted to hold prison officials accountable for their actions.[75] Several women who had given testimony in the 1973 hearings also joined the lawsuit.[76] It was a tenacious, racially diverse coalition of incarcerated women and

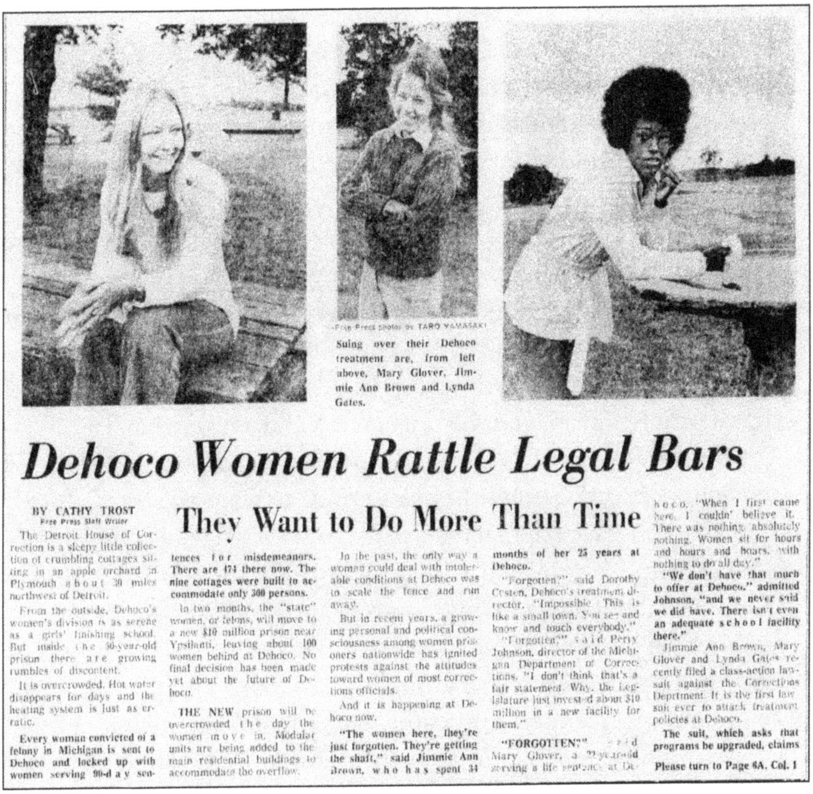

Free Press photos by TARO YAMASAKI

Suing over their Dehoco treatment are, from left above, Mary Glover, Jimmie Ann Brown and Lynda Gates.

Dehoco Women Rattle Legal Bars

They Want to Do More Than Time

BY CATHY TROST
Free Press Staff Writer

The Detroit House of Correction is a sleepy little collection of crumbling cottages sitting in an apple orchard in Plymouth about 30 miles northwest of Detroit.

From the outside, Dehoco's women's division is as serene as a girls' finishing school. But inside the 30-year-old prison there are growing rumbles of discontent.

It is overcrowded. Hot water disappears for days and the heating system is just as erratic.

Every woman convicted of a felony in Michigan is sent to Dehoco and locked up with women serving 90-day sentences for misdemeanors. There are 471 there now. The nine cottages were built to accommodate only 300 persons.

In two months, the "state" women, or felons, will move to a new $10 million prison near Ypsilanti, leaving about 100 women behind at Dehoco. No final decision has been made yet about the future of Dehoco.

THE NEW prison will be overcrowded the day the women move in. Modular units are being added to the main residential buildings to accommodate the overflow.

In the past, the only way a woman could deal with intolerable conditions at Dehoco was to scale the fence and run away.

But in recent years, a growing personal and political consciousness among women prisoners nationwide has ignited protests against the attitudes toward women of most corrections officials.

And it is happening at Dehoco now.

"The women here, they're just forgotten. They're getting the shaft," said Jimmie Ann Brown, who has spent 34 months of her 25 years at Dehoco.

"Forgotten?" said Dorothy Costen, Dehoco's treatment director. "Impossible. This is like a small town. You see and know and touch everybody."

"Forgotten?" said Perry Johnson, director of the Michigan Department of Corrections. "I don't think that's a fair statement. Why, the Legislature just invested about $10 million in a new facility for them."

"FORGOTTEN?" said Mary Glover, a 22-year-old serving a life sentence at Dehoco. "When I first came here, I couldn' believe it. There was nothing, absolutely nothing. Women sit for hours and hours and hours, with nothing to do all day."

"We don't have that much to offer at Dehoco," admitted Johnson, "and we never said we did have. There isn't even an adequate school facility there."

Jimmie Ann Brown, Mary Glover and Lynda Gates recently filed a class-action lawsuit against the Corrections Department. It is the first lawsuit ever to attack treatment policies at Dehoco.

The suit, which asks that programs be upgraded, claims

Please turn to Page 6A, Col. 1

Figure 2.2. *From left to right*: Mary Glover, Jimmie Ann Brown, and Lynda Gates photographed in the yard of Huron Valley Correctional Facility for Women shortly after they, along with several Jane Does, filed the *Glover v. Johnson* lawsuit in federal court. Cathy Trost, "Dehoco Women Rattle Legal Bars," *Detroit Free Press*, June 6, 1977. © Photographs by Taro Yamasaki—USA TODAY NETWORK.

lawyers who filed their complaint in the spring of 1977. The plaintiffs, "Mary Glover, Lynda Gates, Jimmie Ann Brown, and several Jane Does," demanded gender equality in Michigan's prisons.[77]

Glover was the country's first class-action lawsuit filed by incarcerated women claiming that the lack of prison programs violated their right to equal protection.[78] The incarcerated women who filed *Glover* claimed that the prison discriminated against them on the basis of sex, which violated the prisoners' right to equal protection and due process under the Fourteenth Amendment. This pushed the prisoners' rights movement in a new direction. Most prison litigation used the Eighth Amendment's protection against cruel and unusual punishment to enlist the federal courts in ordering sweeping changes to state prison systems. The cases attempted to raise standards in state prison systems by addressing a range of issues, from sanitary living conditions to education, work, law libraries, and employment.[79] Incarcerated women built upon this precedent by adding questions of sex and gender to the legal strategies of the prisoners' rights movement. Women claimed that the state, by denying them access to the courts and to equal programming to that of men, had violated their constitutional rights to due process and equal protection. In federal court, incarcerated women fused their own activism and experience with feminism and the prisoners' rights movement.[80]

The women's complaint was also a product of their lawyers' social and professional networks. *Glover* began when American law schools finally started accepting women in large numbers. Their original complaint alleged that the prison violated Title IX of the Education Amendments of 1972 because the state had offered significantly inferior vocational and educational opportunities for female prisoners compared to male prisoners. Michigan received federal funding for higher education in men's prisons, and incarcerated men could enroll in college courses, but no such opportunities existed for women. The state argued that programs for women, who made up a small proportion of the prison population, would be too burdensome and expensive. Discovery and negotiations before trial dragged on for months.

When the trial finally began, incarcerated women amended their complaint. They had recently been moved into the state prison, Huron Valley Correctional Facility for Women, while an overflow population rotated in and out of the Kalamazoo County Jail. In addition to their Fourteenth Amendment claim, the women claimed that the jail did not accommodate free expression of religious practices, a violation of the First Amendment, and that the conditions of their confinement amounted to cruel and unusual punishment, a violation of the Eighth Amendment. The plaintiffs later dropped their Title IX claim and focused the court's attention on their Fourteenth Amendment claims to due process and equal protection.[81]

The coalition convinced a federal judge that the women's prison maintained discriminatory policies. Federal judge John Feikens of the

Eastern District Court of Michigan was a Republican with a commitment to civil rights. Born in New Jersey in 1917, he moved to Michigan to attend Calvin College, a Dutch Christian Reformed liberal arts college in Grand Rapids. He received his law degree from the University of Michigan in 1941. He served as the chairman of the Civil Rights Commission in Michigan in 1963, the organization's inaugural year. Richard Nixon appointed Judge Feikens to the Eastern District Court of Michigan in 1970. Attorney Charlene Snow thought Feikens had a strong commitment to civil rights that was guided by his faith. Snow also reflected that Feikens had little patience for witnesses who supplied indirect answers to questions. When he thought a witness was trying to talk their way out of an answer, he interrupted testimony to tell that person "which way the wind was blowing." Snow described him as a meticulous judge who preferred direct, unequivocal language in his courtroom.[82] After two years of litigation and hearings, Feikens held that women should have equal access to programs that incarcerated men received across a growing network of prisons. In the 1979 opinion, he described the basic legal dilemma:

> The critical factor in this analysis is gender. It is clear that the State has provided for the separate incarceration of male and female prisoners, and that Huron Valley is the principal facility devoted to the custody of female prisoners. Thus, a female felon in the State of Michigan will be sent to Huron Valley by reason of her gender alone and will necessarily have access only to these programs currently available at that location. A male prisoner, on the other hand, can be classified or later transferred to a wide variety of prison facilities in the State and [in] general will have access to more opportunities than his female counterpart.[83]

Incarcerated women had convinced Feikens of the merits of their equal protection argument, and he ordered gender equality in prisons. Feikens wrote, "With the broad goals of rehabilitation and reintegration in mind, I find that, in general, the relationship between them and the actual practice at Huron Valley falls short of the requirements of equal protection under the Constitution. Significant discrimination against the female prison population occurs in several areas of programming at Huron Valley in violation of the Fourteenth Amendment and must be corrected."[84] Feikens issued a series of structural injunctions that ordered the prison to comply with constitutional standards.

The 1979 decision was a major victory for incarcerated women in Michigan and the nation. It was an attempt to reconceptualize the social, legal, and political status of incarcerated women.[85] Magid exclaimed, "This is a victory for women prisoners everywhere. . . . It's the first case in the country that's designed to improve the conditions [for] all incarcerated women."[86] Magid and Snow wrote to the plaintiffs, "We as your attorneys want you to understand that you have won, since this is the first big lawsuit in the country brought on behalf of women prisoners."[87] Incarcerated women forced the federal courts to review gender-based discrimination and rehabilitation in state prisons.[88] *Glover* served as a model for incarcerated women who brought similar lawsuits in Kentucky and Nebraska, while other states carried out reforms to head off lawsuits like *Glover*.[89]

The *Glover* decision contained three components that would change the way the women's prison operated. First, Judge Feikens held that women should have equal opportunities in schooling and job training to what male prisoners received. Feikens outlined how incarcerated women should have access to a range of programs that were available to incarcerated men in Michigan. Magid told the press, "We found that the programs available to women were so superficial as to give them no skills at all." She added, "The women had to take a custodial training course, for example. Part of that was instruction on how to clean a toilet. Male inmates do not have to take that course."[90] A home economics course was the only vocational training regularly offered in the women's prison. The final exam asked incarcerated women to cook a meal for four people. Incarcerated men, on the other hand, could participate in apprenticeship programs that focused on industrial jobs and were backed by the United States Department of Labor.[91] Magid noted, "Our position was that most of these women are going to get out of prison. Most of them are going to have to support families. They at least deserve an opportunity to gain skills so they can have a chance at a decent job at decent wages."[92] Magid and Snow underscored why it was important that women be prepared for reentry and be able to support themselves upon release.

Second, Feikens found deeply disturbing the prison's use of the Kalamazoo County Jail as a temporary solution to overcrowding and ordered the MDOC to stop using the jail as an overflow facility. Feikens agreed with the incarcerated women that placing prisoners in jail amounted to an inappropriate method of incarceration. Magid and Snow told prisoners, "We believe that the use of the Kalamazoo County Jail is so awful that almost any other plan, even adding more modular [trailers] at Huron Valley, would be better for all women prisoners."[93] Feikens agreed wholeheartedly. He toured the Kalamazoo County Jail in the middle of the trial to assess the conditions the women had described and became irate as he walked through the jail. Years later, Snow recalled Feikens's impression of the jail. At the time, women were forced to go to the bathroom or change sanitary napkins under the gaze of male guards, and in the middle of the tour, Feikens warned the sheriff that if the jail did not install shower curtains around the toilet within forty-eight hours, Feikens would do it himself.[94] In the jail, women were caged in crowded cells designed to be dehumanizing for detainees.[95] Legal scholars Malcolm Feeley and Edward Rubin have analyzed how the use of jails for prisoners has been problematic historically, and the incarceration of women in Kalamazoo in the 1970s illustrates several of these issues. Jails were designed to hold people who had not yet been convicted, and they offered fewer medical resources, educational courses, and job training.[96] *Glover* detailed how this was particularly detrimental to women. The court held that housing state prisoners in a county jail violated Michigan law.[97]

Third and finally, Feikens ruled that the women needed equal access to the courts. This ruling built on emerging gender-equality doctrine. Throughout the 1970s, the United States Supreme Court had asserted the prisoner's right to access the courts, but the cases came from men's facilities.[98] A large population of imprisoned women was a new phenomenon, and Feikens recognized that this new, growing subset of the prison population needed access to the courts. The 1979 decision ordered the women's prison to offer wages, higher education, and job training equivalent to what incarcerated men received.[99] The decision forced the prison to establish a new paralegal program for women.[100]

With *Glover*, incarcerated women and their attorneys carved a path for future prison litigation based on gender equality.[101] In a memorandum to the named plaintiffs, Magid and Snow reiterated, "Soon this case will be written in the lawbooks so that other attorneys around the

Figure 2.3. Photograph of one of the first paralegal classes of incarcerated women at Huron Valley, circa early 1980s. Program from the Detroit Chapter National Lawyers Guild 45th Anniversary Annual Dinner Celebrating the Struggle Against Women's Oppression, May 22, 1982. Courtesy of the National Lawyers Guild Detroit and Michigan Chapter.

country can use it to bring similar cases."[102] Glover remembered how the prison erupted with cheers when the prisoners received the news.[103] Incarcerated women and their attorneys viewed the legal victory as an extension of the women's movement because they had used the ideology of gender equality to critique the prison. Attorney Charlene Snow stated, "It is imperative that equal rights for women permeate all aspects of the criminal justice system, especially as it affects the women who are locked up in prisons and jails throughout the country."[104] Years later, Mary Glover reflected on the legal victory and, laughing, exclaimed, "We were all feminists!"[105] Incarcerated women, Snow, and other lawyers in the Detroit area understood *Glover* to be part of the women's movement.

In 1982, the Detroit Chapter of the National Lawyers Guild celebrated the *Glover* decision at its forty-fifth anniversary dinner. The event's program also included photographs of women advocating for the Equal Rights Amendment outside of the Republican National Convention in Detroit in 1980, the year that Ronald Reagan became the candidate. Black and white women raised their fists and wore buttons with slogans like "ERA YES" at a protest of the convention. Another photograph captured a different rally outside the 1980 Republican National Convention where men held large signs that read, "Womans Libbers E.R.A. Lesbians, Repent, Read the Bible While Your Able."[106] There was also a photograph of the first paralegal class at Huron Valley with a note from the prisoners thanking their attorneys: "Women prisoners everywhere with deeply felt gratitude proudly honor and give tribute to our attorneys: Judith Magid and Charlene Snow." They added, "Whose Excellent contributions in Protecting Prisoner's Rights are the finest in the country."[107] Leftist lawyers and activists connected the prisoners' rights movement to the struggle for equal rights for women and raised funds at the dinner to support incarcerated women in Michigan.

The excitement over the legal victories for incarcerated women was cut short as the relationships between incarcerated women and MDOC employees hardened and MDOC officials subverted interpretations of the *Glover* decision. In May 1980, Warden Gloria Richardson, one of several superintendents named as defendants in *Glover*, unveiled new regulations that turned the idea of gender equality against incarcerated women. Before the change, incarcerated women wore their own clothes and jewelry, but she reduced the amount of personal property women could possess, explaining that male and female prisoners should follow the same rules. Feikens had introduced the concept of parity in *Glover*, yet the 1979 decision acknowledged that incarcerated women have some specific needs, such as medical care and access to programs from which they had historically been excluded. Richardson twisted the concept of parity into gender neutrality by telling women they would have to accept the negative aspects of equal treatment.[108] Richardson aligned herself with the MDOC's adverse reaction to the prisoners' rights movement.

Incarcerated women were outraged, and Richardson gave them a target for their discontent. She misleadingly credited Glover for the new rules. Charmaine Cornish, Carroll Beverly, and Mary Glover protested. They argued that the new policy had nothing to do with the lawsuit, but "rather (Richardson's) own malice" toward incarcerated women.[109] They believed Richardson had created this policy as a form of retaliation against the named plaintiffs.[110] This was one of the many ways in which the MDOC refused to implement the reforms the women had proposed.

The change in property rules was also an attack on incarcerated women's femininity. Black feminist scholar Patricia Hill Collins has argued that "hegemonic femininity" is defined by gender difference, an idea that many of the incarcerated women subscribed to in their behavior and presentation of themselves. Women use their bodies in ways that are dissimilar to the way men use theirs: women's dress, sexuality, and reproductive abilities all constitute important criteria for evaluating femininity.[111] By stripping incarcerated women of their ability to express their femininity through makeup, jewelry, hairstyles, or clothing, Richardson degraded the women. She policed their ability to present themselves in gendered ways, even with the limited resources in prison.

The MDOC advanced an impoverished interpretation of feminism and parity that endured into the 1980s, supporting Richardson's gender-neutral rules. As Angela Davis has pointed out, "Demands for parity with men's prisons, instead of creating greater educational, vocational, and health opportunities for women prisoners, often have led to more repressive conditions for women."[112] A striking example of this occurred in 1983, when Tekla Miller was the deputy warden of Huron Valley Women's Prison. A journalist from the *Ann Arbor News* interviewed Miller about a prisoner who had attempted to escape. The woman had climbed the barbed wire fence surrounding Huron Valley, and officers apprehended her on the other side. The journalist asked Miller how many shots were fired, and she replied that none had been fired. The MDOC policy prohibited guards from blasting warning shots or shooting a female prisoner. Miller relayed the conversation to Director Johnson and later related that "[Johnson] was not pleased, nor was he looking forward to being interrogated by the press about his policy exception which made it look as though the department coddled women prisoners."[113] After this incident Johnson revoked the exception for incarcerated women. Miller, who considered herself a supporter of liberal feminism, interpreted the change as a victory for the parity movement.

Miller had started her corrections career at a time when the agency hired very few women. She began as a probation officer with the Oakland County Circuit Court in 1971 and was promoted to warden of Huron Valley Men's Prison in 1989. In her memoir, *The Warden Wore Pink*, she chronicled the gender-based discrimination, racism, and harassment she encountered at every stage of her career. At the same time, she rarely interrogated criminal legal institutions and their relationship to the feminist arguments for equal opportunity in *Glover*. Miller's interpretation of parity reveals how MDOC officials adopted a depleted logic of equality to amplify power dynamics in prison. In 1983, concerned with the bad press, prison officials permitted guards to shoot fleeing female prisoners after firing a warning shot.[114]

Incarcerated women continued documenting harassment and other grievances as the *Glover* case cycled in and out of federal courts. Glover covertly collected women's letters describing retaliation from prison employees. Guards used sexual assault, solitary confinement, and physical violence to dissuade prisoners from filing complaints in the prison or in court. Glover would walk along the track and women would join her to discuss the retaliation they encountered. She recorded complaints on anything available—notepads, old t-shirts, burlap laundry bags—and hid them in her mattress or laundry bag until she could safely move them out of the prison, delivering them either to lawyers or to Rosemary Sarri, a professor at the University of Michigan's School of Social Work. When Sarri visited the prison, often with little advance notice, she walked with Glover through the prison, which signaled to the guards and prisoners that grievances were being heard by people on the outside.[115]

Incarcerated women turned to the courts to end the harassment they received in retaliation for filing *Glover*. In June 1980, Glover testified that she received an inferior job because of the lawsuit although in the federal court hearing, prison officials denied Glover's claim that kitchen work was "considered the lowest job at Huron Valley."[116] She also complained that guards wrote tickets at an alarming pace: Glover's violations included reporting to the kitchen two minutes late one day and five minutes late another day that week. She believed no other prisoner was timed so closely for work shifts. Other forms of harassment were more menacing. Women were placed in solitary confinement, had privileges removed, and navigated threats of violence and degrading treatment. Feikens issued a temporary injunction prohibiting harassment of women named in the lawsuit. Prison guards, who acted with impunity, were largely undeterred.[117]

The Legacy of the Prisoners' Rights Movement for Women

Incarcerated women interpreted the gains of the women's movement, gave testimony to state legislators, and made their arguments in federal courts. *Glover* was a significant victory for gender equality in 1979; however, the implementation was uneven for the incarcerated women as prison officials repeatedly resisted the court's decrees and denied the prisoners' allegations. The legacy of *Glover* became fragile in subsequent decades as MDOC officials relied on interpretations of the decision that were hostile to women's equality and advancement in society.

Despite the efforts of the incarcerated women and their attorneys, many of their demands were never met. The litigation established programs that proved vulnerable. As criminologist Nicole Hahn Rafter has argued, "The parity movement's efforts to improve programs have an Achilles heel: they rely on institutional solutions. The gains of today can be eradicated by overcrowding tomorrow."[118] The history of the prisoners' rights movement for women illustrates this trend while also highlighting how gender equality hinged on broad political and cultural acceptance. In 1994, President Bill Clinton signed the Violent Crime Control and Law Enforcement Act, which made prisoners ineligible for Pell Grants.[119] The state reduced programming for men, giving prison officials a way to offer fewer education and job-training programs for women.[120] In 1999, Feikens found that the prison had adequately addressed the issues raised in the *Glover* lawsuit. The women appealed to the Sixth Circuit, but it affirmed that the main complaints raised in the 1970s had been resolved.[121]

Mary Glover was forty-eight years old when Governor Engler commuted her sentence, and she was released from prison in 2002. She went to a halfway house in Grand Rapids. She had prayed for release since she had first stepped into the Detroit House of Correction, but still, reentry was challenging, and there was little support for people navigating the obstacles reentry entailed. Glover recalled, "On my way out the door they handed me three condoms and five dollars. So that was their idea of what I really needed. . . . You know, I'm gay."[122] While she expected little of her jailers, the insult of that final encounter must have stung.

The prisoners' rights movement for women, despite its shortcomings, cemented pathways for reform and raised political consciousness. Incarcerated women engaged in constant power struggles as they fought for gender equality in prison. Through critique and action, coalitions of incarcerated women, attorneys, and activists underscored the contingency of mass incarceration. State officials pursued policies and practices that supported mass incarceration, but mass incarceration was not inevitable. Through activism, incarcerated women and their advocates imagined alternatives to overcrowded prisons and programs that would help women pursue education or meaningful skills in prison. Women fought mass imprisonment with arguments for equality and opportunity as they negotiated the terms of their increasingly significant role in Michigan's prison regime.

3

Contesting Feminism

Self-Defense, Activism, and Clemency for Women in Michigan

Warm, humid summer weather had settled into Lansing, Michigan, by the end of July 1979. Juanita Thomas, a Black woman, was a member of the cleaning staff at Michigan State University, where she had worked for ten years. On Thursday, July 26, she left work at 1:30 a.m. and drove to her mother's house to pick up her three teenage children. She piled them into her car, drove them home, and put them to bed. Her boyfriend of seventeen years, Willie Hammond, was out. Thomas was not too concerned as Hammond, a Black man who had lived with Thomas for six years would sometimes leave for a few days and party before returning to Thomas's apartment. Thomas tried to track him down on Friday, July 27, and Saturday, July 28. Neighbors were spreading rumors that he was putting moves on a white woman at a local bar, and on Friday, neighbors told Thomas that Willie was hanging out on a landlord's porch with two other women.[1]

Juanita Thomas was born in rural Mississippi in 1942. She moved to Lansing with her mother and brother when she was thirteen years old. They lived across the street from the Hammond family, who were also Black migrants from Mississippi. When Thomas was nineteen years old, fourteen-year-old Willie Hammond joined his family in Michigan. Thomas and Hammond started sleeping together, and Thomas had a baby girl by the end of Hammond's first year in the Midwest. Thomas and Hammond fell in love quickly and maintained their relationship into adulthood. They both grew up in working-poor families, and they struggled with poverty as adults.[2]

Hammond's violence against Thomas was no secret. Neighbors described the many times he chased her out of their apartment and pursued her in the street. He would whip her, and he once fired a gun, narrowly missing her, while she visited a friend. Hammond tried to choke her with a bicycle chain when she was working at Michigan State University, and her coworkers witnessed the attack. Hammond would "hit her and follow her and sabotage her car, then promise never to hurt her again."[3] Thomas once purchased a set of new furniture with a loan. A few days later she came home to discover that Hammond had slashed the upholstered couch and chairs with a butcher knife. Police, employers, and social service agencies knew that Thomas was a survivor of intimate partner violence. Police documents revealed many visits to Thomas's home and frequent calls, and some officers were friendly with Thomas when they ran into her at the grocery store. Police arrested Hammond only once—for whipping Thomas with a bicycle chain. He served ten days in jail and returned home.[4]

On Saturday, July 28, 1979, Thomas and Hammond reunited and went out together. When they returned home, Hammond passed out and Thomas phoned Hammond's mother and chatted with her about the weekend. (Thomas often checked in with Hammond's mother, whom she had known since her childhood.) In the early morning hours on Sunday, July 29, Hammond tried to force Thomas to perform oral sex. She refused and they fought. Hammond tried to stab her with a letter opener. Missing her, Hammond then bit Thomas. She reached for a knife she had hidden under the bed and stabbed Hammond repeatedly. Thomas ran into the street partially dressed and screamed for help. Police arrived quickly and detained Thomas after finding Hammond's body in the apartment. In the spring of 1980, Thomas was on trial for murder.[5]

Thomas's criminal case activated a broad coalition of feminist groups, activists, incarcerated women, artists, and anti–death penalty attorneys. Feminist organizations contended that a woman has a right to self-defense, especially when confronted with sexual violence. Activists and incarcerated women worked to portray Thomas's story in a way that was legible to women across class, race, and geographic boundaries. Finally, nationally prominent anti–death penalty attorney Andrea Lyon and her team of clinical students at the University of Michigan worked with the coalition to secure Thomas's freedom. The establishment of the Michigan Women's Justice and Clemency Project and passage of the Violence Against Women Act in 1994 helped bring Thomas's time in prison to an end. The history of Thomas's case reflects the ways in which incarcerated people, activists, and criminal defense attorneys focused attention on both intimate partner violence and Black women's growing significance and poor treatment in courts and prisons. This broad coalition of activists with different resources, strengths, and goals raised awareness of violence against women and critiqued the criminal legal system.

This chapter explores the history of the complicated relationship between criminal legal reform and feminist coalitions in the late twentieth century. Incarcerated women and activists pursued legal advocacy while confronting a political landscape committed to tough-on-crime policies. Historian Danielle McGuire's retelling of the civil rights movement refreshes the well-known narrative of the civil rights movement by centering sexual violence against Black women and their activism to document and prevent rape and preserve bodily integrity.[6] In this chapter, I apply a similar approach of centering Black women and feminist activism in the historical rise of mass incarceration. The chapter reveals how coalitions that worked to raise awareness of intimate partner violence challenged the terms of women's confinement. The feminist activism and carceral reform work produced uneven results in the 1970s and 1980s. The shortcomings of initiatives to raise awareness of violence against women highlight the many ways that gender, race, and class were entangled and shaped women's experiences in criminal legal institutions.

Angela Davis has used the term "carceral feminism" to describe the demand to criminalize and imprison people who "engage in gender violence," and in the 1980s and 1990s, "carceral feminism" mobilized different groups to endorse punitive measures against people who were violent against women.[7] As criminologist Beth Richie has explained, "By likening [intimate partner violence] to other forms of assault, we believed that the issue would be taken more seriously by criminal justice authorities, social service providers and the general public. . . . This helped to lead to some important legal changes and shifts in public consciousness."[8] This chapter explores how women convicted of violent crimes used the discourse and strategies of antiviolence movements to fight for carceral reforms, sentence reductions, and freedom. Through high-profile cases, clemency requests, and state postconviction petitions, incarcerated women inserted themselves in national conversations, critiquing criminal legal institutions through feminist frameworks. Incarcerated women leveraged feminist ideology that grew out of the antirape and battered women's movements to seek reform. The establishment of shelters for women and children, antiviolence legislation, and incarceration of people committing family violence established institutional reforms that were fortified in the legal and carceral landscape. The activism in this period illustrates a complementary and capacious understanding of the feminist movements in the late twentieth century.

Development of the Battered Women's Defense

Thomas's criminal trial took place in the midst of significant shifts in the way Americans understood self-defense for survivors of intimate partner violence. In the mid-1960s, American women began to speak more publicly about violence in heterosexual relationships, and informal conversations among friends and within communities raised awareness of violence against women. In her scholarship on Black women, violence, and the criminal legal system, Beth Richie has described how, "in daycare centers, around kitchen tables, and in other everyday gathering places, women began to talk about their experiences of abuse in their homes, and because there were no other options available, they began to help one another." The shelters for women experiencing intimate partner violence that opened in the early 1970s were often managed by survivors. This grassroots activism was soon followed by formal legal changes. Attorneys defending women who fought back or killed assailants developed the "battered women's defense." The term "battered women's defense" captured a set of legal strategies deployed by attorneys in the late 1970s and 1980s, grounded in the assertion of a woman's right to defend herself from physical and sexual violence. Psychological ideas at the time contended that the effects of intimate partner violence amounted to "battered women's syndrome," and advanced the notion that women who survived enduring abuse had a unique response to threats of violence.[9] Psychologist Lenore Walker contended that women in abusive relationships became codependent on their partners, which explained why they stayed in the relationship. Carol Wharton, a sociologist at Michigan State University and leader of the Battered Women's Defense Committee, a Lansing-based group that provided shelter and services for women and children experiencing family violence, explained, "The battered woman and her assailant are in a relationship of extreme psychological dependency: most battered women continue

their relationships with their abusive mates because of emotional attach-
ments, hoping that the abuse will stop."[10] The battered women's defense
hinged on the legal definition of self-defense. Attorneys applied it to a
range of cases where women killed abusive partners or to help explain
why women resorted to violence to protect themselves even after enduring physical and sexual abuse in a long-term relationship.[11]

In North Carolina in 1974, a case mobilized a wide-ranging and dedi-
cated coalition of supporters that shifted the way Americans talked about
incarcerated women and sexual violence. Joan (pronounced Jo-Anne)
Little, a Black woman, stood accused of murdering a white jailer who
sexually assaulted her while she was incarcerated. Little was twenty years
old and was the only woman incarcerated in the Beaufort County Jail
in Washington, North Carolina. In 1970, Washington, the county seat,
had over twelve thousand residents, 38 percent of whom were Black. The
KKK, whose membership had surged in the area in the 1960s, terrorized
Black people in Beaufort County. Little, whom police had targeted in the
past, was jailed on shoplifting charges. Clarence Alligood, the night jailer,
was a sixty-two-year-old white man who stood five feet eight inches tall
and weighed two hundred pounds. As he sexually assaulted Little, she
fought back and stabbed him with an ice pick he stored in his office. A
policeman who was detaining a Black woman for intoxication found Alligood's body, naked from the waist down, in Little's cell at 4:00 a.m. on
August 27, 1974. Little fled and a week-long search ensued. She turned
herself in with the help of local civil rights attorneys.[12]

Little's case resonated with antirape organizations and Black organizers
who had been involved in the civil rights movement. Different chapters
of the Joan Little Defense Fund mobilized across the country. Rosa Parks,
who had moved to Detroit after she led the Montgomery bus boycott, led
a fundraising drive for Little in Michigan. Parks had started her activist
career investigating rape and sexual violence of Black women in Alabama
in the 1940s, and her commitment to antiviolence and antirape work was
central to her activism in the civil rights movement. The Joan Little Defense Fund and the Southern Poverty Law Center, a civil rights organization based in Montgomery, Alabama, raised a combined five hundred
thousand dollars on Little's behalf. The funds helped secure private investigators, legal advice, and experts on body language to select jurors—all of
which was crucial for a fair trial and led to an acquittal for Little.[13]

Little's case made national headlines, sparking debates about Black power, feminism, and prison abolition. Danielle McGuire has analyzed how a collection of social-justice organizations came together to support Little: women's liberation organizations argued that a woman had a right to self-defense and freedom from sexual violence; Black Power groups interpreted Little's case as a terrible example of police violence and the injustices of criminal courts in the South. Furthermore anti–death penalty activists saw Little's case as a chance to highlight the endemic problems of capital punishment in America. After seventy-eight hours of deliberation, a jury acquitted Little. Little's treatment in the criminal legal system drew national attention to the many flaws in policing, courts, and corrections that splintered over issues of class, race, and gender.[14]

A Michigan criminal case that went to trial shortly after Little's acquittal also changed the way many Americans talked about domestic violence. Francine Hughes, a white woman, went to trial in 1977 for killing her ex-husband in Ingham County, the same court where Thomas would be tried in 1980. Born in 1947, Francine married her husband when she was sixteen years old. She dropped out of Jackson High School, and the couple lived in the small, rural town of Dansville. They had four children. James Hughes, who went by Mickey, was a white man who had been working in a nursing home when they got married. He never finished high school and struggled to keep a steady job. In the first seven years of their marriage, the Hugheses moved twenty-two times. Francine discovered that her husband was having an affair, filed for divorce, and received welfare benefits. However, Mickey got in a serious car accident and required intense care during his recovery. Eventually, he returned to live with Francine.[15]

Mickey Hughes had been drinking heavily on March 9, 1977, the day he died. He threatened to "get even" with Francine, who had allegedly been seeing another man. Mickey beat Francine and then forbade her from making dinner for their four children. Mickey tore up Francine's textbooks for her secretarial courses, burned them, and demanded that she drop out of school. She called the police. Two deputies arrived and reported that they did not see an assault, so they left the Hugheses' home. When Francine tried to make dinner, Mickey resumed beating her. He threw the meal on the floor, threatened her with a knife, and raped her.[16]

That evening, Francine poured gasoline around the bed where Mickey was passed out, and lit it on fire. As Hughes described the incident, "I walked into the bedroom . . . with the gas can and I started pouring it around on the floor. There was an urgent whisper saying, 'Do it! Do it! Do it!' over and over and I just kept on." Mickey Hughes died in the fire. One neighbor saw the flames licking the house and thought that Francine or one of the children might be in danger. When she saw the damage, neighbor Alice Quemby concluded, "He's killed her." With her children in the car, Hughes drove directly to the Ingham County Jail and told police she had killed her ex-husband. Harry Tift, the Ingham County sheriff's detective, had seen many "domestic killings," the term used at the time, and he had told Hughes that if she had acted in self-defense she was unlikely to be charged with first-degree murder. At trial, Hughes argued that she killed her husband in self-defense because she was a battered woman and had gone temporarily insane. Ten of the twelve jurors were women.[17]

Newspaper coverage of the trial drew class, gender, and cultural boundaries by comparing white people in northern and southern states. The *Lansing State Journal* described the couple in the following way: "Francine Moran and Mickey Hughes grew up in Michigan, but their roots were in the hills of Kentucky. Their parents were from that area, and the attitudes persisted."[18] The paper reported that the couple grew up in families where men were "strong and silent" and "hit each other (often) and women (occasionally)." Each set of parents had had little education and had married as teenagers. Their children followed along similar paths. The coverage of the Hughes family reinforced a regional binary that was solidified in some ways by the civil rights movement of the 1950s and 1960s. As historian Matthew Lassiter has argued, the emphasis on de jure segregation in the South in the 1950s and 1960s "shaped the trajectory and limited reach" of the social movement and reinforced the myth of an exceptional South.[19] As applied to the Hugheses' case, the rhetoric of southern exceptionalism mapped boundaries around morality and class among white people in Michigan.

Narratives of regional differences between northern and southern states perpetuated myths that also served a political purpose. They suggested that intimate partner violence was not a deep-rooted problem in the Midwest, but something isolated and imported from the South. The narratives affirmed "family values" and critiqued Mickey Hughes for violating the patriarchal expectation that he should provide for his family, but eschewed discussions of family violence. Elizabeth Pleck has argued that the "family ideal," defined as a commitment to domestic privacy, family stability, and conjugal and parental rights, was the most significant obstacle to domestic-violence reform in America.[20] Journalists detailed how Mickey Hughes refused to work to support his family. "The real problem was Mickey's shiftlessness. He kept changing jobs, changing apartments. In the first six months [of their marriage], they moved six times."[21]

Francine Hughes's trial established a rallying point for feminist groups, and they urged courts to embrace the battered women's defense, arguing that Hughes had been living in fear of her ex-husband and that the murder was not premeditated. The *Lansing State Journal* followed the activists' demands for new legal applications of self-defense, particularly for women in abusive relationships. Hughes's court-appointed attorney, Aryon Greydanus, told the jury, "Whatever Francine Hughes did, it was done in the context of her experience."[22] Greydanus referred to the abuse Hughes had endured. In his opening remarks at trial, Greydanus described Hughes as a battered woman who had acted in self-defense.[23] Feminist organizers set up the Francine Hughes Defense Committee. The group advocated on her behalf, collected funds for the trial, and raised awareness about interpersonal violence. The committee brought together a coalition of different legal and feminist organizations. The Lansing chapter of the National Lawyers Guild, the New American Movement, and Sisters for Human Equality contributed resources.[24] One of the founding members, Daria Hyde, recalled, "We wanted to tie the situation into the battered women's movement to show hers was not an isolated incident. . . . A lot of people sympathized with Francine . . . feminists, church-going people. They saw it (her situation) was not humane." Throughout the trial, the Francine Hughes Defense Committee sent Greydanus literature on the battered women's syndrome.[25] Peter Houk, the Ingham County prosecutor, contested that the case was a straightforward murder case and not "a women's rights case."[26]

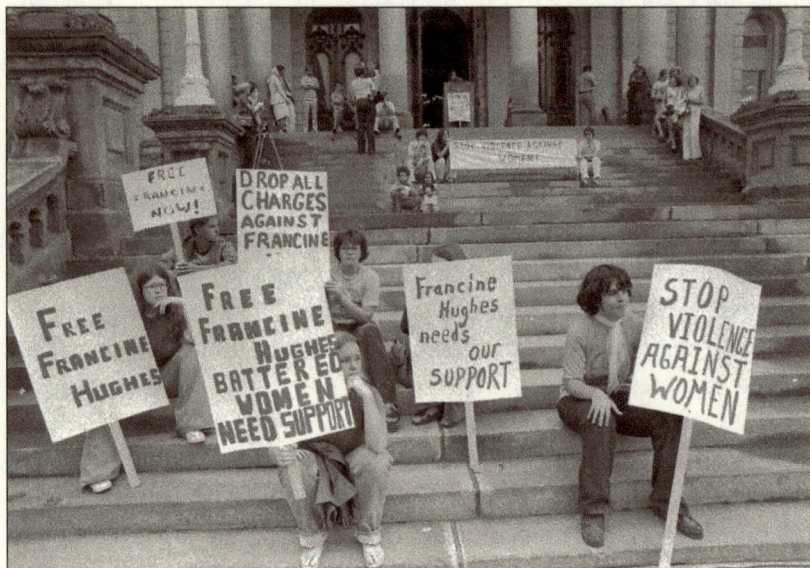

Figure 3.1. A rally in support of Francine Hughes held on the steps of the state capitol in Lansing, Michigan, September 1, 1977. Vickki Dozier, "40th Anniversary of 'Burning Bed,'" *Lansing State Journal*, March 5, 2017. © Lansing State Journal File Photos—USA TODAY NETWORK.

The trial judge stepped down from the case after making a remark that showed bias: at the arraignment Judge Michael Harrison asked, "What kind of a woman kills her husband?"[27] The remark underscored a lack of knowledge regarding intimate partner violence, as well as a paternalistic view of women's role in the family—which was, apparently, to endure whatever abuse their husbands inflicted. Judge Ray Hotchkiss replaced Judge Harrison. Judge Hotchkiss prohibited the prosecutors from pursuing both a first-degree murder charge and the charge of felony of arson that resulted in a murder, which frustrated the prosecution. They went forward with the first-degree murder charge, which carried a mandatory sentence of life without the possibility of parole.[28]

After a dramatic trial the jury found Hughes not guilty by reason of temporary insanity. The verdict renewed debates over gendered narratives of women who fought back against assailants. The Hughes trial also provoked a national conversation about implementing more protections for women in cases of intimate partner violence. Some feminist groups hailed the acquittal as a major victory for the battered women's movement. Others criticized the insanity defense and argued that it reinforced the stereotype of an irrational woman unable to rationally confront violence to preserve her life and bodily integrity. Hyde, a founding member of the Francine Hughes Defense Committee, reflected, "It was obvious she cared a lot for her kids. She was a loving person and she had tried in a thousand ways to change the situation." Hyde spoke to the long-term pattern of violence in the Hugheses' home and advanced a humane interpretation of Hughes, who had also been failed by the criminal legal system.[29]

Francine Hughes became a symbol of the anti–domestic violence movement in the 1980s. Faith McNulty, a writer for the *New Yorker*, wrote a book about Hughes entitled *The Burning Bed*. It was adapted

Figure 3.2. Francine Hughes and her attorney, Aryon Greydanus, walk into the courtroom to hear the verdict on November 3, 1977. Vickki Dozier, "40th Anniversary of 'Burning Bed,'" *Lansing State Journal*, March 5, 2017. © Lansing State Journal File Photos—USA TODAY NETWORK

for a made-for-television film and aired on NBC in 1984, with Farrah Fawcett playing Francine Hughes and Paul Le Mat playing Mickey. Over seventy-five million viewers, a massive audience at the time, tuned in. The film revitalized attention to and public debate about domestic violence and the battered women's defense, and "burning-bed syndrome" became a popular and controversial term. The show made Hughes an icon of feminism, but she did not welcome the spotlight. She told *People* magazine, "I don't feel like I have to explain myself to anybody, and I don't need pity or sympathy. I'm just an ordinary person." Nonetheless, her story inspired action. Social-service agencies and law enforcement started to develop policies aimed at decreasing and preventing intimate partner violence. In 1977, fewer than a dozen shelters for battered women existed in the United States. By 1984, over seven hundred shelters had opened around the country.[30]

Focusing on Francine's interpretation of events, *Burning Bed* largely omitted the work of the Francine Hughes Defense Committee. Notably, some women who worked for the committee became committed to helping victims of intimate partner violence in their careers. Kate Young, who was a member of the Francine Hughes Defense Committee, reflected, "The trial really had a big impact on me. It made me realize how serious domestic violence was and how important it is to make alternatives for the women." Young became the assistant director of the Domestic Violence Prevention and Treatment Board. She and other members established the Council Against Domestic Assault (CADA), which managed shelters for women and children who were victims of domestic violence.[31] By 1980, CADA had established a twenty-four-hour counseling and crisis line and ran a temporary home for women and children in Ingham County. Jo Nol, a member of CADA, explained, "Our purpose is not to help women leave their husbands. Our purpose is to help a woman do what she wants to do."[32] Nol emphasized how their work provided space and time for women to evaluate their options in a peaceful setting. In the wake of the Hughes trial, feminist groups also identified and supported women facing criminal charges after enduring years of violence. Even though the Francine Hughes trial and emerging activism around violence against women raised public awareness of formerly private problems, most survivors who killed partners in self-defense were convicted and incarcerated.[33]

The Trial of Juanita Thomas

In the midst of increasing awareness of intimate partner violence and the development of carceral feminism, Juanita Thomas was put on trial for the murder of Willie Hammond in 1980. Peter Houk, the same elected Ingham County prosecutor who had lost in the Hughes trial, presented the state's case against Thomas. In 1984, Houk gave an interview for *People* magazine in which he stated that he could not sit passively by while there was "open season on men."[34] The hunting reference served as a sharp rebuke to the work of activists, incarcerated women, and defense attorneys who had organized to create a fuller picture of female defendants facing criminal charges for killing abusive partners. Feminist groups like CADA supported Thomas through her trial. Thomas confronted racialized views of criminality and of Black women that created more obstacles to freedom than Hughes had experienced in the same county. But while race played a significant role in the trial, class and sexuality also shaped Thomas's ordeal. As Kimberlé Crenshaw has demonstrated, the intersectional ways in which race, gender, class, and sexuality operate are crucial in constructing the experiences of women of color in the criminal legal system, and all of these factors charted the course of Thomas's trial and incarceration.[35]

In 1980, only approximately 5 percent of Lansing's population was Black, and Thomas's trial was held in Mason, a town that was 98 percent white.[36] Thomas was frustrated by the composition of the all-white jury, two men and ten women, and she objected to the way in which the court assembled the jury and conducted *voir dire* of the potential jurors. Thomas wanted her attorney to be the one to conduct *voir dire*, and she also submitted questions designed to determine jurors' views on race. However, the court denied Thomas's requests. The judge conducted *voir dire* and did not ask the questions she submitted, which, Thomas argued, put her at a disadvantage.[37] Thomas recalled how "it was not a jury of my peers" and emphasized that she didn't think the jurors knew anything about Black culture.[38]

Throughout their seventeen years together, Thomas and Hammond had struggled to stay afloat financially. Hammond's main source of income in the 1970s was his Social Security benefits, which were around four hundred dollars per month. Thomas described how "that was his money. He spent it the way he wanted. He drank it up, bought grass."[39] Furthermore, Hammond would steal from Thomas when he needed cash. Thomas, for her part, maintained a reliable job as a janitor at Michigan State University. The paychecks often did not stretch far enough. Thomas's monthly income in 1979 was between $212 and $218, which barely covered her rent of $210. With three children living at home, she received $145 per month from Aid for Dependent Children. When she was arrested, she had no savings. David Hayes, whom Thomas worked for at Michigan State University, paid 10 percent of her bond, which had been set to $7,500, so that she could be released before the trial. In her affidavit of financial condition, Thomas pleaded with the court to keep Greydanus, the attorney who had represented her at the arraignment and the same lawyer who had represented Hughes. It is not clear whether Thomas knew of Greydanus's success in the Hughes case, but in the small comments box on the financial affidavit she made clear her attempt to secure Greydanus when she wrote, "Please see if I could keep him for a lawyer." Instead, the state assigned defense attorney W. Charles Kingsley to represent her.[40]

Thomas was abused by Hammond for many years prior to his death. Hammond broke Thomas's jaw once and she spent time in the hospital recovering. In 1978, Hammond kicked Thomas while they were outside of a Western Union office and demanded money from her. Later in the year, Hammond poured alcohol over Thomas and punched her in the head.[41] Thomas changed the locks to her apartment two different times, but Hammond busted through the door. Thomas gave up the strategy of changing her locks because it was too expensive to have the door replaced.[42] She later explained, "I knew there was nothing I could do to change him. I was hoping he could change himself. I think in his own destructive way he did care."[43] Thomas called the Lansing Police Department many times. She described how police encouraged her and her children to spend the night in the station so that Hammond could calm down. Thomas was fighting for acknowledgement in a system that did not yet recognize intimate partner violence.

Thomas's memory of their last fight was patchy, but she was adamant that she acted in self-defense when she killed Hammond. She remembered talking to his mother on the phone. After she hung up, Hammond tried to force her to perform oral sex despite the fact that the couple had an agreement that she would not perform oral sex after he had been out for a day or more. She refused. She remembered,

> He reached on the dresser which was near the bed. There was a letter opener on it. He got it and I reached under the bed, got the butcher knife out and just started to hit him again and again. All I wanted to do was get out of the house, not kill him. I got to the bedroom door. Somehow he was still hold-ing me I remember hitting him again. I ran down the stairs out of the door. It was storming bad. I was thinking he was still after me. I ran someplace, knocked on some door then I fell only had on panties and bra. I was later told some man in court I never remember seeing before say he call the po-lice and covered me with his coat. I could not remember who I was. I been told one of the police knew who I were.[44]

Several witnesses testified that they had seen Thomas covered in blood, wearing only her underwear, running from her apartment, and drop-ping to the ground while moaning, "He wouldn't stop." Officers from the Lansing Police Department testified that they found Thomas partially dressed and "speaking incoherently." Thomas told police, "He made me do it; he came after me, I killed him, I know I killed him. . . . I had to do it, he wouldn't give me my clothes, he came after me. I had to stab him, he is dead." Five hours after police detained her she repeated similar statements in a recorded interrogation.[45] In her statement to police, she also described how the argument started when she found her son had a swollen black eye and Hammond had stolen twenty-one dollars from him. Thomas stated, "He got his eye messed up and he won't admit who did it. . . . But I know."[46]

Through the mid-twentieth century, the criminal legal system upheld stereotypes of Black women as lascivious, hypersexual, and deserving of punishment. Thomas's trial illustrated the harm those pernicious de-pictions caused. In his closing arguments the prosecutor took time to poke holes at Thomas's memory of her ordeal. He suggested that Thomas would have been unable to stab Hammond if she were pinned on her back on top of their bed. The prosecutor told the jury, "Maybe one of the most significant physical pieces of evidence in this case is Juanita Thomas herself. We've heard a lot in the case about Willie Hammond; mean guy, not a nice guy; strange, he's a fighter, has fought with knives, he's a mean guy. . . . Does she have any injuries? She has a small surface, it doesn't even bleed, cut on the palm of her hand."[47] The prosecutor suggested that Thomas should have had more scars, bruises, or physical injuries from the night Hammond died. Ultimately, he questioned Thomas's credibility.

Feminist groups in Michigan worked on public education about intimate partner violence and lent support to Thomas during her trial. The Battered Women's Defense Committee (BWDC) was a group of fifty people from Detroit, Lansing, and Ann Arbor. The group held press conferences and rallied in Lansing to demonstrate their support for Thomas. Spokespersons for BWDC argued that the prosecution needed to "understand the circumstances of Ms. Thomas as a battered woman."[48] Instead, the prosecution argued that Thomas had not fought with Hammond as she described but killed him in his sleep. Two of Hammond's sisters, Kimberly Swinton and Phyllis Walker, testified that they had heard Thomas threaten to kill Hammond on the day he died. During the cross-examination, the defense attorney tried to establish Hammond's prior acts of violence toward Thomas, but the court ruled that the questions were irrelevant.[49]

The trial lasted three weeks. The jurors deliberated for one evening and the following morning. They returned with a guilty verdict for first-degree murder on June 23, 1980, and Thomas was sentenced later in the summer to life without the possibility of parole, the mandatory penalty.

Years later, when a team of attorneys put together a state postconviction petition for Thomas, they learned that many jurors were not aware of Hammond's prior arrest record. Police records revealed that he had been arrested more than thirteen times regarding allegations of violence. Furthermore, on the day when jury selection began, a Lansing detective had ordered the destruction of a bloody screen from Thomas's bedroom. Police had noticed the blood stains on the screen, which prompted them to enter the apartment on the night Hammond died. Photographs of the crime scene omitted the bedside table where Hammond had allegedly kept the letter opener and the window where the screen had been. The members of the jury were unaware of the destruction of evidence by the state when they reached their verdict. This physical evidence would have bolstered Thomas's version of the fight. The prosecutor theorized that Hammond had been asleep when

Thomas stabbed him, but the photos of the blood stains on the screen and the dresser presumably would have shown splatters suggesting that Hammond had been standing upright and pinning Thomas down as she stabbed him. The evidence could have been central to demonstrating that Thomas had told the truth and her memory of events could be supported by the physical evidence.[50]

Race infused the trial while demonstrating the pernicious aspects of a "color-blind" legal system.[51] Thomas reflected, "I had an all white jury. That's not a jury of my peers. I never had a chance."[52] Criminologist Nicole Gonzalez Van Cleve has investigated "color-blind" justice and after a decade studying the Cook County Criminal Court in Chicago, concluded that "race is everywhere but nowhere," meaning that while racial prejudice was not overtly present in court proceedings, it informed the norms, culture, and practices of the administration of justice. The courtroom practices amounted to what she calls a "racial degradation ceremony," in which mostly white professionals, judges, and employees reinforce race through "structural arrangements, in the policing of racial boundaries, in the recoding of rhetoric, and in the delineation of defendants." The courtroom proceedings construct narratives of defendants who are "deserving or undeserving."[53] Gonzalez Van Cleve's conclusions can be applied to other courtrooms around the country, such as the one in which Thomas was convicted. Thomas was surrounded by white professionals, and a white jury sentenced her to life in prison.

Ingham County had a history of racial oppression, which is illustrated by the treatment of Malcolm X, who spent much of his childhood in Ingham County. In 1931, Earl Little, Malcolm X's father, was killed in a streetcar accident in Michigan. His death certificate called it a suicide although his family believed the Black Legion, a white-supremacist group, was involved in the death. Thereafter the state sent Malcolm X to foster care and reform schools, and for two years he attended Mason High School, where his experience informed his early views on race relations.[54]

Mason and nearby towns in central Michigan supported KKK activity through the 1970s. KKK former grand dragon and chaplain Robert Miles lived in the town of Howell, less than thirty miles east of Mason. In 1971, Miles and four other white supremacists tarred and feathered Dr. Richard Wiley Brownlee, a principal of Willow Run High School who worked on integrating Ypsilanti schools. In 1972, Miles was linked to the firebombing of ten buses belonging to Pontiac schools as the city launched a school integration plan.[55] Such episodes of racial terrorism offer some windows into white attitudes about Black people in central Michigan in the seventies and demonstrate why Thomas may have been skeptical that she would receive a fair trial. The racial history of Ingham County hung over white jurors judging Black defendants.

The feminist groups that had rallied to support her at trial faded away once she began her sentence. She explained, "I did not have money to do better. The women from the battered shelter was aid to me. I started to feel they only wanted to be in the news. Once I went to prison they soon forgot about me real quick. I don't think no one in the system cared what happen to me being (abused). It was black on black and we wasn't married."[56] Thomas had identified some of the intersectional ways in which power operated in the courtroom. As a Black woman with little money, Thomas had also been stuck with a state-appointed attorney who did little to mount a rigorous defense. He rarely objected at trial, did not conduct a proper investigation, and infrequently asked questions during cross-examination.[57]

Figure 3.3. Juanita Thomas serving a life sentence. Jim Rasmussen, "Behind Bars for Life: Woman Who Killed Boyfriend Still Seeks Justice," *Lansing State Journal*, August 1, 1988. Credit: © Greg DeRuiter—USA TODAY NETWORK.

The state sent Thomas to prison at a time when Michigan, like other states, imprisoned a rapidly growing population of women. In 1985, the Michigan Department of Corrections (MDOC) held 530 women in two women's prisons and a camp: Huron Valley Correctional Facility, Florence Crane Correctional Facility, and Camp Pontiac. By 1987, Michigan prisons housed 925 women.[58] Through newsletters, work with filmmakers, and the efforts of activists, incarcerated women sustained interest in their cases and shed light on prison conditions.

Black magazines also paid attention to the ways race and gender shaped cases of battered women claiming self-defense. In 1981, *Ebony* magazine published an article that analyzed battered women's syndrome. The article focused on Thomas: "The case of a 37-year-old Lansing, Mich., Black woman could be indicative of the judicial system's attitude toward women who are backed into a corner and feel they have to protect their lives."[59] The article emphasized the disproportionate impact of intimate partner violence on women of color. It also drew attention to how gender intersected with race. Most prosecutors and judges were men, and, *Ebony* reported, many men struggled with "accepting the notion that battered women have the right to take whatever action is necessary to protect their lives." Sarah Gorman, administrative director of CADA in Lansing, stated, "That attitude has been reflected in many court cases where women have injured or killed their abusers."[60] From prison, Thomas continued to be a cause célèbre for intimate partner violence and incarcerated women.

Carceral Feminism and Antiviolence Movements

In the mid-1990s, the punitive turn and its connection to feminism accelerated. The Violence Against Women Act (VAWA) had origins in George H. W. Bush's administration, and President Bill Clinton signed the federal legislation in 1994. VAWA is just one part of the massive Violent Crime Control and Law Enforcement Act, the largest criminal legal bill in American history. Commonly known as the crime bill of 1994, this omnibus legislation committed more than ten billion dollars for the construction of new prisons. It also put in place a federal "three strikes" law and promoted hiring and expanding resources for thousands of police officers. The law also ended federal funding of higher education in prisons, which had been a lifeline for many incarcerated people. VAWA established the Office of Violence Against Women in the Department of Justice and was designed to protect survivors of domestic violence while punishing those who engaged in violence against women. In some ways it marked a major victory for anti–domestic violence activists, but it also expanded the carceral state because it relied on the criminal legal system to respond to intimate partner violence. Emily Thuma argues that the passage of VAWA "is perhaps the starkest example of how the claim to crack down on individual perpetrators of violence against women became a critical lever of legitimacy for expanding the carceral state."[61] Much has been made of how the late-twentieth-century antiviolence movements contributed to the growth of mass imprisonment. To complement this narrative, it is also worth examining how women in prison used the new legal landscape to petition for their release.

The antiviolence movements changed the culture within women's prisons in three important ways. First, the movement raised awareness and gave women opportunities to discuss trauma and violence in their personal histories. Second, at the height of "law-and-order" politics, incarcerated women reframed the label of convicted criminal by claiming histories of intimate partner violence. They compiled evidence for legal appeals, postconviction petitions, and clemency applications. Third, incarcerated women used the legal system to confront and condemn sexual violence within prisons.

Some of these changes are apparent in the case of Violet Allen. Allen, a white woman, was incarcerated at Robert Scott Correctional Facility in Plymouth, Michigan. She was thirty-six years old in 1997 and had served eighteen years of her life sentence. Like many women convicted of violent crimes, Allen had been abused as a child, and the state removed her from her family. At sixteen, she married James Allen. Violet described how she fell for her husband quickly, but she also wanted desperately to escape foster care. She recalled, "He was the type of person I thought I really wanted to spend the rest of my life with, to get away from all the abuse." After they got married, things changed. James became controlling. He would follow his wife when she left the house. He accused her of gaining weight and made her walk laps around their home. When he was at work, she was not allowed to leave the house. She explained, "It seemed normal to me because he would also say, 'I'm only doing this because I love you.'. . . That's what my mom and stepfather used to say, too." For two years, Allen survived beatings. Later, she described her life as that of a "prisoner" trapped at home.[62] After a bad fight, Allen shot and killed her husband after he threw their infant daughter across the room. Allen shared a cell with Francine Hughes as the two women awaited their own trials. As described earlier in this chapter, Hughes was acquitted for killing her abusive husband, but in 1977, the court sentenced Allen to life without the possibility of parole for a first-degree murder conviction.[63]

By the mid-1990s, Allen noticed how discussions of abuse were more common among prisoners: "In [1977], this was a taboo subject. I never knew so many other women were in this situation. No one talked about it. No one helped me. What's my mother's favorite saying? 'You made your bed, now you lie in it.'"[64] Before the 1970s, there was almost no public discourse of intimate partner violence. Police records referred to an instance of such violence as a "domestic disturbance," and social workers and counselors used the term "family maladjustment" to describe violence in the home.[65] As women became more aware of the dynamics of intimate partner violence and its impact on their lives, they began to seek redress from courts that had neglected histories of abuse during their initial trials. In 1990, it was estimated that seventy women in Michigan were incarcerated for killing abusive partners, and Allen and other incarcerated women filed petitions asking Governor John Engler to reduce their sentences.[66]

Activism by incarcerated women and their advocates fueled public debates regarding the criminal legal system's response to domestic violence. Allen's petition for clemency had over one thousand signatures. Her attorneys had never presented evidence of intimate partner violence at her trial, which, she argued, prevented her from having a fair chance at a reasonable prison sentence. Prosecutors countered with the theory that Allen killed her husband because he planned to remove her as the beneficiary to the couple's insurance policies.

Allen's petition for clemency was part of a national trend. From 1978 to 1995, the National Clearinghouse for the Defense of Battered Women, a nonprofit organization in Philadelphia, documented eighty-seven cases in twenty-one states of women receiving clemency because of a history of domestic violence.[67] In 1990, Ohio governor Richard Celeste had staff members investigate how domestic violence was a factor in twenty-eight cases where women were incarcerated for murder or assault of an abusive partner, and he commuted the sentences of twenty-five women and pardoned one woman. After learning about the prevalence and effects of domestic violence among incarcerated women, Celeste rented out his own home to become Ohio's first battered women's shelter.[68]

Antiviolence movements of the 1990s raised awareness so that incarcerated women and their jailers relied on new discourses for unpacking gender-based discrimination. Still, activists and incarcerated women often discussed gender violence in terms of universal experiences of women, sometimes ignoring their racial and class differences. In a speech given at the 1996 National Conference for Women in Criminal Justice and Juvenile Justice in Grand Rapids, Michigan, former MDOC director Perry Johnson addressed the notion that the women's movement had gained traction in a way that campaigns for racial justice had not. Reflecting on why women had successfully brought gender issues to light in prisons, Johnson concluded, "I think it was because discrimination against women was given an official legitimacy that racial and ethnic discrimination never had. Racial and ethnic discrimination was a dirty little secret that was unofficial and denied, but gender discrimination was the official policy of the state and its department of corrections."[69] In this statement, Johnson acknowledged the de facto racial segregation upheld in Michigan prisons even though state law deemed it illegal.

Anti–domestic violence movements empowered women to talk about sexual abuse, and incarcerated women framed these issues as problems unique to women's prisons. Building upon the federal legislation and grassroots movements to condemn gender violence, federal agencies and international human rights organizations launched investigations into allegations of rampant sexual violence in state prisons. From 1994 to 1996, Human Rights Watch investigated allegations of abuse in women's prisons in Michigan, and in 1995 the Department of Justice (DOJ) concluded an investigation that had explored how women in prison were vulnerable to the pervasive culture of sexual violence. The DOJ and Human Rights Watch were troubled by the number of male guards in women's prisons in Michigan. In Robert Scott Correctional Facility for Women, 104 of 222 prison guards were men in 1995. In Florence Crane Correctional Facility for Women, 84 of 125 correctional officers were men.[70] DOJ investigators concluded that the MDOC tolerated male guards who sexually harassed, assaulted, and violated women's rights to privacy in women's prisons. Human Rights Watch corroborated the DOJ's findings. Human Rights Watch investigators convinced MDOC officials to cooperate. The MDOC permitted investigators to interview staff and incarcerated women, and supplied information upon request. Human Rights Watch concluded, "Rather than seeking to end such abuse, the Michigan Department of Corrections has consistently refused to acknowledge that there is a problem of sexual misconduct in its women's prisons."[71]

Michigan officials vehemently denied the women's charges of widespread sexual abuse by male guards. Correctional officers claimed that the investigators from DOJ used "reports that are misleading and outright false."[72] MDOC director Kenneth McGinnis stated, "I remain stunned that the nation's chief law enforcement agency would resort to publicizing such outrageous, unverified claims as those contained in the letter from [assistant US attorney general and future governor of Massachusetts] Deval Patrick to Gov. Engler."[73] International human rights organizations denounced the intransigence of state officials but did little to bring about improvements in women's prisons, even with new discourses that provided opportunities for survivors to have their prison terms reviewed. The conclusions and consequences of these investigations will be discussed further in chapter 5.

Clemency for Incarcerated Women

In the 1970s and 1980s, the state convicted and incarcerated most women who were survivors of intimate partner violence and had committed crimes in self-defense.[74] In the mid-1990s, Juanita Thomas, along with dozens of other incarcerated women who had survived intimate partner violence, petitioned the Michigan Parole Board and Governor John Engler for clemency. Thomas explained, "I'm not saying I shouldn't have gotten some time, but not life. There's nothing to justify killing somebody. But I shouldn't have gotten life. I feel I have paid my debt to society."[75] Thomas and other incarcerated women continued their fight for justice by reconfiguring social-justice goals and expanding upon the gains of feminist groups in the antiviolence movements.

Some women who were released from prison devoted their efforts to correcting miscarriages of justice for incarcerated women. Susan Fair was a survivor of intimate partner violence and had been serving a life sentence until she was released from prison in 1991. She began working with attorneys at the ACLU of Michigan to establish the Michigan Battered Women's Clemency Project. Fair collected data on women convicted of murder who had killed their partners and had been in violent relationships. She identified women convicted of homicide who might have benefited from the battered women's defense in their initial trial. Her experience in prison allowed her to quickly relate to incarcerated women and build trust. Fair teamed up with University of Michigan professor Carol Jacobsen and attorney Lynn D'Orio to start writing clemency petitions.

Violet Allen filed the first petition for clemency with the support of the ACLU of Michigan Battered Women's Clemency Project.[76] In May 1995, Governor Engler denied Violet Allen's petition. The Michigan Parole Board granted hearings at their discretion before making a recommendation to the governor's office, and they declined a hearing for Allen. Neither Engler nor the parole board fully explained the decision. A spokesman from Engler's office stated that Allen's prison disciplinary record had "several blemishes." Lynn D'Orio, Allen's attorney, stated, "It just looks like the governor is not really behind women's issues like he'd like the rest of the state to believe."[77] Five more women applied for clemency. Their petitions were denied.[78]

The Michigan Women's Justice and Clemency Project was a coalition of artists, lawyers, and formerly incarcerated women. They wrote petitions and testified at hearings for twenty-six women in Michigan. Carol Jacobsen, a filmmaker and professor at the University of Michigan, was the director of the organization and a survivor of domestic violence. Jacobsen described how the Clemency Project had "assisted a number of women in obtaining paroles on their earliest possible release date, a small victory in a state where the parole board is noted for its history of denying paroles and feeding the bloated prison industry."[79] The initiative had a waitlist of seventy-five incarcerated women seeking clemency. The Michigan Parole Board had rejected over one hundred requests from incarcerated women between 1991 and 2008. The team of former prisoners, attorneys, and activists flagged one hundred cases for additional research.[80]

The work of the Michigan Women's Justice and Clemency Project converged with grassroots prison organizing that was sustained by prison newsletters and publications produced by incarcerated women across the country. A collective of incarcerated women and women who were free who made up the Women Free Women in Prison Collective published the prison newsletter *No More Cages*. The newsletter was, in part, a response to the experience of a Black incarcerated woman, Carol Crooks. Crooks had survived several beatings by guards and spent time in solitary confinement in Bedford Hills, the women's prison in New York. Black and Latina incarcerated women in New York protested in what came to be known as the "August Rebellion" of 1974. For two and a half hours, approximately seventy women demonstrated and held seven staff members hostage.[81] Almost two dozen women were promptly transferred to Matteawan Complex for the Criminally Insane, an infamous prison in the Hudson River Valley.[82] Sociologist Juanita Díaz-Cotto has demonstrated how the rebellion was significant because it generated publicity, which "called attention to the plight of women prisoners."[83] Their protest highlighted how male guards physically attacked and intimidated incarcerated women. The Women Free Women in Prison Collective supported defense campaigns for incarcerated women and organized demonstrations and education programs that shed light on conditions in women's prisons. Published in New York and reaching a national audience, *No More Cages* was a bimonthly newsletter that fueled aspects of the prisoners' rights movement for women in the 1980s. It also helped incarcerated women forge interracial coalitions that confronted the oppression of confinement.[84] *No More Cages* described its purpose: "We went into the prisons for the women themselves, because their oppression overwhelmed us and screamed for action. We went in with a lot of caring and love, and a deep commitment to revolutionary change."[85] Juanita Thomas's case gained renewed interest after she was featured in *No More Cages*.[86]

Because of Thomas's perseverance, her case finally reached an attorney with the expertise and resources she deserved. An attorney who had been working pro bono on Thomas's case after her direct appeal failed wrote an impassioned and desperate letter to Andrea Lyon. He had taken the case, hoping to correct the injustices Thomas endured, but in four years he had not finished reading the transcripts. He was a sole practitioner and could not commit the time needed for a proper investigation.[87] Lyon was a Chicago-based death penalty defense attorney who had earned the nickname the "Angel of Death Row" because of her success convincing judges and politicians to reevaluate cases of people sentenced to death. She had been a tireless advocate for death-row prisoners in her twenty-year career. In 1995, she joined the faculty at the University of Michigan Law School as a clinical professor. After reading the letter from Thomas's lawyer, she drove to the women's prison to meet Thomas. Lyon recalled that their first meeting was held at "the aptly named prison in which she lived, Coldwater. . . . It's in the middle of no where. Cut off, desolate, and distinctly unfriendly. Normally I can get a guard to chat with me as I go through the process of being shaken down and searched. . . . But not there."[88] Thomas remembered the meeting fondly: "When I first met attorney Lyon some strange way I felt OK. One thing she did not make promises. She would say I will give my best to your case. And I felt she would. I had been lied to, made promises, they were never kept."[89] After several meetings and some preliminary research, Lyon decided to move forward with an investigation geared toward a state postconviction petition.

Lyon and her team found that many problems had occurred at Thomas's trial and appeal that had never made it into the record. Lyon focused on the failure of Kingsley to mount a strong defense for Thomas. The state had suppressed key pieces of the physical evidence, but Lyon thought that a decent investigation would have revealed this issue. Thomas's attorney might have pushed for, as Lyon enumerated, "any of the *three* defense theories that were supported by the suppressed evidence: self-defense against the threat of imminent death, self-defense against the threat of imminent great bodily harm, and defense against the forcible felony of rape."[90] Emily Hughes, a clinical law student at the University of Michigan, met with Thomas's attorney in 1996. She was surprised by "how obviously he cared for Ms. Thomas as a person and had tried to do his best, but how his best failed her by falling far short of effective assistance of counsel." He wrote Thomas letters when she was incarcerated. Lyon and her team concluded, "This was not a man who had tried to sabotage his client's defense, but it was clearly a man whose pride had prevented him from realizing he was over his head until it was far too late."[91]

In January of 1997, Lyon filed a 6500 motion, the term for state postconviction petitions in Michigan. Judge Glazer in Lansing was assigned to the case and required the prosecutor to answer the petition. The assigned prosecutor took several months to write a response. Lyon thought this might have been the case because her attorney license had a high practice number, which made her appear on paper to be a new lawyer. She had been practicing for over two decades but had only been in Michigan for two years.[92] But the judge and the prosecutor were moved by Thomas's story and legal arguments. The state agreed to Judge Glazer granting the petition and a new trial. In exchange, Thomas entered a plea of guilty to second-degree murder that carried a sentence of thirty to fifty years. She received credit for the eighteen and a half years she

Figure 3.4. Photograph of Carol Jacobsen, Juanita Thomas, and Susan Fair embracing as Thomas left prison in 1998. Photograph taken by Diane Engleman. Courtesy of Carol Jacobsen.

had already spent in prison, which made her eligible for parole immediately. On October 17, 1998, Thomas left prison. The prison gave Thomas a bus ticket and twenty dollars on her way out. The prosecutor had asked the Michigan Women's Justice and Clemency Project to refrain from publicly celebrating her release.[93] Thomas described it as the "sweetest day."[94]

* * *

While there was no clear path, Juanita Thomas and other women in prison challenged unjust punishment practices. Incarcerated women critically engaged with and repurposed feminist arguments that criticized the courts and prisons. In 1999, Violet Allen filed a state postconviction petition and was released from prison after serving twenty-two years of a life sentence.[95] In 2008, Jacobsen described how the Michigan Women's Justice and Clemency Project continued "research[ing] and working on other strategies to challenge violence and gender subordination in the criminal-legal system."[96] In grievance reports, litigation, investigations, and firsthand accounts from incarcerated women, coalitions charted strategies for criminal legal reform.

The organizations, lawyers, and incarcerated activists in Michigan did not always agree upon how to move forward as they sought justice and safety for women. The cases of Francine Hughes, Juanita Thomas, and Violet Allen illustrate the complicated relationships among feminist groups, incarcerated women, activists, and attorneys in the late twentieth century. Feminist activism inspired critiques and shaped the way criminal legal institutions began to reform their treatment of sexual violence and intimate partner violence.

Escaping Death and Serving Life

Retrenchment Politics, Mandatory Minimum Sentences, and Prison Construction

In October 1978, a Detroit judge imposed a mandatory life sentence without parole on JeDonna Young, a twenty-three-year-old Black woman with no prior convictions. She later recalled how her boyfriend, James Gully, had instructed her to put a bag in the trunk of her car before they headed to a restaurant. They had driven three blocks when police surrounded them and found over 650 grams of heroin inside the bag in her trunk.[1] Law enforcement had been watching Gully for some time. Young was convicted as a coconspirator and one of the first people sentenced according to Michigan's new "650 Lifer" penalty. Young maintained she had no idea her boyfriend sold drugs. Looking back, she described herself as young and naive.[2]

Michigan's 650 Lifer Law was one of the harshest drug laws in the country in 1978. The law levied a mandatory life sentence without the possibility of parole to anyone distributing, possessing, or intending to distribute more than 650 grams of cocaine or heroin.[3] The sentence was harsher than what a person received for a second-degree murder conviction and equivalent to a first-degree murder conviction. By the 1980s, states across the country had implemented mandatory minimum sentences for drug offenses and a host of other crimes.

Also in October 1978, police arrested Timothy Alan Dick, a twenty-five-year-old white man, in the Kalamazoo airport for possessing over 650 grams of cocaine. Unlike Young, Dick knew high-level drug dealers and gave information to law enforcement in exchange for a reduced sentence, escaping the mandatory minimum penalty of life without parole. Michigan attorneys handed Dick's case over to federal prosecutors, and he served a two-and-a-half-year prison sentence. After this setback, he became a successful television actor. He went by the name Tim Allen and played the role of the father in the wildly popular 1990s sitcom *Home Improvement*.[4]

The contrast between JeDonna Young's and Tim Allen's cases highlights the dramatic inequalities of mass incarceration in the late twentieth century. Young's experience underscores how race, class, and gender cemented disadvantages within criminal legal institutions. Her story implicates questions of retribution, equal protection, and freedom from cruel and unusual punishment.

Michigan and other states began sentencing people to life without parole in greater numbers when the Supreme Court placed a temporary moratorium on the death penalty in 1972. This shift increased racial, economic, and gender inequality in the criminal legal system.[5] Scholars have described how mandatory minimum laws like the 650 Lifer Law removed judicial discretion and funneled people into prisons.[6] Racialized rhetoric and punitive policing in poor communities of color fueled growing incarceration rates. As Julilly Kohler-Hausmann has shown, law-and-order politics at the federal and state levels targeted historically marginalized people. Politicians deployed language that condemned poor people, people of color, and women, especially those making new political and economic claims in America.[7]

Tough-on-crime policies fostered an unreceptive political climate for prison reform. This chapter examines institutional responses to the prisoners' rights movement and the rise of mass incarceration in Michigan. National debates surrounding the death penalty influenced state criminal legal systems around the country, and they provide an entry point to explore how punitive sentences became popular in the new carceral landscape. Michigan abolished the death penalty in 1847, making it the first state in the union to do so, but state legislators considered reinstating executions in the 1970s. They ultimately rejected the death penalty, but their deliberations opened institutional pathways for harsh mandatory minimum sentences like the 650 Lifer Law. Diminished judicial discretion and long sentences confined thousands of people. Prison construction also accelerated in the 1980s although white communities across Michigan fought against carceral construction by arguing that prisons would destroy industry, tourism, family values, property values, and the environment. The strengthening of mandatory minimum sentences, weakening of civil rights mandates, and hastening of prison construction informed policies with deleterious consequences for incarcerated women. While much of the material in this chapter focuses on prisons in general rather than women's prisons in particular, the punitive turn of the end of the twentieth century ensnared women in the harsh-sentencing and prison-construction boom of that period.

Midwestern Politics of Mass Incarceration

Racism, segregation, and deindustrialization had narrowed opportunities for the growing Black population and laid the foundation for mass incarceration in Detroit. Throughout the 1960s, white people started to inappropriately blame Black Detroiters for crime, poverty, and deindustrialization.[8] On June 23, 1963, Martin Luther King Jr. visited Detroit to lead "The Long Walk to Freedom," which aimed to highlight racialized inequities in housing, schools, and employment for Black Detroiters, while also raising support for civil rights workers in the South. The Detroit Council for Human Rights, a new civil rights organization chaired by Clarence LaVaughn (C. L.) Franklin, a prominent Black Baptist minister, organized the march alongside local civil rights leaders, Walter P. Reuther, the UAW president, and Detroit mayor Jerome Cavanaugh. Two weeks after the murder of Medgar Evers in Mississippi and exactly twenty years following the 1943 racial uprising in Detroit, King delivered an early version of his "I Have a Dream" speech in Detroit in front of approximately 125,000 marchers.[9]

On July 5, 1963, three weeks after the march, Detroit police killed Cynthia Scott, a twenty-four-year-old Black woman, at 3:00 a.m. as she walked home with Charles Marshall, a twenty-one-year-old Black man, who told police he was Scott's boyfriend.[10] Police records described Scott as a sex worker, and some of the news coverage attached too little importance to her fatal encounter with the police.[11] George Edwards, the Detroit police commissioner, gave a televised statement that defended the shooting and described the shooting officer, Theodore Spicher, as a man acting in self-defense. Civil rights groups and legal organizations, including local chapters of the ACLU, the NAACP, the National Lawyers Guild, the Trade Union Leadership Council, and the Wolverine Bar Association, argued that this version of events grossly misrepresented the police encounter that led to Scott's death.[12] As historian Anne Gray Fischer has brought to light, police officers have exercised an extraordinary amount of discretion policing women in public spaces, and urban police sexually profiled Black women and subjected them to a range of punitive actions.[13] This appears to have been the case with Detroit police officer Spicher, a white man, who reported that he shot Scott twice in the back as she walked away from him. Eyewitnesses detailed how police had harassed her, tried to arrest her, and then shot her as she fled. Her killing revived activism seeking to end police brutality against Black people in Detroit. The NAACP, the Congress of Racial Equality, and Black churches organized rallies and demanded police reform. Rosa Parks, who had moved to Detroit after the Montgomery bus boycotts, participated in the protests.[14]

On the heels of major victories of the civil rights movement, like the Civil Rights Act of 1964, the Voting Rights Act of 1965, and the Supreme Court decision in *Loving v. Virginia*, 388 U.S. 1 (1967), prohibiting "miscegenation" laws, people of color expressed growing frustration and disappointment in northern cities where white supremacy continued to shape housing, schools, job opportunities, policing, and punishment.

On July 23, 1967, Detroit erupted in an uprising that became one of the most violent of the decade. Police raided an unlicensed bar, commonly known as a "blind pig," on Twelfth Street, in the middle of one of the largest Black communities in Detroit. Police detained eighty-five people outside while they called for back-up. The Detroit Police Department (DPD) employed forty-seven hundred officers, and only two hundred policemen were on duty in the early morning hours of the raid. Normally, police would have closed the unlicensed bar and encouraged patrons to go home, but at around 4:00 a.m., an hour into the raid, approximately two hundred people gathered and violence erupted between police and community members. The raid escalated into chaos. Mayor Jerome Cavanaugh ordered police not to shoot people looting. After several days, the Michigan State Police and the National Guard arrived, and the rebellion ended on July 28. Forty-three people died, and police arrested 7,231 women and men, most of whom were Black, on various charges connected to the uprising.[15]

Detroit's uprising was one of many across the country that drew national attention and heightened a demand among politicians and voters for punitive policing and long sentences. Dan Berger argues that political elites used the northern uprisings to increase the militarization of police and expand the punitive power of the state.[16] For example, the Watts rebellion of 1965 had encouraged renewed scrutiny of racism and brutality among police in Los Angeles. California responded by developing militarized police SWAT units that quickly became popular in other states.[17] The DPD established a paramilitary vice unit called STRESS (Stop Robberies, Enjoy Safe Streets) that targeted Black people.[18] Between 1971 and 1973, the DPD killed approximately 108 people, most of whom were unarmed Black males. The violence galvanized a broad social-justice movement when STRESS officers killed two Black boys. The coalition of civil rights, Black power, and radical leftist organizations labeled STRESS a "murder squad." Police responded to the criticism by throwing their support behind mayoral candidate John Nichols, the DPD commissioner and a STRESS supporter, but grassroots activism helped elect Detroit's first Black mayor, Coleman Young, who campaigned on police reform in 1973. Young abolished STRESS, but the state continued to arrest and incarcerate a disproportionate number of Black and Brown people in Detroit.[19]

The expansion of punitive policing accompanied a crime panic in Michigan. In 1977, the *Detroit Free Press* reported, "The crime rate dropped in Detroit last year but not enough to nudge the city from the top spot in most categories of FBI crime statistics for America's 10 largest cities."[20] Media coverage and racialized rhetoric around crime fueled crime panics, even in low-crime areas of Michigan. Researchers at Michigan State University (MSU) found that "crime is considered a major community problem in virtually all areas of Michigan, including the Upper Peninsula, and strong support for more anti-crime spending exists throughout the state." Participants in the MSU study listed crime rates as the most important factor in considering which community to call home.[21]

The rhetoric surrounding crime and punishment contributed to anti-Black politics in Detroit. A popular narrative cited 1967 as the turning point for Detroit from a wealthy white city to one that was majority Black, lacking jobs, and riddled with crime. Historian Kevin Boyle has analyzed how journalists supported this narrative in part because it allowed white people to dodge any responsibility for white flight and segregation.[22]

Courts also shielded white suburbs from legal challenges to segregation in the 1970s, and this also permitted causal factors for mass incarceration to flourish in Detroit. The Supreme Court's decision in *Milliken v. Bradley*, 418 US 717 (1974), dismantled an integration plan for Detroit Public Schools in a 5–4 decision that prohibited the federal courts from enforcing school desegregation in Detroit. Governor Milliken, a Republican, was named in the case, and the state's position blunted desegregation plans and facilitated segregation in urban areas. The white suburban school districts argued that the segregation was not the result of intentional discrimination and therefore the federal courts should not intervene in the same way the courts had forced school integration in southern states. In his dissent, Justice Thurgood Marshall, the only Black justice on the court, wrote, "The very evil that *Brown* was aimed at will not be cured but will be perpetuated."[23] The logic of *Milliken* permitted white people to avoid questions of racial justice while protecting them from legal arguments against segregation. Michelle Alexander has demonstrated how courts permit segregation because of "color-blind" law in the post–civil rights era. Such policies privileged white property owners in wealthy suburbs over Black urban residents with less capital, and racial segregation depleted the tax base and political power in communities of color. Racial tensions hardened as police brutality, deindustrialization, and segregation went unchecked despite protests for social justice and legal fights for equality that reached the United States Supreme Court. After the police killing of Cynthia Scott in 1963 and the riot of 1967, the DPD created STRESS units that targeted Black people and expanded punitive policing and harsh punishment. Problems with criminal legal institutions were compounded by the depletion of political and economic resources, which contributed to a growing wedge along racial lines and bolstered support for tough-on-crime politics in Michigan. The state created conditions in which mass incarceration would thrive.[24]

Death Penalty Debates

Supporting harsh penalties provided a way for some voters to act upon heightened concerns about crime. In 1967, state legislator Stanley Rozycki, a Democrat from Detroit, proposed bringing the death penalty back to Michigan. Referring to the riots that summer, Rozycki argued that the death penalty should be an option for punishing "abominable killings by thugs."[25] Rozycki's phrasing illustrated the coded ways white people conflated race and crime by the late 1960s. The proposal never made it out of the state legislature, but Michigan residents would consider the death penalty and welcome harsh sentences in the 1970s.

The modern era of the death penalty began in the mid-1970s with *Furman v. Georgia*, 408 U.S. 238 (1972), in which the court held that states administered capital punishment arbitrarily by sentencing people to death for a variety of convictions, including rape, kidnapping, and homicides. The justices held that the arbitrary justifications for capital murder convictions violated the Eighth Amendment's ban on cruel and unusual punishment.[26] *Furman* created a moratorium on the death penalty, and capital punishment supporters moved quickly to rewrite capital punishment statutes in state criminal codes. In Michigan, state legislator Joyce Symons, a Democrat from Allen Park, sponsored a resolution that would have allowed the state to impose the death penalty for a small category of homicides. Symons proposed a state constitutional amendment that would sentence to death people convicted of kidnapping, using explosives, murdering first responders, or being snipers, but the resolution never made it out of committee.[27] Symons proposed the amendment after Detroit police officer Gerald Riley tried to stop a bank robbery but was fatally shot in December 1972.[28] Symons believed in deterrence and argued that the bank robber might have decided not to shoot Riley if he had thought his own life might be in jeopardy once he was captured, even though by the 1970s researchers had successfully shown that deterrence did not work.[29]

After several failed attempts by state legislatures, the Supreme Court approved Georgia's revised death penalty statute in *Gregg v. Georgia*, 428 U.S. 153 (1976). The Supreme Court reinstated the death penalty with stricter applications, arguing that it did not amount to cruel and unusual punishment and requiring state prosecutors to prove an aggravating element that made homicide more heinous than a first-degree murder. Aggravating circumstances varied among states and typically included killing a public official, a law enforcement officer, a child, or multiple victims. Committing an additional crime in the course of a murder, such as rape or armed robbery, could also elevate the charges to capital murder in some states.

Gregg also ushered in the bifurcated trial structure, which increased the likelihood of the defendant receiving a death sentence. The trial had two phases: a guilt phase and a penalty phase. During the guilt phase, prosecutors could magnify the harm of the crime by exploring the impact of the aggravating circumstances. Only after a defendant was convicted of capital murder and had entered the penalty phase could defense attorneys introduce mitigating factors to persuade jurors to give the defendant a sentence of life without parole. In the penalty phase, good defense attorneys narrated forces outside of the defendant's control that might convince a jury and judge that his or her life was worth saving. Compelling life histories highlighted that exposure to violence, mental illness, or poverty was a common mitigating factor. However, only defense attorneys with time, resources, and a commitment to ensuring a fair trial pursued thorough investigations for their clients.

As American lawmakers rewrote criminal codes to permit the death penalty, other countries abolished capital punishment. Canada's prime minister Pierre Trudeau and his Liberal Party successfully guided the House of Commons to abolishment of the death penalty in June 1976. The close vote of 133 in favor of abolition and 125 against concluded a long, contentious debate over the punishment in Canada.[30] Detroit shares a border with the province of Ontario, and Canada's abolition of the death penalty generated discussion of the death penalty in Michigan, where death penalty supporters confronted prison leaders who wanted the state to uphold its abolitionist tradition. The editorial board of the *Detroit Free Press* wrote, "We understand the frustration that has led so many states to restore the death penalty. We share the belief that *something* has to be done about the violence and wanton contempt for human life that prevails in much of our society.... But the way to respond to it, or so it seems to us, is not by having the state participate in the violence by resorting to executions."[31]

Shifts in policies surrounding crime and punishment in the United States also created challenges for wardens and directors of departments of corrections in state prison systems. Perry Johnson, the director of the MDOC and key defendant in *Glover*, championed rehabilitation in prisons. Johnson was born in rural Alberta, Canada, in 1931 and moved with his parents to Lakeview, a small town in central Michigan, as a child. He attended Michigan State University, where he studied social work and embarked on a counseling career in 1955 at the State Prison of Southern Michigan, a maximum-security men's facility nicknamed "the Big House," in Jackson. He quickly climbed the promotional ladder, serving as the warden from 1970 to 1972. In 1972, he became the director of the MDOC.[32]

When the *Gregg* decision was handed down, Johnson worked with other criminal legal and community leaders to argue that Michigan should maintain its opposition to the death penalty. Johnson, along with Arthur Brandstatter, the dean of the School of Criminal Justice at Michigan State University, and Richard Devor, a senior minister at the Central Methodist Church in Detroit, joined a panel discussion hosted by the Michigan Committee Against Capital Punishment to unpack *Gregg*. Concerned that voters would seek the death penalty in a heightened tough-on-crime political culture, the three men reached similar conclusions from their respective fields. Johnson, in his unequivocal style, stated, "The death penalty may be legal, but it's a bad idea."[33] Johnson acknowledged the desire for vengeance on behalf of victims, agreeing that "retribution does indeed have its place in the criminal justice system." But, he argued, "Persons convicted of first-degree murder in Michigan are given very severe punishment for their crimes. Life in prison is not an easy way out."[34] Johnson argued that reform was possible for all prisoners, revealing his training in social work. Johnson knew that people convicted of murder were unlikely to commit another homicide. He stated, "Of the 395 convicted first-degree murderers paroled in Michigan between 1938 and 1974 not one has been returned to prison for committing another first-degree murder."[35] Johnson argued that executing people would be an expression of the state's capacity for violence.

Governor Milliken maintained his opposition to the death penalty while also appearing tough on crime. In a memorandum, Milliken's staff stated, "The merits of the argument that capital punishment is not a deterrent and that capital proceedings would fall hardest upon minority groups and indigents should be thoroughly articulated. A position on this issue would have to be dissected from the greater issue of crime in the streets and a program that indicates toughness or firmness in dealing with crime in general would have to be set forth which would clearly refute any inference that the Governor was soft on crime for opposing the repeal of the death penalty."[36] He only planned to voice his opposition if a referendum to amend the state constitution to allow the death penalty was presented to voters. However, the proposals for the death penalty never left the state legislature. Michigan's criminal legal system found other ways to condemn criminality.

In Georgia and other states, racial discrimination transformed but remained a central feature of criminal legal practices. In 1987, the Supreme Court decided *McCleskey v. Kemp*, 481 U.S. 279, a death penalty case from Georgia. Warren McCleskey, a Black man, had been convicted of killing a white police officer and was sentenced to death. He argued that his sentence violated his rights to equal protection and protection against cruel and unusual punishment. McCleskey and his lawyers relied on sociologist and law professor David Baldus's social-scientific study, which found that defendants convicted of killing white victims were more likely to receive a death sentence in Georgia. Black defendants accused of killing white victims were four times more likely to be sentenced to death compared to Black defendants accused of killing Black victims. The study demonstrated racial bias in Georgia's death penalty and suggested racial bias throughout the criminal courts. In a 5–4 decision, Justice Powell, writing for the majority, stated, "In light of the safeguards designed to minimize racial bias in the process, the fundamental value of [the] jury trial in our criminal justice system, and the benefits that discretion provides to criminal defendants, we hold that the Baldus study does not demonstrate a constitutionally significant risk of racial bias affecting the Georgia capital sentencing process."[37] Because attorneys could not prove racial bias in McCleskey's case, the justices discounted evidence of general racial bias in the justice system. However, in any criminal case, there are many people making decisions at various stages, from arrest to conviction. Police, prosecutors, attorneys, juries, and trial judges share decision-making responsibilities, and proving how judges, jurors, prosecutors, or police intentionally discriminated against one defendant is nearly impossible.[38]

The 650 Lifer Law and Mandatory Minimum Sentences

President Lyndon Johnson had been the first president to declare a war on crime in 1964, but each subsequent administration expanded on that rhetoric of state power. By 1980, Ronald Reagan campaigned for the presidency on a neoconservative platform that argued that educational, familial, and religious institutions were under threat from expanding civil rights and the role of government articulated in Johnson's Great Society initiatives. When Reagan was elected in 1981, he scaled up the war on drugs. Reagan encouraged Congress to criminalize drug use and significantly increase penalties for drug possession. Nancy Reagan launched the "Just Say No" initiative that targeted children.[39] The Reagan administration amplified the racialized rhetoric of tough-on-crime politics that had been deployed in the Nixon administration and declared a war on drugs in 1982.[40] The war on drugs during the Reagan administration tightened connections between the federal government and the states.[41] Michigan deployed long sentences, like life without parole, as a tool in the war on drugs. Michigan politicians and criminal legal authorities had rejected the death penalty but were liberal with enforcing mandatory minimum sentences.

Two state legislators proposed attaching drug-treatment plans to mandatory-minimum bills. Democratic state legislators George Cushingberry and Monte Geralds introduced the bills, which, Cushingberry argued, were "the key to making our streets safer."[42] The massive public health package included a proposal for police to easily gain access to wiretaps for suspected drug dealers. It also imposed mandatory minimums for people convicted of possessing large amounts of cocaine or heroin, and an additional qualification would allow a judge to find a defendant "addicted and guilty," a condition that would send a person to a drug treatment program rather than prison.[43] The mandatory minimums created a sentencing scheme that instructed judges to sentence a person convicted with one hundred grams or less of heroin or cocaine to one year in prison or a drug-detoxification program. A judge would sentence a person to ten years in prison if the defendant had 100 to 225 grams of drugs. A defendant would receive a twenty-year sentence if convicted with 225 to 650 grams. The harshest sentence was a mandatory life sentence without the possibility of parole for people convicted with 650 grams or more of heroin or cocaine, which later became known as the "650 Lifer Law."[44] In April 1977, state legislators gathered overwhelming support for mandatory minimum sentences for drug crimes, and the State House passed the mandatory sentencing bill by a vote of eighty-four to eleven. A companion bill prohibiting the application of good time for prisoners on a mandatory sentence for a drug conviction passed with a majority of eighty-seven in favor and eleven opposed.[45] The drug bill package moved to the state Senate.[46]

State legislators modeled Michigan's mandatory minimum laws after New York State's Rockefeller Drug laws, which had imposed mandatory minimum sentences since 1973. State legislator Paul Rosenbaum, a New York native and a Democrat representing Battle Creek, sponsored the final version of the 650 Lifer Law. Rosenbaum then wrote a harsher version of the penalties that removed sentencing discretion from the trial judge. In 1978, he introduced the final version of the 650 Lifer Law.[47] The bill passed in the state Senate with a 27-7 vote in February 1978, and it was returned to the state House.[48] In May, lawmakers concluded months of fiery debates over the bill package, which targeted users and pushers of heroin, cocaine, and other drugs. A journalist reported, "Tempers flared on the House floor when Rep. Jeffery Padden spoke out against the measure. He claimed similar crackdowns in other states have succeeded only in swelling the prison population."[49] Padden, a Democrat from Wyandotte, could not convince fellow lawmakers. Supporters of the bill repeatedly interrupted him, yelling that he was out of order.[50] Governor Milliken signed the bill into law on Friday, May 12, 1978, and called drug abuse "the lowest form of crime."[51]

Some lawyers and judges argued that the 650 Lifer Law would violate a prisoner's constitutional rights against cruel and unusual punishment, and started to test the argument in state courts. Oakland County circuit judge James Thorburn dismissed the drug-possession charges against defendant Vernon McCarty and held that the 650 Lifer Law was a violation of a person's Eighth Amendment rights prohibiting cruel and unusual punishment. However, on Friday, February 19, 1982, the Michigan Court of Appeals upheld the mandatory minimum sentence, reversing Judge Thorburn's decision. The state appeals court referred to the 650 Lifer Law as a "well thought-out" initiative by the legislature "to prevent offenders from doing further harm, and to deter others."[52] The 650 Lifer Law had little impact on stemming the flow of drug trafficking and drug use in Michigan.[53] Instead, it put into place a harsh stance against people convicted of crimes and increased demand for prison beds.

At the national level, the Reagan administration capitalized on the political momentum and racial resentment white people expressed to facilitate the war on drugs. The media created a crack hysteria in the 1980s, with devastating consequences for Black people entangled in criminal legal surveillance. Congress passed the Anti–Drug Abuse Act of 1986, which mandated a minimum sentence of five years in prison for a person convicted of having five grams of crack cocaine, the equivalent weight of about two small packets of sugar and approximately ten to fifty doses. In comparison, a five-year sentence was mandated for someone convicted with five hundred grams of powder cocaine, approximately one hundred times the amount for crack. This amount of powder cocaine would have produced anywhere from twenty-five hundred to five thousand doses. Since crack was more prevalent in Black communities whereas higher-priced cocaine was more prevalent in white communities, this discrepancy ensnared many more Black than white people in the criminal legal system. It was not amended until 2010 when President Obama signed the Fair Sentencing Act, which significantly reduced the disparity between the amount of crack and cocaine required to trigger the mandatory minimum sentence.[54]

With the war on drugs, prisons swelled with people serving long sentences, and Rudolph H. Stahlberg, the regional administrator of the Corrections Commission of Southeastern Michigan, acknowledged that overcrowding had driven a wedge between prison staff and the incarcerated.[55] Staff were overburdened, and prisoners were fed up with being underserved. Incarcerated people on life sentences were not eligible for transfers to work camps or community centers. "Lifers," as they called themselves, took an adversarial stance toward their jailers while correctional officers railed against aspects of the ongoing *Glover* litigation.[56] Nonetheless, aligning themselves with national political trends, Michigan's politicians forged ahead with mass incarceration. Facing an overcrowding crisis, the MDOC proceeded to build new prisons, although those plans were contested in the host communities.

Carceral Construction

Women were the fastest-growing segment of the incarcerated population in the United States throughout the 1980s. In 1979, 12,995 women were incarcerated in the United States. By 1989, the female prison population had grown to 40,612, an increase of 212 percent. In comparison, the male prison population had increased from 301,462 to 671,752, a 122 percent increase.[57] Table 4.1 shows the growth in the population of incarcerated women in Michigan.

Problems multiplied as the number of women sent to prison outpaced the number of open beds. In January of 1980, warden Gloria Richardson assigned new prisoners to trailers scattered across Huron Valley's grounds. Although temporary housing made it difficult for prisoners to establish a routine and settle into prison life, overcrowding made modular housing not only necessary but also in constant demand. Also, the MDOC converted a former reform school for boys in Coldwater, Michigan, to a women's prison and a work camp, the Florence Crane Correctional Facility.[58] When incarcerated women were moved into the prison,

TABLE 4.1. Michigan Female Prison Population, 1978 to 2016

Year	Number of Female Prisoners	Year	Number of Female Prisoners
1978	621	1998	2,052
1979	628	1999	2,027
1980	634	2000	2,131
1981	630	2001	2,149
1982	624	2002	2,267
1983	660	2003	2,198
1984	683	2004	2,113
1985	814	2005	2,111
1986	1,018	2006	2,170
1987	1,183	2007	2,080
1988	1,333	2008	1,957
1989	1,586	2009	1,755
1990	1,688	2010	1,869
1991	1,734	2011	1,909
1992	1,842	2012	1,989
1993	1,798	2013	2,059
1994	2,021	2014	2,123
1995	1,842	2015	2,273
1996	1,920	2016	2,242
1997	2,056		

Source: Carson E. Ann and Joseph Mulako-Wangota, Bureau of Justice Statistics (Count of total jurisdiction population), generated using the Corrections Statistical Analysis Tool (CSAT), Prisoners, http://www.bjs.gov.

their first task was to clean the abandoned buildings. Mary Glover was transferred to Florence Crane to relieve overcrowding at Huron Valley. She recalled, "Florence Crane was a decrepit rat hole that was the worst of the worst."[59]

MDOC directors looked for new locations to build prisons for its rapidly expanding population. In response, many Michigan residents revived adversarial rhetoric similar to what they used in debates about the death penalty. They conducted letter-writing campaigns, signed petitions, and attended town hall meetings to voice opposition to prison placement in white, rural parts of the state. Racialized media portrayals of the war on drugs fueled local challenges to prison construction, which complement sociologist John Eason's findings that community leaders seek to manage stigmas associated with prison towns and shield their communities from hosting poor people of color, either incarcerated or visiting imprisoned family members.[60] The fact that Michigan residents pushed back in complex ways against prison construction runs counter to the received wisdom that many American communities, especially those experiencing decline, embraced prison construction, believing it would secure a stable economy for communities grappling with the fallout of deindustrialization.[61] The tension between the state's push for prison construction and local resistance across predominantly white areas of Michigan highlights the resolve of state officials to expand the state's criminal legal institutions and hold a growing prison population.[62]

MDOC director Johnson diverged from the national trends in which prison administrators embraced politics of fear and retribution. Johnson worked to incorporate the voices of prisoners in administrative meetings. He looked abroad for new models of rehabilitative programming and proposed regional prisons that would help prisoners maintain connections to their home communities. He gave incarcerated men and women some autonomy and space to participate in administrative meetings through incarcerated representatives. At the same time, Johnson navigated the preferences of people across Michigan who wanted prisoners housed in far-flung corners of the state.

Amid heated debates about crime and punishment, Johnson launched his plan for regional prisons, which was designed to help prisoners maintain connections to their home communities. Johnson proposed smaller prisons across the state that would hold five hundred or six hundred incarcerated people and offer a full range of security categories, from minimum to maximum security levels. The plan would have overhauled the model of large, maximum-security facilities that held thousands of prisoners, many of whom were incarcerated far away from their home communities,[63] such as the State Prison of Southern Michigan, in Jackson, which held fifty-five hundred male prisoners in 1981, making it the largest walled prison in the world.[64] Johnson envisioned regional prisons "located near the community from which the offender comes, and [in which] he would typically serve his entire institutional sentence, progressing through security levels, at that one facility."[65] (Johnson referred to most prisoners as male.) According to the regional plan, prisoners would be incarcerated close to home. Johnson's statements demonstrate a desire to have incarcerated people be invested in their home communities and to maintain connections to employers, schools, and family members. Johnson urged the MDOC to build prisons close to major cities that could accommodate prisoners with different security levels. More importantly, he knew that most prisoners, 75 percent, would be released to their homes within three to four years. Johnson explained, "This is true even though Michigan prison terms are longer than the national average." In Johnson's estimation, about half of all prisoners, many on probation or parole, returned to their home community within two years. He was eager to break the assembly-line process by which the criminal legal system incarcerated and released people, often without regard for meaningful change. Johnson contended that regional prisons would have a major impact on recidivism rates by helping returning citizens maintain personal and professional relationships while serving their sentence, with the goal of making reentry a smoother process.[66] Johnson believed that a regional prison could leverage community resources and recruit staff more effectively than remote, rural facilities. Finally, Johnson thought that regional facilities might be more environmentally responsible than large, maximum-security prisons. Smaller facilities could be efficient with energy and rely more on local resources, compared to large prisons that were expensive to operate and often drew resources and employees from the region with long commutes. Furthermore, regional prisons would reduce the cost of transferring prisoners to different prisons across the state. The MDOC moved prisoners from maximum-security to minimum-security facilities as people grew older or approached their release dates, and Johnson hoped that people could remain in a single regional facility for their entire sentence. Johnson was convinced that regional facilities were a cost-effective proposal.[67]

The search for new prison sites alarmed residents in rural areas and inflamed anti-Black politics. Rural residents viewed prisoners as a threat to their public safety, their home values, regional tourism, and their ability to enjoy the outdoors.

In letters to state leaders, residents argued that prison construction threatened white, middle-class social and economic structures. In 1977, the MDOC floated the possibility of building a minimum-security prison camp in Holland, Michigan, and residents responded with vitriol.[68] A married couple merged environmentalism with law-and-order politics in their pleas to Director Johnson. They wrote, "Please, for our peace of mind, can't you possibly find a more isolated prison facility? We agree that there must be rehabilitation facilities, but why ruin some of our last remaining dunes? We are trying to raise our family in a wonderful small community. Why must we expose them to an undesirable element?"[69] Other Holland residents opposed the construction of a prison camp, a facility for low-security-level prisoners, after they became frightened that property values would plummet. A homeowner living on the border of the proposed site wrote, "Now with the news of the prison camp we are literally sick, we feel our dreams for a safe quiet beautiful home and living surroundings are in jeopardy—not only for us but our children and grandchildren."[70] In Allegan County, a mostly white area south of Grand Rapids and Holland, a resident expressed his concern that a prison would disrupt wildlife conservation. He listed ways it might be dangerous to house prisoners close to seasonal hunting grounds and stated that the closest state police station was a forty-five-minute drive from the proposed prison site. Furthermore, a married couple worried that a prison would deplete the understaffed sheriff's office and local fire department in Allegan County. The husband wrote, "I believe these are all valid reasons. . . . I feel there are much lower populated areas in the state than Allegan County."[71] He added, "The intent of the State Land was for Hunting not for a Prison Camp and please [let's] keep it that way."[72]

Other residents justified their objections within the often racialized and gendered ideal of "family values." Most of the letter writers were white men. When women signed the letters they often signed as wife of the primary writer. The letters reflected patriarchal family structures. They wrote about potential crimes that prisoners might commit in areas beyond the prison camp. Michigan prison camps were minimum-security correctional facilities that held incarcerated people with good disciplinary records or people who were scheduled to return to their home communities within a year. The incarcerated people worked long hours, usually in agriculture or manufacturing. Prisoners serving life sentences or those with records of disciplinary problems remained in high-security prisons. Nonetheless, many residents in southwest Michigan had convinced themselves that a prison camp would give incarcerated people opportunities to commit new violent crimes. Emils Avots wrote to Director Johnson on behalf of his Latvian church. The church ran children's camps and family camping on land that was one mile away from a proposed prison site. Avots wrote, "The close location will ruin our camping work. The close prison camp will lead to problems, much theft, vandalism, rapes, kidnapping and other problems. This situation also will drive away families from camp [out] of the fear for their [children's] safety."[73] Another writer stated, "This area has a lot of wildlife and a very good hunting area, and because of the danger of unguarded prisoners in the area this all would have to come to an end."[74] Some people described some of their worst fears to Johnson: "Also less than two miles from a K–6 Elementary School, this makes it easy for a prisoner to sneak over to the school, molest a child, and walk back to the prison camp with very little chance of proving who committed the crime. This prison camp endangers the whole Hamilton area!"[75] The letters reflected stereotypes of incarcerated people who were defined by their crimes.

Letter writers anticipated economic pitfalls and the potential stigmas associated with becoming a prison town. The Fennville City Commission drafted a resolution that listed potential burdens on the community if it hosted a new prison. City commissioners worried that a prison would require more police and firefighters and would be economically detrimental for tourism in their southwest corner of the state. Finally, the commissioners argued that the use of state land for a prison contradicted the county's land use planning and zoning codes. They saved their emotional appeal for the final lines of the letter: "We do not believe that a successful family park can be provided and maintained with a prison immediately adjacent to it."[76]

John Eason has described how towns and small cities in rural areas started to compete to become prison sites because of the removal of mills, agriculture, factories, and military bases that had anchored communities in the first half of the twentieth century. However, many residents in white communities of southwest Michigan articulated a "not in my backyard" perspective despite economic uncertainty. The letter campaign suggests they anticipated struggles in managing "the spoiled identity" that impacted morale and economic opportunities in potential prison towns.[77]

On the southeastern shores of Lake Michigan, several small business owners bemoaned prison construction by describing the fickle nature of the tourist economy. An alliance of business owners in Allegan County wrote to Governor Milliken, "As you know, Allegan County is one of the most economically depressed per-capita Counties in the State of Michigan. Further, the tourist trade is an important economic factor to all of the retail businesses in Allegan County and the bulk of that tourist trade comes from campers, hikers, hunters, fishermen, snow-mobiles, horsemen and others. To place a minimum security prison camp in this area would be an economic disaster."[78] Another business owner, Herb Eldean, described how his family enjoyed state land for hiking in the summer and cross-country skiing in the winter. He feared that he would no longer be able to enjoy the outdoors if the state built a prison close to his home. He equated incarcerated people to "leeches" on state funds and concluded, "The area in question would be much better utilized as a state or county nature center for all the taxpayers to enjoy."[79] Eldean was concerned not only for his family's use of state parks but also that a new prison might discourage tourism. He emphasized his role as a local business owner and taxpayer, distinguishing his social standing from his perception of the incarcerated population. Another resident corroborated his contempt for prisoners by writing, "How you can turn over such property, justifiably to those who have broken their right to be free citizens, is hard to understand."[80] In his view, the MDOC's overcrowding crisis "didn't happen overnight and just because the management of this department over the years has not been far sighted enough to see the growing need and plan for it, is no reason why another serious mistake must be made now."[81] The mistake, in this resident's view, would be to use property hugging Lake Michigan shoreline for a prison camp.

Johnson was frustrated by the opposition to regional prison construction plans, which, he argued, offered an alternative to the prison regime crystallizing in Michigan. In an internal MDOC memorandum, Johnson contended, "If we give in to the resistance of local communities whose unrealistic fear of institutions borders on the pathological, then we will never achieve a regionalized corrections system. We will instead hand on to the next century the legacy of a prison system designed in the last, and a burden to the present."[82] Johnson believed that the expansion of regional facilities would encourage communities to engage with incarcerated people and set them up for successful reentry. He explained, "So long as our facilities are centralized and remote, it is both fiscally and psychologically inviting for the community to solve the problem presented to it by the offender by exiling him."[83] Johnson acknowledged how it must be tempting for local government officials to send lawbreakers to prisons in far-flung parts of the state. However, he wanted local residents to engage with prisoners while they lived close to home: "The point here is that this is much easier to do psychologically when the destination of the prisoner is an abstraction—'the state prison system'— than when it is an institution which the judge has visited; which has a common administration over the probation staff in his or her court; and whose administrators belong to the same civic groups as the leaders in the police, prosecutors' and judges' communities."[84] Undeterred by local complaints and Johnson's arguments for regional prisons, the MDOC moved forward with new construction of traditional prisons that did not embrace the regional model.

In the 1980s, Johnson laid the groundwork for the largest prison construction initiative in Michigan history. The plan would cost the state $421 million. In the first nine months of 1985, the state increased the number of beds in its prisons by 1,785, bringing the total prison bed capacity to 14,299. The MDOC made room for a projected population of 22,000 prisoners by the mid-1990s. The MDOC built barn complexes that would house hundreds of prisoners, and the state launched large remodeling projects for five existing prisons in Coldwater, Ionia, Jackson, Marquette, and Northville. Furthermore, county jails on the east side of the state prepared to house more prisoners for longer sentences.[85] Michigan's push to increase its carceral capacity was a common response to the prisoners' rights movement and court orders that demanded solutions to overcrowding, violence, and sanitation problems in prisons.[86] Since the 1980s, states and the federal government have built more than fifteen hundred new prisons, vastly increasing their carceral capacity.[87] Prisons have reorganized local economies and geographies. They have repurposed state land and employed thousands of people as guards, administrative staff, and drivers transporting friends, families, and employees to and from the prisons. Nonetheless, Michigan's prison boom was not always a welcome change in local towns and communities. The decision of state officials to build more prisons despite objections demonstrates how Johnson was outmatched politically; ultimately, he could not drum up support for community-based alternatives to large, sterile, and bureaucratic prisons as lawmakers responded to the racialized crime hysteria and war on drugs by building more space to incarcerate.

The Decline of Prisoners' Rights and Reform

Sociologist Juanita Díaz-Cotto has demonstrated how state prison officials became more intransigent and less receptive to reform after massive rebellions by Black and Latinx prisoners in the 1970s and 1980s.[88] Her conclusions align with similar trends in Michigan, where MDOC director Johnson's efforts to improve the operation of prisons were met with resistance. The prisoners' rights movement encouraged Johnson to reflect on the structure of prison governance in Michigan. Johnson had studied the political shifts within prisons, and he incorporated elements of participatory governance in the 1980s. In cases like *Glover*, incarcerated women had complained that there was no grievance procedure and that the classification of female prisoners felt arbitrary and random. Johnson agreed with their complaints and devised ways to allow incarcerated people to document grievances, negotiate policies, and take on more responsibility while incarcerated. In doing so, he gained the respect of many incarcerated women. Glover affectionately called Johnson "Uncle Perry" when she saw him in court.[89] He advanced the idea that prisons functioned best when prisoners and staff felt invested in the institution. He developed what became known as the participatory model in prison governance, which allowed for limited self-representation by incarcerated people.[90] Johnson believed that prisons should incapacitate dangerous men and women, but also help "our clients become independent and responsible citizens."[91]

For Johnson, rehabilitation and punishment were bound together in correctional work. He shirked the popular idea that prisons were no longer organized around rehabilitation, arguing that "we must turn to a new practice of corrections in which living experiences have purpose."[92] Johnson developed a prison governance model aimed at imposing the least amount of punishment necessary to maintain a secure, effective prison. This model directly contrasted with the "control" model, a term used by criminologists to refer to a focus on discipline, incapacitation, and a hierarchical prison structure.[93]

Over time, reform launched by prisoners became more difficult in American prisons. State prison systems became large, sterile, bureaucratic institutions that proved even more hostile to incarcerated people. In response to prisoner-led challenges to confinement, Congress passed the Prison Litigation Reform Act in 1995. The act was designed to transfer control of prisons back to the state—out of the hands of activist federal judges—and discourage prison lawsuits that senators described as "frivolous."[94]

In Michigan, state officials discussed rehabilitation through prisoner participation in prison governance, but also warehoused people in overcrowded facilities. The participatory penal governance in Michigan did little to improve prison life during the era of mass incarceration. Confinement was punishing, isolating, and torturous for those trapped inside correctional facilities.[95] Mass incarceration unraveled Johnson's plans for regional prisons and robust rehabilitative programs. While the rhetoric of prison reform supported Johnson's plans, he ultimately lacked the resources and political support to actualize his ideas. He continued to build more facilities and campaigned for rehabilitative programs, hoping to secure federal funding. In 1983 he pleaded, "The shortage of prison bed space, as well as the high cost of maintaining prisoners, give support to the argument that imprisonment should be reserved for those too dangerous to remain at large, with community alternatives used for the nondangerous."[96] Johnson urged MDOC officials to gain insight from penal systems in Europe: "There is already some precedence for such a system in Scandinavian countries where the concept of a 'day-fine' has been in use for some while. Under this concept, offenders are not fined a certain number of dollars, but rather the income from a certain number of days."[97] The penal code would have had to be rewritten and approved by lawmakers for such a proposal to gain traction in Michigan. Johnson suggested, "Probably a proposal of this kind is more palatable to the public than to some members of the criminal justice community, for whom it may represent a radical departure in practice."[98] Johnson argued that state prisons could benefit from alternatives, even in an age of mass imprisonment.

In 1984 Johnson presented his proposal to a conference of the American Correctional Association, where he sought support from other state prison leaders. A program of selective incapacitation addressed what he thought were two major problems with punishment in the 1980s. First, Americans' preference for sending all criminals to prison overburdened state criminal legal systems. Johnson explained, "This unnecessarily endangers the public when high risk cases are placed in the community; and it overburdens the prison system, and raises ethical questions when low risk offenders are imprisoned."[99] Second, states sent people to prison when it was not necessary for public safety.[100] Day fines seemed an appropriate alternative penalty for Johnson, and he argued that midwestern states would be particularly well suited for such a program.[101]

At the same time, the reality of Michigan's prison regime could not match Johnson's rhetoric. Johnson directed wardens to make room for female prisoners at several other facilities to relieve overcrowding. In September 1984, deputy director of the MDOC Alvin Whitfield assured Johnson, "All major projects are proceeding without major problems this month."[102] Camp Pontiac and Florence Crane housed women to relieve overcrowding at Huron Valley. Camp Pontiac was a minimum-security facility, and Florence Crane was a medium-security prison that was renovated to house only women to avoid further litigation from *Glover* regarding overcrowding. Johnson stepped down as the director of the MDOC in 1984.

* * *

Mass incarceration reconfigured state prison systems and blunted reforms conceived in the prisoners' rights movement. In 1991, the

Supreme Court upheld Michigan's 650 Lifer Law in *Harmelin v. Michigan*, 501 U.S. 957 (1991). Ronald Harmelin was convicted for the first time and sentenced to life without parole for possessing over 650 grams of cocaine. He argued that his sentence was cruel and unusual because the judge was barred from considering mitigating evidence. In a 5–4 decision, the United States Supreme Court held that the Eighth Amendment does not guarantee proportionality between the crime and the sentence. The court held that the punishment was cruel but not unusual.[103] In a dissenting opinion, Justice John Paul Stevens likened Michigan's 650 Lifer Law to the death penalty statutes that the court had found unconstitutional in *Furman*. Had Harmelin been convicted in another state he would have been sentenced to a much shorter term. Stevens argued, "No jurisdiction except Michigan has concluded that the offense belongs in a category where reform and rehabilitation are considered unattainable."[104]

Between 1978 and 1998, Michigan sentenced 240 people to life without the possibility of parole under the 650 Lifer Law, many of whom, like JeDonna Young, were convicted and sent to prison for the first time.[105] In her appeal, Young had argued that her sentence amounted to cruel and unusual punishment, but in 1989, a federal judge affirmed the lower court's decision, upholding Young's sentence.[106] In 1998, Republican governor John Engler approved the state legislature's revisions to the 650 Lifer Law, which allowed people to become eligible for parole after serving fifteen to twenty years.[107] Young received parole in 1999, after she had spent twenty years in prison.[108] She hoped to earn a graduate degree in social work and contribute to Families Against Mandatory Minimums, a national nonprofit organization that supported her release. When considering release for those sentenced under the 650 Lifer Law, the Michigan Parole Board took into account the role that the applicant played in the crime, where the arrest happened, and whether drugs were sold to children.[109] Young's story suggests that she benefited from higher education and job training in women's prisons, which were some of the hard-won legacies of *Glover* and the broader prisoners' rights movement. As we will see in the next chapter, the MDOC would continue to obstruct prison reform, embrace unusually long sentences, and increase the state's prison capacity for women.

5

From Civil Rights to Human Rights

Resisting Violence against Incarcerated Women

After being incarcerated for fourteen years, Stacy Barker, a Black woman, gained a chance at freedom. Before prison, Barker had been an aide worker in an assisted living facility in Southfield, a northern suburb of Detroit. She recalled that she loved the work and was skilled at helping people. One of the residents was Frank Madsen, an eighty-one-year-old white man and retired Lutheran minister who attempted to rape Barker in 1986. She told him to stop. When he wouldn't, she struck him over the head with a small wooden statue within reach, but he continued attacking her. When he cornered her in the kitchen of his apartment, she stabbed him repeatedly with a paring knife. As she tried to defend herself, she killed him. At trial in October 1987, Barker claimed she had acted in self-defense, but the jury deadlocked. She faced a second trial in November and the jury found her guilty of first-degree murder. The judge sentenced Barker to life without parole.[1]

The Supreme Court of Michigan rejected Barker's appeal. The court acknowledged that the trial judge should have given jurors proper instructions by explaining that Barker could use deadly force to defend herself from a sexual assault. Those instructions had been omitted at trial, but Michigan's highest court ruled that the error was "harmless." The court held that it was unlikely a reasonable juror would be convinced Barker acted in self-defense. The court reasoned that the victim was old and "enfeebled." However, at the time of his death, Madsen weighed two hundred pounds, was six feet tall, and was able to move throughout the retirement home while using a cane. Barker was a twenty-year-old survivor who had been abused as a child and the victim of a gang rape as a teenager. When Madsen assaulted her, she was terrified she was about to be raped again. At trial, Barker described how the victim "wrestled her to the floor" and ripped her clothes as he attacked her. In 1999, a federal court overturned her conviction and granted her a new trial.[2]

Barker had established herself as a strategic and resilient prison organizer by the time she faced a third trial. She had filed successful lawsuits against the Michigan Department of Corrections (MDOC) accusing prison guards of sexual assaults and rape of incarcerated women. As a result, guards targeted her for retaliation and abuse. Barker later explained that she was able to fight to curtail violence in prisons because she had a strong support network and was firmly resolved to secure her release. When she began her sentence, she was a mother to a young daughter and motivated to gain her freedom. Members of the local chapter of the Women's Lawyers Association of Michigan attended her new trial in 2001. The organization had awarded Barker with the Liberty Bell to commend her fight against sexual violence for imprisoned women. Her attorney told the *Detroit Free Press* that Barker's activism would have no bearing on her trial but conceded that Barker had "certainly received far greater punishment than simply being incarcerated." In 2001, Barker pleaded guilty to second-degree murder and her sentence was reduced to twenty-one to seventy years, giving her a chance to one day return from prison.[3]

Barker's experience in the criminal legal system illustrates some of the ways retrenchment politics sustained mass incarceration and permitted violence in prisons. In the 1990s, politics of law and order encouraged laws and practices that clamped down on the prisoners' rights movement and women's movements. The 1994 Violent Crime Control and Law Enforcement Act and the 1996 Prison Litigation Reform Act (PLRA), respectively, bolstered the militarization of police and proliferation of prisons across the country. The PLRA made it difficult for incarcerated people to file lawsuits and easy for federal judges to dismiss them.[4] As the national prison population rose above 1.6 million people, there was a dramatic reduction in prison litigation cases. The total number of prison civil rights cases filed went from forty thousand to approximately twenty-five thousand during the first year PLRA went into effect.[5] These shifts also made it increasingly difficult for incarcerated women to document violations of their rights, all but guaranteeing that women would be isolated and vulnerable to state violence.

In the 1990s, state prisons embraced what I call "equality born of retrenchment." This term describes the impoverished applications of equality and of a politics that converged to silence prison litigation and deny prison reform. The equality born of retrenchment was cemented in laws and prison rules that left incarcerated women subjected to rodent infestations, torture, and sexual abuse. However, equality born of retrenchment did not extinguish activism in women's prisons. Incarcerated women, especially Black women and radical feminists, continued to resist, rebel, and petition for different terms of confinement. Stacy Barker and other imprisoned women filed successful lawsuits that changed Michigan's criminal legal regime while revealing the brutality of its prisons. Their prolonged ordeals in the courts illustrate the interconnected ways in which women navigated racial harm, gendered violence, and mass incarceration. Women in prison turned to federal and state courts, the federal government, and international human rights organizations to affirm their rights to privacy, bodily integrity, and dignity. In internal grievances, lawsuits, and investigations, they documented torture and violence, rat infestations, and sexual assaults by guard as they sought reprieve from state violence propelled by mass incarceration.

Sanitation, Infestations, and Medical Care for Women

Basic sanitation in overcrowded prisons compounded poor medical care, mental illness, and gendered violence. As the founder of the Michigan Women's Justice and Clemency Project, Carol Jacobsen, observed, "[Florence] Crane's women's prison is like a medieval dungeon. . . . There are dripping ceilings, rats and mice in the food, bugs everywhere. The women are packed in like sardines. Forty-one women share two shower heads, five sinks and two toilets in a tiny bathroom."[6] Jacobsen's observations were consistent with stories from incarcerated women. At night, Mary Glover heard rats scurrying along floors, roofs, and gutters. Guards working the night shift would barricade themselves in their offices to prevent rats from crawling under their desks, which in turn trapped the rats in the long corridors where women tried to sleep. It also meant that, at night, guards were unlikely to help prisoners with medical issues or intervene if prisoners were assaulted. Prisoners complained that rats and mice infested their lockers and laid claim to food purchased in the commissary. Women confirmed that during meals, they had seen rodent feces in the serving trays.[7]

Prisoners watched rats shuffle between large trash bins perched on cement platforms outside of the kitchen. Mary Glover remembered, "I filed a grievance and it was returned to me almost immediately, saying, in the words of the administrative assistant to the warden, that this was a group grievance and could not be filed by an individual. That this issue needed to be taken up with the warden's forum." Incarcerated women jumped at the invitation to complain, but the warden refused to hire an exterminator. In an act of desperation, Glover called her sister, who lived close to the prison, and she recommended calling the Public Health Department. Years later, Glover discovered that her sister also called the warden's office and told her that the rats were venturing into homes of surrounding neighborhoods.[8]

The prison finally exterminated the rats. Huge trucks hauled away the dumpsters behind the kitchen. Men disembarked and swung large mallets to break up the cement that had sheltered nests and burrow holes. Incarcerated women crowded at the windows. Glover saw the men jumping around, trying to escape the onslaught of rodents. Prisoners delighted in the spectacle: "We laughed and laughed and laughed! Watching men scream and watching the folly of the rats taking over the prison. Which at the time was horrific but was hilarious in its own right because we watched prison guards also squealing and running as they came toward the kitchen. I actually saw food service workers dancing, moving their feet up and down on the back dock as they tried to get away from the rats as they went back home." The humorous interlude quickly turned gruesome: "A decision was made to poison the rats. They had to catch the rats that had come from under the pad. So, they came with black boxes that look like a black lunch box and it had rat poison in them. So these little black rat catch-boxes were placed in the yard all over the facility and the rats were fed some kind of horrible rat killer. And it caused them to bleed. So now we had bleeding rats in the yard and on sidewalks and in doorways. There were bleeding rats all over the place."[9]

Basic standards of sanitation were some of the least of the problems incarcerated women confronted. Incarcerated women documented improper policies for receiving new prisoners, which led to significant infestations and illness. Edward Trudeau, a field investigator in the Office of Legislative Corrections Ombudsman in Lansing, shared his findings with MDOC director Robert Brown after examining the Reception and Guidance Center (RGC) at Huron Valley Correctional Facility for Women. The RGC processed new prisoners before they were assigned to general population housing. Trudeau interviewed women who were living in the gym while they waited for a housing assignment. Some women were recent transfers, but other women had been living there for several weeks. "All of the prisoners were concerned about their health because of being thrown together with prisoners coming directly from county jails who had not properly been processed into the system." Incarcerated women were especially frustrated because pubic lice had spread rapidly throughout the unit. Prison staff ordered all inmates to take showers with Kwell, a chemical poisonous to lice, and wash their linens. Trudeau concluded that the plan might have been "too little, too late." Women enrolled in classes together, shared bathrooms, ate in common dining halls, and congregated in common areas in a generally overcrowded institution, and Trudeau lamented, "There is the possibility that the crabs have, by now, infested the entire facility."[10]

Other women entered Huron Valley in dire need of medical attention. One woman arrived on July 13, 1988, and prison officials put her in a top bunk bed in a dorm with the general prison population. She was addicted to drugs and had "numerous abscessed areas on both legs which, prior to coming to prison, doctors had tried to correct with skin grafts." She was incarcerated in the middle of her convalescence, and the grafts never attached properly. Trudeau wrote, "This prisoner has large, open, postulating sores on both legs from her ankles to her hips. Further, she has one finger on her left hand that has the same type of ulceration and has turned black." When the woman had been quarantined as a new prisoner, she had received relatively decent medical care. Her limbs were dressed in clean gauze each day. However, when the prison moved her to the general population living quarters, her treatment ended. Her condition rapidly deteriorated, and she couldn't even find clean dressings for her wounds. Other prisoners told Trudeau that the woman "should not have been placed on a top bunk in her condition, that she should not have to withstand the embarrassment of exposing the condition of her body to the other prisoners while trying to take a shower or to clean her wounds." Trudeau took this information to the assistant deputy warden, Roy Rider, who eventually found a bed for her within the same building as the prison medical staff. Her condition gradually stabilized after her requests for daily medical visits were granted.[11]

The harms incarcerated women endured highlight the chaos of prisons and the contingency of mass incarceration. In 1988, attorney Charlene Snow wrote to a clinical lawyer at the University of Michigan, urging him to file lawsuits to improve healthcare for women in prison. Snow summarized, "The fact of the matter as I have observed it, is that healthcare for women prisoners is almost non-existent."[12] In 1976, the United States Supreme Court held that "deliberate indifference by prison personnel to a prisoner's serious illness or injury constitutes cruel and unusual punishment contravening the Eighth Amendment" and established a constitutional right to healthcare for incarcerated people.[13] Despite these legal protections, incarcerated women struggled to access basic medical care. Pamela Disbrow began her prison sentence in 1987. She told guards that she had been having trouble hearing and never received medical attention. In 1995, her conviction was overturned and she was released. She visited a doctor only to learn that she had permanently lost most of her hearing although her condition had been preventable.[14]

Linda Hamilton, a white woman serving a life sentence, also struggled to access medical care. In 1976, Hamilton had caught her husband raping their four-year-old daughter. They were living in the state of Washington, and Hamilton reported the rape to the closest hospital and the military police, where her husband was serving in the army. She tried to escape with her children, but her husband intervened and held them hostage in their house. Hamilton eventually escaped with her children by driving across the country so they could live closer to family in Michigan, but her husband followed her. She explained to a friend her fears for her and her children's safety, and shortly after that conversation her husband was found dead, killed by an unknown person. Hamilton was convicted of first-degree murder. The rape and abuse were never raised at Hamilton's trial. In prison, Hamilton slowly lost her ability to see and never received proper medical attention. Hamilton was diagnosed with a thyroid eye disease, which can cause eye dryness and protrusion. A rare number of people with the disease might become blind, especially when symptoms do not receive adequate treatment.[15] The Michigan

Women's Justice and Clemency Project supported Hamilton's clemency case. In 2009, Governor Jennifer Granholm signed her petition. When Hamilton gained her freedom, she was legally blind.[16]

Fatal medical neglect was not unheard of in women's prisons. In 1987, Darlene Lake collapsed in front of a guard during a severe asthma attack. Several minutes later, a nurse walked up and moved Lake, by then unconscious, into a wheelchair. The prison transferred Lake to a hospital too late. She died of complications from the asthma attack.[17]

Grievance reports and requests for internal hearings were the main tools prisoners used to document prison brutality, and incarcerated women kept count of who won disputes within the prison. In 1991, they noticed a racialized pattern. At Florence Crane Women's Correctional Facility, a prisoner asked field investigator Keith Barber, "Why can't we beat tickets in Coldwater, especially Black females?"[18] Tickets were a disciplinary tool prison staff used to document infractions of the rules. Individual records went into an incarcerated person's file, and parole board members would often look at disciplinary records to help determine whether a person was ready for release. Incarcerated people could request a hearing, especially if they disagreed with the allegation or if they believed they were treated unfairly. Barber eschewed any discussion of racism and explained how each officer must evaluate individual cases on their own merit: "There are many reasons why a prisoner may not be able to beat a ticket and each would require individual analysis to determine if the hearing officer reached a reasonable conclusion. The hearing officer is supposed to decide a case based on a preponderance of evidence, meaning that the disposition should reflect whatever the majority of the evidence indicates."[19] The prison denied the possibility of racial bias in the enforcement of its rules. The prison's refusal forestalled incarcerated women critiquing institution-wide problems and forced them to reflect individually on their circumstances.

Male Prison Guards in Women's Prisons

The dynamics between incarcerated women and prison guards became particularly adversarial after the MDOC permitted men to work in women's prisons in the 1980s. The MDOC had racially integrated prison staff and the prison population in the mid-twentieth century, but employees remained segregated by sex until the late 1970s.[20] In his memoir, former MDOC director Perry Johnson described the exclusion of women as discriminatory and exploitative, writing, "For years, women at SPSM [the State Prison in Southern Michigan in Jackson] worked alongside male officers at the information desk and in the inmate visiting areas, as well as searching female visitors, and they did this all on clerical pay."[21] Female guards successfully argued that their prohibition from working in men's facilities barred them from promotions, perpetuating unequal pay and treatment in the workplace. A federal judge was persuaded by the guards' claims, and women gained the right to work in men's prisons in 1982.[22] Likewise, men began working in women's prisons after male officers threatened to sue the MDOC in 1985, claiming that they were targets of gender-based discrimination because they were prohibited from working in women's prisons.[23] In 1987, approximately thirty male officers worked at Huron Valley, comprising 25 percent of the workforce in the prison.[24]

Officers received little training when they switched prisons, reflecting an assumption that men's and women's prisons demanded a uniform set of skills. This also revealed the MDOC's approach to muting acknowledgment of gender difference for incarcerated women. The MDOC pursued gender parity in its staffing, training, and confinement practices, affording women little room to assert gender differences or capacious applications of equality that could have acknowledged unique experiences of women.

Bringing men to work in women's prisons with little training opened the door to corruption and sexual abuse. Prison reports and grievances illustrate how male officers and incarcerated women used sex as a bargaining tool. Some incarcerated women discussed how offering sexual favors would improve their living conditions, commissary account, or material comforts difficult to find in prison.[25] Meanwhile guards sexually profiled prisoners and described abundant opportunities to engage in sexual activity with incarcerated women. Henry Parker, a guard who transferred from a men's prison, took a brief training course before he began working at Huron Valley. His supervisors instructed the incoming cohort of male guards to "be wary of inmates trying to manipulate [their] behavior with sex." Parker claimed that incarcerated women solicited him for sexual favors constantly during his first few weeks. Parker interpreted the exchange as a test of his self-control and masculinity. "They are trying to see if you are a weak person. It's more so with women because women feel that you're a man so, naturally, when it comes to sex, you aren't supposed to turn that down. They go after a man even harder than a man will go after a woman."[26] Such comments illustrated power dynamics within the prison that were entangled with harmful racialized and gendered narratives of overly sexualized women of color, who were also disproportionately incarcerated.[27]

Female MDOC employees also experienced sexual harassment at work because the internal reporting system encouraged silence. The MDOC required employees to complete a grievance report that documented the allegation and named the accused person. However, just filing an initial report was a risky step most women were unwilling to take. Retaliation, job insecurity, and public shaming served as serious deterrents. In 1986, six female employees at Florence Crane women's prison complained to three different supervisors that Robert Barto, the prison chaplain, had been sexually harassing them. Patricia Balasco, the director of prisoner services and one of the few Black women in a leadership position, verified the women's complaints. She confirmed how each woman had experienced behavior or comments "offensive to them." However, Balasco could not discipline Barto without a formal report, and all six women refused to file one. They had decided either to avoid Barto or to tell him how he had made them feel. Balasco concluded, "When the women indicated to Barto that the words, invitations, or actions were not appreciated or welcomed the behavior did not continue."[28] The prison passed responsibility along to female MDOC employees for changing male behavior in the workplace.

Incarcerated women documented an increase in sexual harassment and assault from male employees when they started working in women's prisons. In Huron Valley, male guards regularly assaulted incarcerated women. Sequita Eaves recalled how upsetting it was to regularly witness sexual assaults: "You had some good guards, and you had the most part of them, they were really bad. . . . They treated you really, really bad. At the time when I was in prison the guards were having sex with the women, and all. It was just a big thing." Eaves said, "They were just really nasty. They were really nasty."[29] MDOC administrators required evidence to discipline employees, but accusations were difficult to prove.

Perhaps aware of how the women's prison offered fertile ground for a scandal, Huron Valley warden Tekla Miller, a white woman, bluntly claimed that most accusations of guards harassing women were unfounded. "I've had a lot of problems with the men . . . because when we first started having the men it naturally was a great game for the women prisoners to say, 'Oh, he's writing me letters,' or 'I'm being assaulted.' And we have investigated every accusation whether it's on a male officer or a female officer and 99 percent have proven false." [30] Nonetheless, in 1987, Miller fired two male guards because they were having sex with prisoners. [31] Sex with incarcerated women violated prison policies and state law, although the dismissal of a small number of guards did not stem the rising number of allegations of sexual violence in 1990s. [32] In 1991, field investigator Keith Barber reviewed the flood of allegations of sexual violence in women's prisons: "It is difficult to prove in many cases that an officer has lied on, or was obscene to, a prisoner, giving the perception that the officer gets away with it. Based on my experience, supervisors and the warden generally do not tolerate such behavior, however, sufficient evidence must be presented. . . . Most frequently allegations of this nature concern a one on one situation. It is difficult, if not impossible, to enforce disciplinary action against an employee based on that, even if the allegation is believed to be true by the administration." [33] This problem of proof also surfaced when incarcerated women asked the prison for disciplinary sanctions against guards who were routinely "obscene and crude." MDOC officials issued a single, standard response: "Our office reviews each complaint of this nature on an individual basis. . . . The issue cannot be easily raised without proof." [34] The MDOC's refusal to act and reluctance to accept women's accounts of sexual assault exacerbated frustrations among incarcerated women. Incarcerated women's versions of events were recorded, but the prison largely dismissed or denied allegations of gender violence.

In 1988, attorneys heard reports of guards restraining prisoners as a form of punishment and torture. The incarcerated women had sent a number of complaints detailing how guards were using "top of bed" restraints on women at Huron Valley, and the Office of Legislative Corrections Ombudsman in Lansing tried to get more information from Warden Miller. In a letter to Miller, investigator Trudeau asked, "A complaint has been received that prisoners are stripped naked prior to being placed into 'top of bed' physical restraints. Is this true?" Three prisoners—Shelly Williams, Linda Bouck, and Patricia Nolley—told the ombudsman's office how they were neglected by medical personnel and denied access to a toilet for hours. The women described how the guards forced them into "leg irons, handcuffs and belly chains which are connected by [chains] to eye bolts embedded in a concrete slab in the ceiling." The women described the restraints as degrading, cruel, and unusual punishment. The Office of Legislative Corrections had the option to encourage prohibition of this treatment but expressed indifference. The ombudsman suggested that the prison use soft, leather restraints in place of metal bolts and chains.[35]

As the civil rights of incarcerated women became increasingly fragile in the 1990s, women reframed their right to bodily integrity as a human right. They drew the interest of legal agencies and international organizations that helped put pressure on state prisons to reform or abolish certain practices.[36] When the state offered flimsy responses to reports of sexual abuse and torture, incarcerated women framed the violence as human rights violations.

Sexual Violence and Torture

Incarcerated women told harrowing stories of sexual violence in prison. Human rights activists raised awareness of abuse and torture in state prisons and leveraged international law to pressure states to end brutal practices, especially in facilities that confined children and women. In the 1990s, the DOJ, Amnesty International, and Human Rights Watch investigated patterns of sexual assault in state prisons around the country. An array of reports exposed tolerance of longstanding violence within women's prisons. These and other organizations started to put pressure on state prisons to end abuse of incarcerated women at a time when community members, courts, and activists dismantled torture regimes in other areas of the criminal legal system.

In 1994, the United States Supreme Court ruled that the prison would be liable if officials were aware of "substantial risk of serious harm" and did not attempt to protect prisoners.[37] Dee Farmer was a Black transgender prisoner who was born biologically male and identified as female. After a 1986 conviction for credit card fraud, a federal court sent

Farmer to a men's prison in Wisconsin where prison officials placed her in solitary confinement for long stretches to protect her personal safety. Farmer was transferred to a federal maximum-security prison for men in Terre Haute, Indiana, where an incarcerated man brutally raped her at knifepoint. Farmer argued that federal officials knew she was likely to be raped in a men's prison, which violated her Eighth Amendment protection against cruel and unusual punishment. All nine justices agreed with Farmer. In a separate concurrence joined by Justice John Paul Stevens, Justice Harry Blackmun described how the case "sends a clear message to prison officials that their affirmative duty under the Constitution to provide for the safety of inmates is not to be taken lightly."[38] For many incarcerated women, the ruling did little to curtail sexual violence in prisons.

The PLRA, signed by President Clinton in 1996, delivered another blow to the flagging prisoners' rights movement. The PLRA blunted activist intervention of federal judges in state prisons because it erected four major obstacles for incarcerated people filing lawsuits. Legal scholar Margo Schlanger has written extensively about the PLRA and analyzed some of the major ways it discouraged lawsuits, all of which applied to incarcerated women in Michigan. First, the act required prisoners to exhaust the internal grievance procedures before turning to the courts. Prisoners in Michigan knew that the grievance system favored the officers, but under the PLRA, a judge could easily dismiss a lawsuit if the prisoner failed to go through the internal grievance system. Second, prisoners had to pay filing fees in the federal courts. The PLRA created barriers for incarcerated people who were unable to pay the fees by establishing a complex fee formula. Prisoners could still file *in forma pauperis*, which would allow them to ask the federal court to waive the fee, but such a filing introduced a different problem: a third obstacle created by the PLRA was the "three strikes" rule mandating that if a prisoner had three cases dismissed when filing *in forma pauperis*, they would be ineligible to pursue further claims in federal courts. (There was an exception to the "three strikes" rule if the prisoner alleged that they would suffer extreme physical injury if the complaint was not resolved.) Finally, incarcerated people could only allege that the prison was causing emotional harm or injuring their mental health if they could also prove they were suffering physical harm.[39]

After decades of intervention by federal courts on behalf of prisoners in state facilities, politicians and prison leaders across the country interpreted the PLRA as a victory for states' rights. Historian Robert Chase has analyzed how states responded to prisoner-led legal challenges with a militarized carceral apparatus that embraced prison construction and harsh disciplinary regimes. In response to prison-conditions litigation grounded in Black power and civil rights movements, the PLRA curtailed new lawsuits that fought the penal practices in states. The PLRA limited federal intervention in prison cases by placing an expiration date on a federal court's involvement: two years after a court order unless the court found that the violation persisted.[40]

With the PLRA, legal scholars and politicians claimed that local officials could regain control of state prisons. For example, two academics extolled the benefits of states managing their own prisons and called the PLRA an "unexpected and much-needed legislative gift" and "a watershed in the struggle over whether judges or elected mayors and legislators should have the power to make municipal policy." An op-ed in the *Detroit Free Press* disregarded the well-being of incarcerated people in its protest against federal involvement in state prison management: "In Michigan, for example, a federal court controls the warmth of the prison food, the brightness of prison lights, the comfort levels of prison air and water, the availability of electrical outlets in prison cells and the professional credentials of prison barbers."[41] Such descriptions fed deceptive public perceptions of prisons as regulated, clean, and welcoming, while reports from incarcerated people revealed the opposite. When the PLRA was passed, federal court orders intended to improve prison conditions and limit incarcerated populations in overcrowded facilities became vulnerable.

Facing mounting legal roadblocks, incarcerated women pursued different methods to resist and reform Michigan's carceral regime. Two major lawsuits sought to change the culture of women's prisons and protect women from sexual violence and harassment. In 1996, incarcerated women in Florence Crane and Robert Scott filed a lawsuit in federal court, *Nunn v. Michigan Department of Corrections*, in which they alleged that male guards targeted them for a range of sexual abuses and harassment. They claimed that guards retaliated against women who filed grievance reports and violated their rights to privacy. They described how male guards physically threatened and assaulted them. These issues were compounded by a lack of training and discipline for male guards who subjected women to abuse. Over thirty incarcerated women named themselves as plaintiffs. Also in 1996, incarcerated women sought injunctions on policies that made them vulnerable to abuse, mistreatment, and violations of their privacy when they filed a second massive class action lawsuit in state court, *Neal v. Michigan Department of Corrections*.[42] Deborah LaBelle, an attorney who worked on the *Glover, Nunn*, and *Neal* lawsuits, described how, when she was working to increase access to education and vocational training in prison as a part of *Glover*, "I noticed more women started to report abuse." There were incarcerated girls as young as fourteen years old who had been placed in women's prison who told their attorneys that guards were sexually assaulting them.[43]

Nunn and *Neal* underscored a shift in discourse from civil rights to human rights for incarcerated women. Incarcerated women exposed abuse that was tolerated in Michigan prisons at a time when other torture regimes were exposed. The infamous use of torture by the Chicago police under Jon Burge's leadership was dismantled because of the persistent work of a local coalition of attorneys, activists, community members, and victims.[44] In 1994, the United States ratified the Convention Against Torture nearly a decade after the United Nations General Assembly had adopted the text. This was largely a symbolic gesture since the Reagan administration had created a series of loopholes so that the United States could ratify the document, demonstrating a commitment to human rights abroad while evading the legal consequences through several conditions and amendments.[45] For example, in 1992, the United States became a party to the United Nations International Covenant on Civil and Political Rights, but clarified that the United States was committed to the prohibition of "cruel, inhuman and degrading treatment or punishment" only to the extent outlined in the Eighth Amendment's ban on cruel and unusual punishment in the US Constitution.[46]

Human Rights Watch (HRW) investigated conditions in women's prisons in the United States from 1994 to 1996 and concluded that Michigan's prisons tolerated rampant sexual violence. Investigators spoke with incarcerated women, returning citizens, attorneys, MDOC employees, and prisoner' rights advocates and found that the MDOC permitted a "systematic campaign of retaliation" for women named in lawsuits. Investigators documented rapes, sexual assaults, privacy violations, and verbal harassment, which had become routine by the mid-1990s. The DOJ conducted an investigation and made similar findings. HRW issued a second report on Michigan's prison in 1998 concluding that the state permitted rape, sexual assault, harassment, violations of privacy, and other forms of degradation.[47]

Connections to human rights work proved crucial to documenting abuse and strengthening calls for decarceration. Stacy Barker's life sentence started in 1987. For the first seven years of Barker's prison term, she maintained the lowest security classification by avoiding disciplinary tickets and never testing positive for illegal substances. She also pursued an undergraduate degree in behavioral science through correspondence courses. At the same time, she grew adept at using the courts to protect her rights and as a form of survival. In 1995, she won a civil lawsuit after a male guard sexually assaulted her for nearly two years, and a monetary settlement was delivered in June. In September, guards began calling Barker a "set-up queen."[48] The nickname was a riff on the racialized caricature of a "welfare queen," a term that supported a misleading narrative and criminalized Black women.[49] Barker began suspecting that guards were targeting her for retaliation after her legal victory against the abusive prison guard. Guards would search Barker's room and claim to have found drugs, a razor, and other contraband, which Barker believed were planted by the officers. Her security level changed, and the prison placed her in solitary confinement for 275 days, from October 1995 to August 1996. Women placed in punitive segregation confronted the most restrictive aspects of Michigan's penal regime. Barker was locked in her cell for twenty-three hours each day. She was permitted only three showers each week and lost her chance to attend classes or work in prison. She could not use the phone, and visits were permitted only by appointment.[50]

In January 1997, a correctional officer sexually assaulted Barker and another plaintiff in *Nunn*. This time, Barker did not report the abuse to her attorney or to the medical team in the prison. Another incarcerated woman wrote to Barker's attorney because she had seen Officer Portman enter Barker's cell. In February, Barker reported to the prison psychiatrist that guards were raping her. The prison transferred her to the psychiatric hospital in Huron Valley, where the staff members harassed her and once again called her the "set-up queen." In October, Barker attempted to take her own life. She described to HRW investigators how, when guards found her, three male guards removed her clothing and put her in a top-of-bed restraint with no sheet or blanket. Guards left her in the five-point restraint over a prison bed for nine hours. The prison then placed her on suicide watch, where she was kept within four feet of an officer for twenty-four hours. Typically, suicide watch lasted three to five days, according to the prison policies in 1997. For Barker, the prison watched her in this way for close to a month. After twenty-nine days, the prison transferred Barker to Florence Crane and placed her in a housing unit that was staffed by another guard accused of sexual assault in *Nunn*. In the court hearings for *Nunn*, a former female prison guard stated that she heard other MDOC employees "talking about punishing Barker." The former guard spoke on the condition of anonymity because she feared retaliation.[51]

Michigan officials went to great lengths to deny, block, and remove further inquiry into the conditions of women's prisons. US assistant attorney general Deval Patrick, who led the Civil Rights Division at the DOJ, wrote a twelve-page letter to Governor John Engler in 1995 stating, "The sexual abuse of women inmates by guards, including rapes, lack of adequate medical care, including mental health services, grossly deficient sanitation, crowding, and other threats to the physical safety and well-being of inmates violates their constitutional rights."[52] However, Engler refused to give the DOJ access to Michigan prisons.

Newspaper coverage of the tension between the state and federal government conveyed skepticism regarding the incarcerated women's claims of sexual abuse and assault. State legislators called the allegations of abuse "serious but doubtful." Gerald Law, a Republican state legislator from Plymouth, Michigan, the former hometown of the old Detroit House of Correction, stated, "These women aren't in prison because they tell the truth. Some of them expect this is a holiday."[53] In 1997, the DOJ returned to Michigan to investigate the record of abuse in women's prisons. The federal investigators tried to conduct interviews with prisoners and guards at women's prisons, but the unwillingness of state officials to assist in the investigation hampered their work.

Ronesha Williams, a woman incarcerated at Robert Scott Correctional Facility for Women, began a one-to-three-year sentence determined to fly under the radar of guards and fellow prisoners, but in July 1997, Williams decided to tell DOJ investigators that a prison guard had raped her in May. After she reported the rape, the prison transferred her to Florence Crane, where she was placed in a housing unit managed by a guard named Thomas Hauk. Williams complained of excessive pat-and-frisks from Hauk, a defendant in *Nunn*, and other officers working the housing unit. During one search, an officer threatened her. He accused her of recording each pat-and-frisk in her notebook and told her that he "better not show up in relation to the law suit." Williams was scheduled for a transfer to community release in May 1998, but in February Hauk wrote four minor misconduct tickets against Williams, and the tickets blocked her from her release. Williams told HRW investigators that she regretted reporting the rape. She had no idea the report would make her life so troubled, and she came to believe she might have had a real shot at leaving prison had she remained silent about the guard who raped her.[54]

The retaliation against prisoners who reported sexual violence silenced many incarcerated women. One plaintiff in *Nunn* went by Jane Doe to avoid retaliation. Doe accused an officer of exposing himself and making sexual demands in July 1997. She sought counsel from the prison chaplain to work through the episode without reporting it through the internal grievance system. On his own initiative, the chaplain reported Doe's allegation to prison administrators, and Doe believed prison guards targeted her because of the chaplain's report.[55]

In 2000, the parties from *Nunn* reached a settlement with Michigan officials, which required the MDOC to maintain a policy prohibiting sexual harassment, misconduct, and retaliation. The MDOC stated that it would conduct background screenings of potential employees and investigate allegations of sexual misconduct.[56] In the following years plaintiffs complained that sexual abuse and harassment continued. The court issued its final agreement in 2007, barring male guards from supervising female housing units.[57]

Retrenchment politics in Michigan produced new restrictions on prisoners' rights that compounded the sexual violence. In *Neal v. Michigan Department of Corrections*, incarcerated women alleged that the state permitted sexual abuse and harassment in women's prisons that violated the state's main civil rights laws.[58] In 1999, Michigan legislators passed a law that excluded incarcerated people from the Elliot-Larsen Civil Rights Act of 1976 and the Persons with Disabilities Civil Rights Act of 1976, Michigan's main civil rights laws.[59] The Elliot-Larsen Civil Rights Act prohibited discrimination "based upon religion, race, color, national origin, age, sex, height, weight, familial status, or marital status." The Persons with Disabilities Civil Rights Act granted access to public services and prohibited discrimination against people with disabilities.[60] LaBelle, an attorney who represented the women in *Glover*, *Neal*, and *Nunn*, argued in an opinion piece for the *Detroit Free Press*, "The assault on prisoners' civil rights is a misguided reaction to a few cases that have brought public attention to serious claims about the mistreatment and abuse of female prisoners and the denial of program participation to the disabled."[61] The editorial board of the *Detroit Free Press* affirmed LaBelle's conclusions when it wrote, "Prisoners' rights do not rank high with many people. But this isn't about TV sets and workout rooms. It's the right of a prisoner who can't walk to have a wheelchair, or of a prisoner who's female to remain free of sexual assault, or of a prisoner who's elderly and sick to receive decent health care."[62] LaBelle contended that the prioritization of the victim in the criminal legal system caused many Americans to reject the application of universal human rights for incarcerated people. She argued, "Treatment of prisoners in the United States . . . has always been diminished by the construct that those detained in jails and prisons, in addition to the loss of civil and political rights associated with violating laws, are reduced to a lesser human status."[63] LaBelle accused the state of trying to end ongoing prison litigation by claiming that female prisoners did not have civil rights. She argued, "The Michigan Court of Appeals has ruled in the past that Michigan's civil rights law, like the federal civil rights acts it is based upon, applies to prisoners. But rather than respond to the women's claims in the *Neal* case, the Michigan Department of Corrections has supported removing the law's protections for prisoners. There is nothing unclear about the language and intent of Michigan's civil rights acts. They were intended to ensure the most basic rights for all persons."[64]

The testimony at trial strengthened the conclusions of the human rights investigators. For example, Toni Bunton had been incarcerated at Scott Correctional Facility when she was eighteen years old. By the time she gave testimony in the *Neal* trial in 2009, she had spent sixteen years incarcerated. Bunton was raped eight times in prison, making her one of many incarcerated women who described being raped, assaulted, and groped by male prison guards. She described, "I felt this was part of prison life. I didn't know any different. Nobody sat me down and told me."[65] A female guard gave testimony describing how she had seen male guards go into women's cells or take women into stairwells, but she never reported anything because guards had threatened her with retaliation.[66]

In 2009, the court ruled in the women's favor in *Neal v. MDOC*. Over five hundred incarcerated women were represented in the lawsuit.[67] Jurors had awarded ten incarcerated women fifteen million dollars. In an unusual move, a woman who served on the jury asked to read a statement: "We the members of the jury, as representatives of the citizens of Michigan, would like to express our extreme regret and apologies for what you have been through."[68] For many of the incarcerated women, it was the first time they had received an apology for the sexual violence in prison. It was also an explicit acknowledgment of the violence that is tethered to prisons. By the time the case ended, the parties in *Neal* settled for one hundred million dollars. The *New York Times* reported, "Four hundred more current or former female inmates have claimed for part of a $100 million settlement in the month since the state resolved accusations that prisoners had been raped, groped, and peeked at by male members of the corrections staff."[69] The case was a major victory for incarcerated women, but the culture of violence, neglect, and isolation continued to characterize women's prisons.

Human Rights in Women's Prisons

Human rights organizations placed Michigan's incarcerated women within the national and global context of antiviolence movements and thereby strengthened the women's critiques of the prison. In 1999, Amnesty International published "Not Part of My Sentence," a report that examined the lack of protections for incarcerated women who were raped or victims of sexual assault in prisons. The organization had been pushing for Congress to pass legislation that would criminalize sexual contact between prison employees and incarcerated women. The report found that fear of retaliation among incarcerated populations meant that sexual assault in prison was underreported, and few states offered standard services for survivors. In a follow-up report, Amnesty International found over a thousand cases of sexual abuse against incarcerated women in forty-nine states from 1998 to 2001. The organization concluded that there were few legal protections in place for incarcerated women, making them vulnerable to sexual abuse.[70]

The United States was eager to affirm that torture was something that happened abroad but not within its borders. (International law deemed rape of prisoners a form of torture.) In 2003, for example, President George W. Bush routinely denied reports of torture at the American military prison at Guantánamo. However, his protests were called into question by reports of torture at another prison run by the US military: in April 2004, *60 Minutes II* on CBS and Seymour Hersh at the *New Yorker* broke stories detailing the torture of prisoners by American intelligence and military forces at Abu Ghraib in Iraq. The broadcast and exposé projected gruesome photographs of detainees being tortured. Images captured the bodies of dead prisoners on ice while soldiers smiled or gave a thumbs-up for the camera. Historian Michael Sherry has analyzed how these stories sparked a flood of investigations, discussions, and outrage while Americans tried to make sense of and hold accountable those who engaged in torture abroad. The stories left little doubt for most Americans that torture was happening in military prisons, but few people reflected on conditions of confinement in the United States.[71]

In 2003, amid national debates about torture in prisons abroad, President Bush signed the Prison Rape Elimination Act (PREA). The passage of PREA amounted to national recognition of sexual assault in American prisons. PREA also directed significant research toward "the analysis of the incidence and effects of prison rape in federal, state, and local institutions," with the aim of "provid[ing] information, resources, recommendations and funding to protect individuals from prison rape." The legislation also established the National Prison Rape Elimination Commission to create guidelines for eradicating rape in prisons. The DOJ produced the final PREA Standards, which were based on the research conducted by the commission and went into effect in August 2012.[72] The Bureau of Justice Statistics (BJS), an agency within the Department of

Justice, was responsible for conducting anonymous surveys that hundreds of thousands of incarcerated people completed. The BJS followed up with institutions identified as the best and worst performing to establish the final standards. The result was a consistent and reliable data set that made the causes and impact of sexual abuse in prison undeniable. By the 2010s, the data made it increasingly difficult for prison leaders to accuse incarcerated people of lying about sexual violence.[73]

The reports PREA produced also reveal the racial bias and heteronormativity that infused American discourse regarding sexual violence in prison, especially as it was documented in court cases and human rights investigations. In their work on the history of sex in prisons, historian Regina Kunzel has unpacked the way binaries of heterosexuality and homosexuality or fears of interracial sexual violence have shaped rules and public narratives regarding sex in prisons.[74] The research conducted by the DOJ challenged the logic of widely held prison policies. The federal government's studies found that women were more likely than men to experience prisoner-on-prisoner sexual abuse. Women were also more likely than men to commit sexual assault against other prisoners. The DOJ's researchers found that prison staff would downplay an incarcerated woman's abuse of another woman, perhaps making the institution less likely to intervene. Some prison employees referred to sexual abuse among incarcerated women as a "cat fight" or dismissed it as prisoners replicating the so-called family structure, a key feature of maternal justice from the early twentieth century. In the 2000s, prison employees used the term "family structure" to also describe sexual assault when an incarcerated woman modeled herself after the patriarchal protector of another woman in exchange for sex. The studies found that guards were more likely to assault Black prisoners. Finally, the federal government surveyed juvenile detention facilities, and the statistics revealed that boys were more likely to be victims of sexual assault than girls and that female guards in those facilities were more likely to commit rape than male guards.[75] The findings raised questions for future research but also uncovered the particularly violent character of many women's prisons.

* * *

In the 1990s, incarcerated women shifted their claims and expectations of Michigan's prison regime as they navigated a hostile state legislature, retrenchment politics, and state violence. Rats infested their cells, work-spaces, and dining halls. They fought for some semblance of medical care and attempted to document injustices and degradations large and small. Navigating major legislation that attempted to restrict access to the courts, incarcerated women challenged state violence in prisons by framing their fights for bodily integrity and personal safety as fights for human rights.

The PLRA made it extremely difficult for incarcerated people to file lawsuits, but incarcerated women continued turning to the courts for prison reform. Stacy Barker was a named plaintiff in several major law-suits that challenged incarceration of women. Barker joined the *Glover* lawsuit that fought for parity in educational and vocational training and access to the courts and was ongoing when she entered prison in the 1980s. She was a plaintiff in *Nunn* and *Neal*, two cases that sought to end sexual assault of incarcerated women. She was also a named plaintiff in *Bazzetta v. McGinnis*, in which incarcerated people fought to improve access to visitation privileges—especially for incarcerated parents—and in *Cain v. MDOC*, a lawsuit in which incarcerated men and women chal-lenged security classifications, solitary confinement, access to the courts, and other basic issues of prison life, such as personal property.[76] For her prison activism, guards targeted Barker for harassment, assaults, and administrative segregation. Her sentence was reduced in 2001, but the parole board denied her applications for release. After being incarcer-ated for twenty-two years, she won her freedom in 2009.[77]

The passage of PREA and the subsequent research bolstered the claims of abuse made by incarcerated women. Nonetheless, incarceration rates for women continued to increase. From 2009 to 2018, Michigan was one of eight states where prison population of women grew larger when the men's prison population declined. According to the Prison Policy Initia-tive, the state decreased the men's prison population by 8 percent from 2009 to 2015 and its women's prison population increased by 30 per-cent.[78] The reports from PREA, DOJ, Amnesty International, HRW, and major lawsuits have contributed to twenty-first-century conversations regarding decarceration, prison reform, and prison abolition.

Epilogue

Reconsidering Challenges to Confinement

Sharleen Wabindato has been incarcerated for most of her life. Wabindato is sixty-six years old and an enrolled member of the Little River Band of Ottawa Indians.[1] She was convicted for first-degree murder when she was twenty-two years old. In 1977, her abusive partner, Larry Bates, killed a disabled sixty-year-old white man, Raymond Kozal, in the course of a robbery. Bates, Wabindato, and Val Vega broke into Kozal's modest home in Muskegon, a city on the southeastern coast of Lake Michigan. The trio intended to rob him, but Wabindato's memory of that night is hazy. She had been coerced into drinking and consuming drugs and cannot remember the entire night. They tied Kozal up and then Bates beat him with wood sticks and shot him. Wabindato remembers placing a Bible in Kozal's hand when she realized he was dead. They left the house with only $111. His family found his body the next day. Bates and Wabindato received life sentences. Vega was never charged because he cooperated with the prosecution.[2]

Wabindato was pregnant when she began her sentence and gave birth to a daughter, her second child, in prison. She sent her baby to live with family who had also been taking care of her two-year-old daughter. For the next decade Wabindato described herself as depressed. She sought counseling to cope with the trauma of intimate partner violence and missing her children grow up. Wabindato has petitioned for clemency with the support of the American Friends Service Committee, the ACLU of Michigan, and the Michigan Women's Justice and Clemency Project. Wabindato is one of many women of color who continue to be disproportionately incarcerated, representing mass incarceration's overlapping ties to racial oppression and gendered harm.[3] At the time of this writing, Wabindato remains incarcerated at Huron Valley.

Figure E.1. Photograph of Sharleen Wabindato incarcerated at Florence Crane women's prison in Coldwater, Michigan. Antoinette Martin, "Dear Governor Engler," *Detroit Free Press*, July 26, 1992. © Steven R. Nickerson—USA TODAY NETWORK.

Incarcerated women, lawyers, and activists have pushed back and protested the prison despite the strong political and cultural currents that have sustained penal practices. Wabindato was one of many women serving life terms in prison by the 1990s.[4] In 1992, the *Detroit Free Press* captured her story in an article that implored Governor Engler to grant more clemencies to people sentenced to die in prison. Former governor James Blanchard, who served from 1983 to 1990, had commuted sentences for only six people. A popular narrative circulated among lawyers and journalists that Blanchard was spooked after Governor Milliken released James Ellis, a man who had been serving a life sentence, in 1974. In 1982, eight years after his release, Ellis managed a residential building owned by his church. Tenants were increasingly frustrated with his work, and they held a meeting to discuss removing Ellis from his job. When the meeting ended, Ellis fired on the tenants, killing three people and leaving two others paralyzed. Survivors recalled that before firing into the room, Ellis, whom they had nicknamed "Preacher" because of his religious enthusiasm, announced, "Everybody has had their say. Now I'm going to have my say, clear and loud." Sensational stories like Ellis's encouraged voters to demand that politicians act punitively and sowed seeds of doubt that incarcerated people should be allowed to shed the stigma of a conviction. By 1992, there were 3,112 prisoners serving life without parole in Michigan. In 2017, Michigan held over 3,800 people serving life sentences without the possibility of parole.[5]

After decades of activism, the work of the women who challenged confinement remained unfinished. The *Glover* case marked a fleeting victory in 1979 for feminists working to reform Michigan's carceral regime. For over twenty years, incarcerated women, attorneys, activists, and judges used the courts to remedy oppressive aspects of prisons. The application of parity relied on institutional solutions, as criminologist Nicole Hahn Rafter has demonstrated, but the state created obstacles for meaningful change.[6] Parity, as articulated in *Glover*, championed more programming in women's prisons, including parenting programs, vocational courses, higher education, and paralegal education. It could have inspired innovation but ultimately made reforms vulnerable to shifts in funding and political support. Prison leaders removed programming from men's prisons, which allowed them to disregard the gap in rehabilitative programs in women's prisons.[7] The flow of federal funds for higher education courses in prisons dried up, forcing prisoners to become increasingly resourceful to access the courts, education, and vocational training. Many of the broad coalitions of the 1970s splintered by the 1980s and 1990s.[8] Faced with political opposition and institutional intransigence, prisoners pursued targeted reforms. Incarcerated women and their allies focused on the critical goals of women's health and freedom from sexual violence.

This book has traced the ways activists and incarcerated women tried to dismantle power structures by applying a range of feminist ideals and conceiving of a more humane criminal legal system. Connecting women's histories to carceral studies sheds light on the contingency of mass imprisonment and on multiple paths to end it. A powerful retrenchment period followed prisoners' rights victories but did not extinguish activism among incarcerated women. In Michigan, activists and community members chased a future that would be less reliant on incarceration. Angela Davis argues that an abolitionist framework requires a constellation of options rather than a single alternative to prison. Imagining alternatives to incarceration also necessitates a thorough examination of how punishment has been enmeshed in ideas of race, gender, and criminal legal initiatives.[9]

Currently and formerly incarcerated women are particularly well suited to contribute to a prison abolitionist framework. From inside prison, the incarcerated women chronicled in this book sought acknowledgment of their human rights and carved out space for themselves in coalitions. Universities and nonprofit organizations have supported feminist fights for equality and established bridges between academic and incarcerated communities. For example, in 1990, the MDOC transferred Mary Glover to Florence Crane Correctional Facility because of overcrowding at Huron Valley. There, she connected with activist Buzz Alexander, and they established a performing arts group called Sisters Within Theater Troupe. The group developed theater programs written and produced by incarcerated women. Sharleen Wabindato participated in their workshops and performed. This prison arts program evolved to become the Prison Creative Arts Project (PCAP), which is housed in the University of Michigan's Residential College and offers programs in every Michigan prison.[10] PCAP supports incarcerated artists and raises awareness about incarcerated people by sponsoring exhibits and bringing volunteers, students, and academics inside Michigan prisons.

Many formerly incarcerated women have advocated for social justice in Michigan's carceral spaces after leaving prison. Juanita Thomas was the first woman to be released with the support of the Michigan Women's Justice and Clemency Project. She left prison in 1998 after being incarcerated for over eighteen years. She initially lived with her daughter in Lansing and took care of her young grandson. She had married a man she got to know while she was in prison and gradually adjusted to his companionship. Thomas reflected, "He is older and set in *his* ways." In

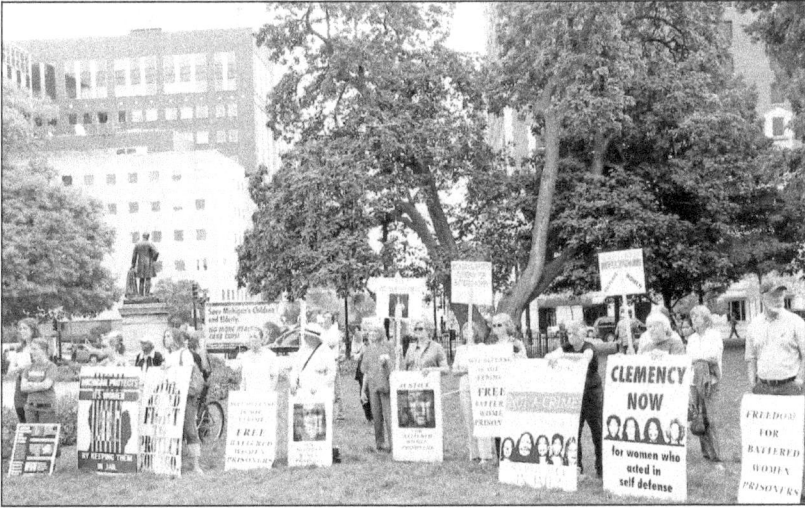

Figure E.2. Rally outside of the Michigan State Capitol in Lansing, Michigan. The Michigan Women's Justice and Clemency Project organized annual rallies from 2001 to 2008. Photography by Diane Engleman. Courtesy of Carol Jacobsen, www.umich.edu /~clemency.

1999 she had a heart attack and her left leg would "go dead" on her, causing her to fall occasionally. Her husband was beaten up that summer and went into debt because of his hospital bills. To calm her mind when she became frustrated with the bills she told herself, "Nothing is bad as prison." After gaining her freedom, Thomas focused on reconnecting with family.[11] Thomas kept in touch with her attorneys and advocates and wrote about her experiences at trial and in prison.[12] The Michigan Women's Justice and Clemency Project, public interest attorneys, and formerly incarcerated people engaged in new projects that documented sexism and racism in prisons and advanced social justice initiatives.

Michigan governor John Engler commuted Mary Glover's sentence, and the state released her from prison in 2002. After twenty-six years in prison, she had spent most of her life locked up. She initially lived in a halfway house in Grand Rapids and worked at a Meijer grocery store. Glover returned to her family name, Heinen. She funneled her frustrations and a sense of obligation into her work on prisons. In 2006, she was a community coordinator for the Prison Creative Arts Project

(PCAP) at the University of Michigan. This experience propelled her to win a Soros Justice Fellowship from the Open Society Foundation in 2011. She worked on reentry for juveniles and adults. In 2012, she completed a master's degree in social work from the University of Michigan. Today, Heinen works as an advocate, teacher, and program coordinator for PCAP. In 2017, Heinen married Melnee McPherson, a Black woman and a retired clinical sociologist and social worker who had also been incarcerated in Michigan. She and her wife live near Huron Valley Correctional Facility for Women.[13]

Stacy Barker, an activist and survivor who had been serving a life sentence, left prison on August 25, 2009. She had been incarcerated for twenty-two years. Initially she did not want to work with returning citizens or prisoners. She described needing time to reconnect with her daughter, family, and friends and focus on herself. She then returned to the work that she loved. She now owns her own company, which provides home caregivers for elderly people in southeast Michigan, similar work to what she was doing when she caught her case. Barker enjoys connecting with the families of elderly people and manages two employees. She has also continued her activism. She is a volunteer with the Westland Youth Assistance Program, where children are referred after encounters with criminal legal institutions or schools in Westland, Michigan. Barker has advocated for women, especially survivors of sexual assault, returning citizens, and incarcerated people from Detroit. She works as an engagement specialist with the nonprofit organization Nation Outside, which supports formerly and currently incarcerated people in Michigan. Nation Outside empowers formerly incarcerated people to vote and to voice their ideas to improve reentry and prison reform through civic engagement. In her work, Barker engages with returning citizens to raise awareness of their right to vote, facilitate access to community resources, and encourage formerly incarcerated people to advocate for prison and reentry reform.[14]

Examining the convergence of feminism, critiques of carceral regimes, and protests in prisons allows us to bring historical perspectives to contemporary conversations regarding decarceration and prison abolition in the United States. By exploring the many ways incarcerated women contested abject prison conditions throughout the twentieth century, this book has traced how women's movements in prisons formed a tributary to the river of resistance against mass incarceration. Incarcerated women sustained social movements to fight for equality, safety, and dignity. Focusing on the intersection of women's movements and mass incarceration in Michigan highlights the significant work of incarcerated women and activists and the brutality of prisons. Together, they advocated for an alternative carceral reality by relying on feminist politics and ideals of social justice.

ACKNOWLEDGMENTS

I first became interested in studying the history of women, prisons, and social justice when I regularly visited women in prison while working for the Equal Justice Initiative in Alabama. Meeting with incarcerated women made me question the origins of women's prisons and how incarcerated people used protest and the law to force changes in carceral institutions. I have benefited from the generosity, enthusiasm, and critical feedback of so many people at countless stages of writing this book. I want to first thank Clara Platter, my editor at New York University Press, for championing this book. I also thank the editorial and production team at NYU Press for the excellent care and attention they gave to the manuscript. I am indebted to Beth Slutsky for her thoughtful reviews and encouraging critiques of the book. I also want to thank the anonymous readers who helped me revise and develop earlier drafts. This is a much better book because of their insights and suggestions.

At Northwestern University, I found an extraordinary scholarly community that challenged me to think about history and mass incarceration in new ways. I thank Michael Sherry for his superb advice, encouragement, and support. He challenged me to think critically about American history while pushing me to be a better writer, researcher, and teacher. Martha Biondi offered excellent advice, collegiality, and reassurance. Her feedback reminded me to stay focused on the stakes of this history. I also thank Kevin Boyle for his suggestions and conversations on writing and teaching, which helped me reevaluate the structure of this book. I am grateful for the excellent faculty members in the History Department at Northwestern who helped me think deeply and creatively about historical research and writing. Their passion and commitment to their work is inspiring. I thank Ken Alder, Michael Allen, T. H. Breen, Deborah Cohen, Kate Masur, Dylan Penningroth, Helen Tilley, and Ji-Yeon Yuh. I also thank the staff members of the History Department including Paula Blaskovits, Annerys Cano, Susan Delrahim, and Eric West. I thank Sarah

Maza, Elzbieta Foeller-Pituch, and the Nicholas D. Chabraja Center for Historical Studies for the time and resources to write and workshop ideas as I completed an early draft of this book. I also thank Jennifer Lackey for reminding me of why it is important to think about and teach in prisons.

In Chicago, I benefited from discussions with many people who helped me develop some of the arguments in this book. At the University of Chicago, conversations with Susan Gzesh helped me think through the importance of writing about women and mass incarceration in Michigan. Her reflections on the legal activists who worked on *Glover* were crucial. I am also indebted to the late Alison Winter, whose unparalleled enthusiasm for legal history inspired me to keep asking questions and returning to the archives. Alison's advice and guidance inspired me to become a historian. Having friends and colleagues willing to talk about American history and criminal legal issues over coffee and meals has enriched my personal and professional life in so many ways. I thank Mariah Hepworth, Alex Hobson, Rebecca Marchiel, and Leigh Soares for sharing ideas and making my time at Northwestern productive, enjoyable, and worthwhile.

Presenting and participating in workshops and conferences forced me to dig deeper into the history of incarcerated women in Michigan. The American history workshop at Northwestern provided a space to take risks, develop a craft, and cultivate a scholarly community. I thank Michael Sherry and Kate Masur for running this workshop. I am grateful for my colleagues and friends who offered critical feedback on early chapter drafts, including Ashley Johnson Bavery, Kyle Burke, Myisha Eatmon, Michael Falcone, Matthew June, Amanda Kleintop, Sam Kling, Melissa Santana-Rivera, Aram Sarkisian, Ian Saxine, and many more. I presented draft chapters of this book at academic conferences where commentators helped me refine my arguments and analysis. I thank Michael Allen, Andrew Baer, Chad Broughton, Felicia Kornbluh, Michelle Nickerson, and Reuel Schiller for their questions, critiques, and suggestions. I had the opportunity to present my research at the Center for Equity Education as I approached the final stages of writing this book. I thank Colleen Schoenfeld and Nicholas Modglin for facilitating a generative conversation about gender equality and prison education in Michigan.

My colleagues at the University of Florida welcomed me into an interdisciplinary community where I was able to expand and develop some of the ideas that have been at the core of this book. I thank Brenden Beck, Abigail Fagan, Rebecca Hanson, Tiffany Jenson, Nicole Jones, Jessica Kahler, Charles Peek, Stephen Perz, and Barbara Zsembik for their feedback, support, and encouragement. I also thank the staff of the Sociology and Criminology & Law Department for their help navigating research during the pandemic, including Lisandra Harkeli, Stephanie Hathcox, and Kelly Senker. For their friendship and advice at critical stages of writing and revising, I thank Elizabeth Dale, Jodi Lane, Barbara Mennel, Lauren Pearlman, and Joseph Spillane. Baylee Bennett and Caitlin Bozarth were excellent undergraduate research assistants who provided timely, creative, and interesting perspectives on the histories of women, incarceration, and antiviolence movements. Conversations with graduate and undergraduate students at the University of Florida helped me think about mass incarceration, gender, and race in new and productive ways.

This book was completed as I was moving to the Department of Criminal Justice at Indiana University–Bloomington, and I am grateful for my once and future colleagues' questions and engagement. The Center for Law, Society & Culture at the Indiana University Maurer School of Law gave me the chance to present my work, and I thank Jody Madeira, Victor Quintanilla, and Deborah Widiss for their insightful feedback at the workshop. In the Department of Criminal Justice, I am indebted to Jonathan Brauer, Natalie Kroovand Hipple, Roger Levesque, Richard Lippke, Miriam Northcutt Bohmert, Bruce Sales, and Marla Sandys for their encouragement, feedback, and support while completing this book. I am grateful for Ellen Dwyer's mentorship and enthusiasm for this project. I am incredibly fortunate to be a part of the dynamic group of scholars in Bloomington.

I would not have been able to complete this book without the help from the staff and archivists at different institutions devoted to preserving historical records. I am grateful for the librarians at the Walter P. Reuther Library at Wayne State University, the Bentley Historical Library at the University of Michigan, the Burton Historical Collection at the Detroit Public Library, the State Archives of Michigan, and the

National Archives in Chicago. I want to especially thank archivists who scanned files during the pandemic, which helped me keep this project moving forward. Staff members from the Ingham County Court and Muskegon County Court helped me access case records, and I thoroughly appreciate their dedication to making files accessible from a distance.

The research for this book was funded by awards, grants, and fellowships from the College of Liberal Arts and Sciences at the University of Florida, the Center for Humanities and the Public Sphere at the University of Florida, the College of Arts and Sciences at Indiana University–Bloomington, Northwestern University, the Nicholas D. Chabraja Center for Historical Studies at Northwestern University, and the Walter P. Reuther Library at Wayne State University. I am so grateful for the support.

Several sections of chapter 2 have been revised and expanded after appearing in the article "'The Influence of the Women's Movement Cannot Stop at the Prison Door': The Prisoners' Rights Movement in Michigan Correctional Facilities for Women," which was published in the *Michigan Historical Review* 47.2 (Fall 2021): 61–88. I am grateful for the editor, Lane Demas, and his work on the journal. Thanks to Central Michigan University and the *Michigan Historical Review* for permission to publish a revised version of this work.

Many materials that capture the history of incarcerated women in Michigan have not yet been deposited in archives. To fill in the gaps and incorporate incarcerated women's perspectives on prisons and state violence, I relied on what Kelly Lytle Hernández, in her book *City of Inmates*, calls "the rebel archive," or the archive of individuals and organizations that fought state violence, power, and punishment. I am grateful for the generosity of Stacy Barker, Sequita Eaves, Tirtza Even, Mary Heinen, Carol Jacobsen, and Charlene Snow. They shared documents, photographs, digital files, memories, and stories about their work on prison reform and abolition. Without their help and dedication to social justice, this book would have told a very different history.

Friends and family have been understanding and encouraging throughout the years it has taken me to research and write this book. Lilly Connett and Luke Rodehorst provided meals, lodging, and friendship during innumerable trips to Ann Arbor. Sharing stories and laughter in their home over the years has been a delight. I hope I can continue to come up with an excuse to invite myself over. Kurt Dewhurst and Marsha MacDowell made East Lansing a home away from home. I owe Emma Kaufman special thanks for her friendship, support, and willingness to talk about the history of prisons. I also thank Maddie Allan, Rose Briccetti, Emily Brown, Eric Gardiner, Mayumi Grigsby, Theodora Rodman, Catherine Schoenfeld, and many other friends for shaping my life in joyful and meaningful ways. My family has been incredibly reassuring and encouraging. I thank Laura Hemphill, Scott Hemphill, Beth Snyder, and Chris Stewart for their steadfast support over the years. My parents, Kris and Betsy Ernst, and my sister, Megan Ernst, have been unconditionally encouraging of and enthusiastic about all my endeavors.

Finally, I thank my husband, Andrew Hammond. Andrew has been there for the highs and lows, and he has never wavered in his love and encouragement. His companionship, humor, and support have kept me going in times of doubt and reminded me of how beautiful our life is together. I am forever grateful. Our son, John, was born in the final years of this project and shows us that life is special and joyous. I am thankful for the many nannies and teachers who took great care of John while I was writing. I hope that when John reads about the history of mass incarceration it will be firmly in America's past.

NOTES

INTRODUCTION

1 Complaint, May 19, 1977, Glover v. Johnson, 478 F. Supp. 1075 (E.D. Mich. 1979), 77cv71229, Box 8, Federal Records Center, National Archives, Chicago, IL (hereafter FRC).

2 Affidavit in Support of Mary L. Doe Request, May 19, 1977, Box 8, FRC.

3 Affidavit in Support of Jane Doe Request, May 18, 1977, Box 8, FRC.

4 Cathy Trost, "Dehoco Women Rattle Legal Bars," *Detroit Free Press*, June 6, 1977.

5 Trost, "Dehoco Women Rattle Legal Bars."

6 Trost, "Dehoco Women Rattle Legal Bars"; Gerald Volgenau, "Sex Bias in Prisons," *Detroit Free Press*, October 21, 1979; Glover v. Johnson, 478 F. Supp. 1075 (E.D. Mich. 1979).

7 Volgenau, "Sex Bias in Prisons"; "Courts," *Battle Creek Enquirer*, July 23, 1976.

8 Lauren G. Beatty and Tracy L. Snell, *Profile of Prison Inmates, 2016* (Washington, DC: Bureau of Justice Statistics of the US Department of Justice, 2021), www.bjs.ojp.gov; Wendy Sawyer, *The Gender Divide: Tracking Women's State Prison Growth* (Northampton, MA: Prison Policy Initiative, 2018), www.prisonpolicy.org; Leah Wang, Wendy Sawyer, Tiana Herring, and Emily Widra, "Beyond the Count: A Deep Dive into State Prison Populations," Prison Policy Initiative (April 2022), www.prisonpolicy.org.

9 Little River Band of Ottawa Indians Tribal Directory, August 2022, https://lrboi-nsn.gov; "Women of the Clemency Project," Michigan Women's Justice and Clemency Project, http://websites.umich.edu.

10 Charlene Snow, "Women in Prison," *Clearinghouse Review* 14 (February 1981): 1068.

11 In 1980, the population of incarcerated women was 26,378. In 2014, the number of women incarcerated reached 215,332. "Incarcerated Women and Girls," Fact Sheet, The Sentencing Project, November 2015, www.sentencingproject.org.

12 By 1999, penal policies pushed the inmate population to 1.273 million men and 90,428 women. E. Ann Carson and Joseph Mulako-Wangota, Corrections Statistical Analysis Tool (CSAT)—Prisoners, Bureau of Justice Statistics, https://csat.bjs.ojp.gov/.

13 Thomas Sugrue, *The Origins of the Urban Crisis: Race and Inequality in Postwar Detroit* (Princeton, NJ: Princeton University Press, 1996). For more on how the migration of people from cities to suburbia further depleted urban communities,

see Matthew Lassiter, *The Silent Majority: Suburban Politics in the Sunbelt South* (Princeton, NJ: Princeton University Press, 2005).

14 Andrew Highsmith, *Demolition Means Progress: Flint, Michigan, and the Fate of the American Metropolis* (Chicago: University of Chicago Press, 2015).

15 Loïc Wacquant, *Punishing the Poor: The Neoliberal Government of Social Insecurity* (Durham, NC: Duke University Press, 2009).

16 Heather Ann Thompson, "Why Mass Incarceration Matters: Rethinking Crisis, Decline, and Transformation in Postwar American History," *Journal of American History* 97, no. 3 (December 2010): 708.

17 Prisoners in Michigan served an average of 4.3 years for all categories of criminal convictions. In comparison, prisoners in Florida served an average of 3.0 years, in Illinois they served an average of 1.7 years, and in New York they served an average of 3.6 years. "Time Served: The High Cost, Low Return of Longer Prison Terms," Pew Center on the States 2009, 13, www.pewtrusts.org.

18 Marie Gottschalk, *The Prison and the Gallows: The Politics of Mass Incarceration in America* (Cambridge: Cambridge University Press, 2006); Elizabeth Hinton, *From the War on Poverty to the War on Crime: The Making of Mass Incarceration in America* (Cambridge, MA: Harvard University Press, 2016); Naomi Murakawa, *The First Civil Right: How Liberals Built Prison America* (New York: Oxford University Press, 2014); Heather Schoenfeld, *Building the Prison State: Race and the Politics of Mass Incarceration* (Chicago: University of Chicago Press, 2018); Jonathan Simon, *Governing through Crime: How the War on Crime Transformed American Democracy and Created a Culture of Fear* (New York: Oxford University Press, 2007).

19 David Garland, *The Culture of Control: Crime and Social Order in Contemporary Society* (Chicago: University of Chicago Press, 2001); Michael Sherry, *The Punitive Turn in American Life: How the United States Learned to Fight Crime like a War* (Chapel Hill: University of North Carolina Press, 2020).

20 Michelle Alexander, *The New Jim Crow: Mass Incarceration in the Age of Colorblindness* (New York: New Press, 2010); Katherine Beckett, *Making Crime Pay: Law and Order in Contemporary American Politics* (New York: Oxford University Press, 1997); Marie Gottschalk, *Caught: The Prison State and the Lockdown of American Politics* (Princeton, NJ: Princeton University Press, 2016); Mary Pattillo, David Weiman, Bruce Western (eds.), *Imprisoning America: The Social Effects of Mass Incarceration* (New York: Russell Sage Foundation, 2004); Wacquant, *Punishing the Poor*.

21 Andrew Baer, *Beyond the Usual Beating: The Jon Burge Police Torture Scandal and Social Movements for Police Accountability in Chicago* (Chicago: University of Chicago Press, 2020); Dan Berger, *Captive Nation: Black Prison Organizing in the Civil Rights Era* (Chapel Hill: University of North Carolina Press, 2015); Garrett Felber, *Those Who Know Don't Say: The Nation of Islam, the Black Freedom Movement, and the Carceral State* (Chapel Hill: University of North Carolina Press, 2019); Kelly Lytle Hernández, *City of Inmates: Conquest, Rebellion, and the Rise of*

Human Caging in Los Angeles, 1777–1965 (Chapel Hill: University of North Carolina Press, 2017); Heather Ann Thompson, *Blood in the Water: The Attica Prison Uprising of 1971 and Its Legacy* (New York: Pantheon Books, 2016).

22 Emily Thuma, *All Our Trials: Prisons, Policing, and the Feminist Fight to End Violence* (Urbana: University of Illinois Press, 2019), 12–13.

23 Cheryl Hicks, *Talk with You like a Woman: African American Women, Justice, and Reform in New York, 1890–1935* (Chapel Hill: University of North Carolina Press, 2010).

24 Kali Gross, *Colored Amazons: Crime, Violence, and Black Women in the City of Brotherly Love, 1880–1910* (Durham, NC: Duke University Press, 2006); Sarah Haley, *No Mercy Here: Gender, Punishment, and the Making of Jim Crow Modernity* (Chapel Hill: University of North Carolina Press, 2016); Talitha LeFlouria, *Chained in Silence: Black Women and Convict Labor in the New South* (Chapel Hill: University of North Carolina Press, 2015).

25 Danielle L. McGuire, *At the Dark End of the Street: Black Women, Rape, and Resistance; A New History of the Civil Rights Movement from Rosa Parks to the Rise of Black Power* (New York: Vintage Books, 2011).

26 Estelle Freedman, *Their Sister's Keepers: Women and Prison Reform in America, 1830–1930* (Ann Arbor: University of Michigan Press, 1981) and *Maternal Justice: Miriam Van Waters and the Female Reform Tradition* (Chicago: University of Chicago Press, 1996).

27 Schoenfeld, *Building the Prison State.*

CHAPTER 1. "WE ARE DEALING WITH WOMEN"

1 Black men worked in wet sanding at Cadillac Motors and in the spray rooms at Dodge Brothers. At Ford, Black people sometimes worked the full scale of production but were often sent to the foundries, where they stoked massive furnaces. Injuries on the job were common. Heather Ann Thompson, *Whose Detroit? Labor, Politics, and Race in Modern America* (Ithaca, NY: Cornell University Press, 2001), 19.

2 Forrester B. Washington and Robert T. Lansdale (comps.), "Section IX: Crime," in *The Negro in Detroit* (Detroit: Detroit Bureau of Government Research 1926), 30–31, https://crcmich.org; Kevin Boyle, *Arc of Justice: A Saga of Race, Civil Rights, and Murder in the Jazz Age* (New York: Henry Holt, 2004), 106–9.

3 Washington and Lansdale, *The Negro in Detroit*, 3–4.

4 Boyle, *Arc of Justice*, 106–7.

5 Boyle, *Arc of Justice*, 8.

6 Washington and Lansdale, "Section IX: Crime," 38.

7 Washington and Lansdale, "Section IX: Crime," 30–31.

8 Haley, *No Mercy Here*, 7.

9 Michigan State Federation of Women's Clubs, *A History of the Michigan State Federation of Women's Clubs, 1895–1953* (Ann Arbor, MI: Ann Arbor Press, 1953).

10 Michigan State Federation of Women's Clubs, *A History of the Michigan State Federation of Women's Clubs, 1895–1953*; Victoria Wolcott, *Remaking Respectability:*

African American Women in Interwar Detroit (Chapel Hill: University of North Carolina Press, 2001).

11 Freedman, *Their Sister's Keepers* and *Maternal Justice*, xiii. For more on maternal justice and prison reform for women in the early twentieth century, see Anne M. Butler, *Gendered Justice in the American West: Women Prisoners in Men's Penitentiaries* (Urbana: University of Illinois Press, 1997); Nicole Hahn Rafter, *Partial Justice: Women, Prisons, and Social Control*, 2nd ed. (New Brunswick, NJ: Transaction Publishers, 1990).

12 Zebulon Brockway, *Fifty Years of Prison Service: An Autobiography* (New York: Charities Publication Committee, 1912), 68.

13 In 1916, the Michigan legislature created appropriations for the women's prison. Alice T. Crathern, *In Detroit . . . Courage Was the Fashion: The Contribution of Women to the Development of Detroit from 1701 to 1951* (Detroit: Wayne State University Press, 1953), 140–41.

14 Jayne Morris-Crowther, "Municipal Housekeeping: The Political Activities of the Detroit Federation of Women's Clubs in the 1920s," *Michigan Historical Review* 30, no. 1 (Spring 2004): 42.

15 WXYZ Team, "Meet Two of the Early Detroit Police Officers Who Worked in the Women's Division," WXYZ Detroit, February 8, 2021, www.wxyz.com.

16 Sugrue, *The Origins of the Urban Crisis*, 23.

17 Sweet delayed moving into the house after watching other Black homeowners forced out of their homes in white areas by armed white mobs. Dr. Alexander Turner, a Black physician, was forced out of his home in June 1925. Vollington Bristol and John Fletcher were also forced out of their homes in white Detroit neighborhoods in July 1925. The Sweet family moved into their house on September 8, 1925. Detroit police were patrolling the home and were notified that the family was moving. For more on Ossian Sweet, see Boyle, *Arc of Justice*; Phyllis Vine, *One Man's Castle: Clarence Darrow in Defense of the American Dream* (New York: Amistad, 2004).

18 Edward Larson, *Summer for the Gods: The Scopes Trial and America's Continuing Debate over Science and Religion* (New York: Basic Books, 2006).

19 Clarence Darrow closing arguments at Sweet trial as quoted in Ben Schmitt, "Danger at the Doorstep," *Detroit Free Press*, March 29, 2004.

20 Boyle, *Arc of Justice*; Renee Lee, "Racial Tensions Cloud Doctor's Tragic Life," *Detroit Free Press*, September 9, 2007.

21 "Crime and Police," in *Report of the Mayor's Committee on Race Relations, Detroit, Michigan* (Detroit: Detroit Bureau of Governmental Research, 1926), 7. https://hdl .handle.net.

22 From Glenn Seymour Taylor, "Prostitution in Detroit" (PhD diss., University of Michigan, 1933) as quoted in Wolcott, *Remaking Respectability*, 111.

23 Taylor, "Prostitution in Detroit," 111.

24 Washington and Lansdale, "Section IX, Crime," in *The Negro in Detroit*, 18.

25 Washington and Lansdale, "Section III, Industry," in *The Negro in Detroit*, 27.

26 Washington and Lansdale, "Section IX, Crime" in *The Negro in Detroit*, 15–16. Historians have explored how Black women have been targeted by racialized and discretionary policing in the early twentieth century. Tera Hunter examines how Black sex workers in Atlanta navigated shifting economies of leisure. Tera Hunter, *To 'Joy My Freedom: Black Women's Lives and Labors after the Civil War* (Cambridge, MA: Harvard University Press, 1997), 154. Historians have also analyzed how sex work confronted boundaries of class and politics of respectability in Chicago and Detroit. Cynthia Blair, *I've Got to Make My Livin': Black Women's Sex Work in Turn-of-the-Century Chicago* (Chicago: University of Chicago Press, 2010); Wolcott, *Remaking Respectability*, 106–11.

27 Simon Balto, *Occupied Territory: Policing Black Chicago from Red Summer to Black Power* (Chapel Hill: University of North Carolina Press, 2019), 70–71.

28 Washington and Lansdale, "Section IX, Crime," in *The Negro in Detroit*, 34.

29 Washington and Lansdale, "Section IX, Crime," in *The Negro in Detroit*, 34–35; Boyle, *Arc of Justice*, 144.

30 "Patrolman Held on Charge of Murder," *Escanaba Daily Press*, February 14, 1925.

31 "Ex-Policeman Acquitted," *Lansing State Journal*, March 24, 1925.

32 Daniel Amsterdam, *Roaring Metropolis: Businessmen's Campaign for a Civic Welfare State* (Philadelphia: University of Pennsylvania Press, 2016), 26–27, 54.

33 Jayne Morris-Crowther, "Municipal Housekeeping: The Political Activities of the Detroit Federation of Women's Clubs in the 1920s," *Michigan Historical Review* 30, no. 1 (Spring 2004): 31–57, 40–41.

34 Morris-Crowther, "Municipal Housekeeping," 34.

35 Mary Church Terrell, "The Duty of the National Association of Colored Women to the Race," 1899, Mary Church Terrell Papers: Speeches and Writings, 1866–1953, mss42549, Box 28, Reel 20, Library of Congress, Washington, DC. https://hdl.loc.gov/.

36 For more on convict leasing, see Edward L. Ayers, *Vengeance and Justice: Crime and Punishment in the Nineteenth-Century American South* (New York: Oxford University Press, 1985); Douglas A. Blackmun, *Slavery by Another Name: The Re-enslavement of Black Americans from the Civil War to World War II* (New York: Anchor Books, 2009); Alex Lichtenstein, *Twice the Work of Free Labor: The Political Economy of Convict Labor in the New South* (New York: Verso Books, 1996).

37 Haley's emphasis in quoted text. Haley, *No Mercy Here*, 120–22.

38 Haley, *No Mercy Here*, 140–41.

39 "Protests to Wilson against Forcing the Suffs to Take Food," *Rutland Daily Herald*, November 10, 1917.

40 Kathryn Coker, "Jailed for Freedom: Virginia's Occoquan Workshouse," Richmond Public Library, rvalibrary.org; Catherine H. Palczewski, "The 1919 Prison Special: Constituting White Women's Citizenship," *Quarterly Journal of Speech* 102, no. 2 (2016): 107–32.

41 "Suffs Greet Their 26 Prison Tourists," *New York Herald*, March 11, 1919; "Woman's Party Heads Meet Here to Plan Week's Suffrage Fight," *New-York Tribune*,

February 4, 1919. For more on the National Woman's Party see Doris Stevens, *Jailed for Freedom: American Women Win the Vote*, reprint ed. (Tillamook, OR: New Sage Press, 1995).

42 Cheryl Hicks analyzes this phenomenon in New York courts in the early twentieth century in her book *Talk with You like a Woman*. See also Ruth Harris, *Murders and Madness: Medicine, Law, and Psychiatry* (New York: Oxford University Press, 1989), which examines trial outcomes in Europe.

43 "Don't Let Baby Know, Plea of Lareta Lee: Girl Robber, Sentenced to from 8 to 20 Years, Finally Breaks Down," *Detroit Free Press*, October 22, 1922, 1.

44 "Lareta Lee Dead, Forgiven by Kin: Funeral to Be Held from Home of Uncle in Alma," *Detroit Free Press*, March 13, 1926.

45 "Girl Bandit to Redeem Name for Boy's Sake," *Detroit Free Press*, Saturday, March 6, 1926.

46 For more on maternal justice from the Progressive Era through the Cold War, see Freedman, *Their Sister's Keepers*, and Freedman, *Maternal Justice*.

47 "Lareta Lee Dead, Forgiven by Kin."

48 "Lareta Lee Dead, Forgiven by Kin."

49 Boyd Simmons, "Death Brought Reform: Women's Prison Jam Recalls Martyr's Plight," *Detroit News*, March 4, 1956.

50 Angela Davis, *Are Prisons Obsolete?* (New York: Seven Stories Press, 2003), 72; Lucia Zedner, "Wayward Sisters: The Prison for Women," in Norval Morris and David J. Rothman (eds.), *The Oxford History of the Prison: The Practice of Punishment in Western Society* (New York: Oxford University Press, 1995), 318.

51 Anne E. Parsons, *From Asylum to Prison: Deinstitutionalization and the Rise of Mass Incarceration after 1945* (Chapel Hill: University of North Carolina Press, 2018).

52 Buck v. Bell, 274 U.S. 200 (1927).

53 *Buck v. Bell*. For more on the eugenics movement, see Dan Kevles, *In the Name of Eugenics: Genetics and the Uses of Human Heredity* (Cambridge, MA: Harvard University Press, 1985).

54 Regina Kunzel, *Criminal Intimacy: Prison and the Uneven History of Modern American Sexuality* (Chicago: University of Chicago Press, 2008), 70; Alexandra Minna Stern, "Sterilized in the Name of Public Health: Race, Immigration, and Reproductive Control in Modern California," *American Journal of Public Health* 95, no. 7 (July 2005): 1128–38, doi: 10.2105/AJPH.2004.041608; Sarah Zhang, "A Long-Lost Data Trove Uncovers California's Sterilization Program, *Atlantic*, January 3, 2017, www.theatlantic.com.

55 "Women's Clubs Fight for Prison Reforms," *Detroit News*, Thursday, March 29, 1956, 16. Folder 5: Office Files—Newspaper Clippings, Box 3, Detroit House of Correction Records, Burton Historical Collection, Detroit Public Library, Detroit, MI (hereafter DHC). In 1918, the Board of Commissioners for the Detroit House of Correction purchased twelve hundred acres of farmland on the border of Northville and Plymouth, towns located thirty miles west of Detroit. The Board of

Commissioners had four members who were appointed by the mayor of Detroit. William B. Cox and F. Lovell Bixby, PhD, "The Osborne Association, Inc. combining National Society of Penal Information, Inc. and Welfare League Association, Inc.—News Bulletin—," June 1934, page 2, Folder 4: Office Files, Box 3, DHC.

56 Superintendent A. Black Gillies to Mayor Edward J. Jeffries, May 21, 1940, page 13. Folder 4: Office Files, Box 3, DHC.

57 "History," City of Detroit, Detroit House of Correction, November 16, 1933, Folder 4: Office Files—History of Detroit House of Corrections, Box 3, DHC. Campbell resigned from her post on the Board of Commissioners for the Detroit House of Corrections to lead the Women's Division. "Prison Job Target for Clubs' Row," *Detroit Free Press*, February 27, 1930.

58 Crathern, *In Detroit*, 235–36.

59 Cox and Bixby, "The Osborne Association," 11–12.

60 Crathern, *In Detroit*, 141.

61 "History," City of Detroit, Detroit House of Correction, Plymouth, Michigan, November 16, 1933. Folder 4: Office Files, Box 3, DHC.

62 A. Blake Gillies, "The Detroit House of Correction," undated (1930s, early 1940s), pages 6–7, Folder 4: Office Files, Box 3, DHC. Gillies was the superintendent from July 6, 1938, to May 6, 1953.

63 Carla Yanni, "The Coed's Predicament: The Martha Cook Building at the University of Michigan," *Buildings and Landscapes* 24, no. 1 (Spring 2017): 38. For more information on the history of college dormitories and the built environment, see Carla Yanni, *Living on Campus: An Architectural History of the American Dormitory* (Minneapolis: University of Minnesota Press, 2019).

64 Yanni, "The Coed's Predicament," 42.

65 Freedman argues that despite labels like "reformatories," these institutions were first and foremost prisons. Freedman, *Their Sisters' Keepers*.

66 Denniston to Campbell, January 5, 1930, Folder 4: Correspondence—Farm, January to March 1831, Box 1I: Farm Correspondence, 1929–1948, DHC.

67 Campbell requested that privileges be restored to Belle Smith and another prisoner, Jean Wilson. Wilson had six reports filed against her in ten months. Denniston to Campbell, February 12, 1931, Folder 4: Correspondence—Farm, January to March 1931, Box1I: Farm Correspondence, 1929–1948, DHC.

68 Thompson, *Whose Detroit?*

69 "History," City of Detroit, Detroit House of Correction, Plymouth, Michigan, November 16, 1933. Folder 4: Office Files, Box 3, DHC.

70 K. H. Campbell to Mr. Edw. Denniston, October 11, 1929, Folder 15: Corres.—Farm, August—October 1929, Box 1H: Construction, Women's Prison 1926–1927, DHC.

71 Campbell to Denniston, October 11, 1929.

72 Campbell wrote, "I advised you some time ago of the condition of the floor in the Laundry, but to date nothing has been done and as the situation is becoming more acute, I am again calling your attention to this matter." Campbell to

Denniston, May 26, 1931, Folder 10: Correspondence—Farm, Mrs. Campbell, April to March 1931, Box 1I: Farm Correspondence, 1929–1948, DHC.

73 Most women had finished a middle school education. Only fifty-eight women had graduated from high school. Annual Report, 1935, page 11, Box 9: Annual Reports, 1916–1959, excerpts from 1862–1872, DHC; Sugrue, *The Origins of the Urban Crisis*, 23.

74 Annual Report 1940, page 8, Box 9: Annual Reports, 1916–1959, excerpts from 1862–1872, DHC. For more on segregation in prisons, see Dan Berger and Toussaint Losier, *Rethinking the American Prison Movement* (New York: Routledge, 2018).

75 Khalil Gibran Muhammad, *The Condemnation of Blackness: Race, Crime, and the Making of Modern Urban America* (Cambridge, MA: Harvard University Press, 2010).

76 Annual Report, 1945, page 2, Box 9: Annual Reports, 1916–1959, excerpts from 1862–1872, DHC.

77 Jos. S. Haefner, Annual Report 1955, page 11, Box 9: Annual Reports, 1916–1959, excerpts from 1862–1872, DHC.

78 Campbell Gibson and Kay Jung, "Michigan: Race and Hispanic Origin, 1800 to 1990," in *Historical Census Statistics on Population Totals by Race, 1790 to 1990, and by Hispanic Origin, 1970 to 1990, for the United States, Regions, Divisions, and States* (Washington, DC: US Census Bureau, 2002), 65. www.census.gov.

79 Boyd Simmons, "Women's Prison Jam Recalls Martyr's Plight," *Detroit News*, March 4, 1956, Folder 5: Office Files—Newspaper Clippings, Box 3, DHC.

80 Charles Manos, "No Retaliation Planned at Dehoco: Pledge Strikers Full Hearing; Clubwoman Who Heads Board Defends Handling of Trouble," *Detroit Free Press*, Sunday, May 12, 1957, A3.

81 Ralph Nelson and Harry Golden Jr., "Free Press Settles Women's Jail Strike," *Detroit Free Press*, May 11, 1957.

82 Nelson and Golden, "Free Press Settles Women's Jail Strike."

83 Nelson and Golden, "Free Press Settles Women's Jail Strike."

84 Nelson and Golden, "Free Press Settles Women's Jail Strike."

85 Commissioners offered a caveat that they might investigate a small number of demands. Nelson and Golden, "Free Press Settles Women's Jail Strike."

86 Manos, "No Retaliation Planned at Dehoco."

87 Manos, "No Retaliation Planned at Dehoco."

88 Highsmith, *Demolition Means Progress*, 58–60. Throughout the 1940s and 1950s, labor unions shaped workplace culture, negotiations, and industry standards. By 1950, the majority of workers in Detroit belonged to labor unions. Unions sometimes compromised on the location of plants and hiring practices and eventually followed factories into the suburbs. Sugrue, *The Origins of Urban Crisis*, 10. For more on the UAW and the labor movement in Michigan see Kevin Boyle, *The UAW and the Heyday of American Liberalism* (Ithaca, NY: Cornell University Press, 1998); Sidney Fine, *Sit-Down: The General Motors Strike of 1936–1937* (Ann Arbor: University of Michigan Press, 1969).

89 The committee included Parker L. Hancock, a warden from the New Hampshire State Prison, Arthur T. Prasse, a commissioner from the Pennsylvania Bureau of Corrections, Joseph E. Ragan, a warden from the State Penitentiary of Illinois, and Clara Thune, the superintendent of the State Reformatory for Women in Minnesota. "Angry Cobo to Investigate Dehoco Conditions," *Detroit Free Press*, August 16, 1957, 4.

90 *Report and Recommendations of the Special Committee to Study the Detroit House of Correction* (Detroit: Common Council City of Detroit, August 1957), 4, https://hdl.handle.net/.

91 *Report and Recommendations of the Special Committee to Study the Detroit House of Correction*, 6.

92 "Angry Cobo to Investigate Dehoco Conditions."

93 This trend aligned with New Deal initiatives to have centralized management over vast bureaucracies. See Lizabeth Cohen, *Making a New Deal: Industrial Workers in Chicago, 1919–1939* (Cambridge: Cambridge University Press, 1990). For prison managerialism see Berger and Losier, *Rethinking the American Prison Movement*; James B. Jacobs, *Stateville: The Penitentiary in Mass Society* (Chicago: University of Chicago Press, 1978).

94 "Angry Cobo to Investigate Dehoco Conditions."

95 Special Study of the Women's Division Detroit House of Corrections, page 1, May 1958, Folder 6: Office Files—Women's Division, Transfer, Box 4, DHC.

96 Special Study of the Women's Division Detroit House of Corrections, page 7.

97 Annual Reports of the Detroit House of Correction, 1950 and 1955, Box 9: Annual Reports 1916–59, DHC; Annual Reports of the Detroit House of Correction, 1960 and 1968, Box 9A: Annual Reports 1960–79, DHC.

98 Annual Report of the Detroit House of Correction, 1960, Box 9A: Annual Reports, 1960–79, DHC.

CHAPTER 2. FROM MASS ACTION TO CLASS ACTION

1 Glover pleaded guilty to second-degree murder and two counts of assault with the intent to commit murder. Tony Hornus, "Mary Glover Given 3 Life Prison Terms," *Argus Press*, August 16, 1976. Glover v. Michigan Parole Board, Supreme Court of Michigan, July 13, 1999.

2 Mary Glover, "A Woman's Life in State Prison," *Michigan Daily*, February 10, 1988, Folder 2: Department of Corrections, Warden's Subject File, Public Information Office, 1985–1988, Box 6, RG 93-115 Corrections—Florence Crane Warden's Subject File, P-S, 1982–1992, Michigan Department of Corrections, State Archives of Michigan, Lansing, MI (hereafter MDC).

3 Glover, "A Woman's Life."

4 See Berger and Losier, *Rethinking the American Prison Movement*; Felber, *Those Who Know Don't Say*; Mona Lynch, *Sunbelt Justice: Arizona and the Transformation of American Punishment* (Palo Alto, CA: Stanford University Press, 2009); Ruth Wilson Gilmore, *Golden Gulag: Prisons, Surplus, Crisis, and Opposition in*

Globalizing California (Oakland: University of California Press, 2007); Schoen-feld, *Building the Prison State*; Thompson, *Blood in the Water*; Robert Perkinson, *Texas Tough:The Rise of America's Prison Empire* (New York: Picador, 2010).

5 Thompson, *Blood in the Water*.

6 See Berger, *Captive Nation*, 10–11; Gilmore, *Golden Gulag*; Perkinson, *Texas Tough*.

7 Alice Echols, *Daring to Be Bad: Radical Feminism in America, 1967–1975*, 30th an-niversary ed. (Minneapolis: University of Minnesota Press, 2019).

8 Baer, *Beyond the Usual Beating*; Thuma, *All Our Trials*; Anne Gray Fischer, *The Streets Belong to Us: Sex, Race, and Police Power from Segregation to Gentrification* (Chapel Hill: University of North Carolina Press, 2022).

9 See Canterino v. Wilson, 546 F. Supp. 174 (W.D. Ky. 1982) and Klinger v. Nebraska, 824 F. Supp. 1374 (D. Neb. 1993).

10 Serena Mayeri, *Reasoning from Race: Feminism, Law, and the Civil Rights Revolu-tion* (Cambridge, MA: Harvard University Press, 2014), 6. For more on differ-ent aspects of the women's movement, see Stephanie Gilmore (ed.), *Feminist Coalitions: Historical Perspectives on Second-Wave Feminism in the United States* (Urbana: University of Illinois Press, 2008); Susan Hartman, *The Other Feminists: Activists in the Liberal Establishment* (New Haven, CT: Yale Univer-sity Press, 2013); Kirsten Swinth, *Feminism's Forgotten Fight: The Unfinished Struggle for Work and Family* (Cambridge, MA: Harvard University Press, 2018).

11 This argument relies on recent interpretations of the women's movement that avoid characterizing its leaders and beneficiaries as white, middle-class women. See Gilmore, *Feminist Coalitions*; Nancy MacLean, *Freedom Is Not Enough: The Opening of the American Work Place* (Cambridge, MA: Harvard University Press, 2006); Mayeri, *Reasoning from Race*; Premilla Nadasen, "Expanding the Bound-aries of the Women's Movement: Black Feminism and the Struggle for Welfare Rights," *Feminist Studies* 28, no. 2 (Summer 2002): 270–301.

12 "Introduction," Hearing of the Subcommittee on Corrections of the Committee on Social Services and Corrections, Detroit House of Corrections, August 23, 1973, Folder 10: Office Files, Box 3, DHC.

13 The city of Detroit maintained the women's prison operations until 1975, when the MDOC was authorized to supervise the prison under H.B. 5015. Perry John-son, "State Officially Takes Over DeHoCo," *Dialogues* no. 6 (November 1975), RG93–115, Folder 1, Box 6: Corrections—Florence Crane, Warden's Subject File, P-S, 1982–1992, MDC.

14 Glover, "A Woman's Life."

15 Hornus, "Mary Glover Given 3 Life Prison Terms."

16 Glover, "A Woman's Life."

17 Glover, "A Woman's Life."

18 Deborah Labelle and Sheryl Pimlott Kubiak, "Balancing Gender Equity for Women Prisoners," *Feminist Studies* 30, no. 2 (Summer 2004): 417–18.

19 Engle was one of several representatives from each cottage. Judith Frutig, "Ex-Bunny Released from Jail," *Detroit Free Press*, July 21, 1970, 4D.

20 Tom Ricke, "The Tragedy of Kathy: A Detroit Girl's Fast Short Trip from Second Avenue to DeHoCo," *Detroit Free Press*, February 1, 1970, 8.

21 Carol Jacobsen, director, *From One Prison . . .* , Paul Robeson Foundation Fellowship and Women in Film Foundation Arbur Fellowship, 1994, VHS.

22 Transcript of Inmate Testimony, Hearing of the Subcommittee on Corrections of the Committee on Social Services and Corrections, 22, Detroit House of Corrections, August 23, 1973, Folder 10: Office Files, Box 3, DHC.

23 Quotation in subtitle from Transcript of Inmate Testimony, Hearing of the Subcommittee on Corrections of the Committee on Social Services and Corrections, 3.

24 For more on the Attica uprising, see Thompson, *Blood in the Water*.

25 Tom Wicker, "The Animals at Attica," *New York Times*, September 16, 1971, www.nytimes.com.

26 David Fathi, "Attica Is Every Prison; and Every Prison Is Attica," American Civil Liberties Union, September 14, 2018, www.aclu.org.

27 James B. Jacobs, "The Prisoners' Rights Movement and Its Impact, 1960–1980," *Crime and Justice* 2 (1980): 429–70.

28 Jacobs, "The Prisoners' Rights Movement."

29 "1954 MAC, R 791.4430(1) States in part: Each institution shall provide programs for rehabilitation to provide residents the opportunity to emphasize their individual strengths and develop the ability to handle responsibility. Programs for rehabilitation shall include, but not be limited to, considerations of job readiness, educational preparedness, mental and physical health, substance abuse treatment, and socialization." Glover v. Johnson, 478 F. Supp. 1075 (E.D. Mich. 1979).

30 "Introduction," Hearing of the Subcommittee on Corrections of the Committee on Social Services and Corrections.

31 The committee consisted of David S. Holmes Jr. (chairman), Howard E. Wolpe, and Warren O'Brien. "Introduction," Hearing of the Subcommittee on Corrections of the Committee on Social Services and Corrections.

32 Transcript of Inmate Testimony, Hearing of the Subcommittee on Corrections of the Committee on Social Services and Corrections, 3.

33 "Introduction," Hearing of the Subcommittee on Corrections of the Committee on Social Services and Corrections.

34 Transcript of Inmate Testimony, Hearing of the Subcommittee on Corrections of the Committee on Social Services and Corrections, 57.

35 "Introduction," Hearing of the Subcommittee on Corrections of the Committee on Social Services and Corrections, 1.

36 "Introduction," Hearing of the Subcommittee on Corrections of the Committee on Social Services and Corrections, Detroit House of Corrections.

37 See Gideon v. Wainwright, 372 US 335 (1963); Miranda v. Arizona, 384 U.S. 346 (1966); Mapp v. Ohio, 367 U.S. 643 (1961); Terry v. Ohio, 392 U.S. 1 (1967). For

more on the rights revolution in criminal legal institutions, see Michael Klar-
man, "Rethinking the Civil Rights and Civil Liberties Revolutions," *Virginia Law
Review* 82, no. 1 (February 1996): 1–67.

38 Jacobs, "The Prisoners' Rights Movement," 440–41; Toussaint Losier, ". . . For
Strictly Religious Reason[s]: *Cooper v. Pate* and the Origins of the Prisoners'
Rights Movement," *Souls* 15, nos. 1–2 (July 2013): 19–38.

39 Wolff v. McDonnell, 418 U.S. 539 (1974).

40 Jacobs, "The Prisoners' Rights Movement," 441.

41 Transcript of Inmate Testimony, Hearing of the Subcommittee on Corrections of
the Committee on Social Services and Corrections, 59.

42 Judith Frutig, "Ex-Bunny Released from Jail," *Detroit Free Press*, July 21, 1970, 4D.

43 Transcript of Inmate Testimony, Hearing of the Subcommittee on Corrections of
the Committee on Social Services and Corrections, 3.

44 Transcript of Staff Testimony, Hearing of the Subcommittee on Corrections of the
Committee on Social Services and Corrections, 119.

45 Sherry, *The Punitive Turn in American Life*; Deborah McDowell, Claudrena
Harold, and Juan Battle (eds.), *The Punitive Turn: New Approaches to Race and
Incarceration* (Charlottesville: University of Virginia Press, 2013).

46 Transcript of Inmate Testimony, Hearing of the Subcommittee on Corrections of
the Committee on Social Services and Corrections, 54; Wilson recorded her race
in the Detroit House of Correction Prison Register, 1974, DHC.

47 "Policeman's Slayer Gives Up to Priest," *Escanaba Daily*, October 30, 1969; "A
Tragic Murder Pinpoints the Policeman's Dual Job," *Detroit Free Press*, October 28,
1969. Fulghan is racially unmarked in the newspaper coverage of her case and the
testimony for the special committee.

48 Transcript of Inmate Testimony, Hearing of the Subcommittee on Corrections of
the Committee on Social Services and Corrections, 54. Male prisoners who held
jobs in Michigan prison industries earned $3.50 per hour in 1981. This was sig-
nificantly higher than the national average prison wage of $0.65 per hour. Snow,
"Women in Prison," 1068.

49 "Recommendations," Hearing of the Subcommittee on Corrections of the Committee on Social Services and Corrections.

50 MDOC managed the women's prison beginning in 1975. Annual Report of the
Detroit House of Correction, 1974, Box 9A: Annual Reports, 1960–1979, DHC.

51 Schoenfeld, *Building the Prison State*.

52 Charlotte Robinson, "Jailer's Goal: Women Prepared for 'Outside,'" *Detroit Free
Press*, July 1, 1976.

53 Robinson, "Jailer's Goal."

54 Barbara Zwald and Charmaine Cornish, "As Our Readers See It: Outdated Ideas
Won't Do for Women Prisoners," *Detroit Free Press*, July 10, 1976; race of women
recorded in the Detroit House of Correction Prison Register, 1973 and 1975, DHC.

55 Zwald and Cornish, "As Our Readers See It."

56 Zwald and Cornish, "As Our Readers See It."

57 Glover v. Johnson, 478 F. Supp. 1075, 1085 (E.D. Mich. 1979), footnote 4.
58 Annual Report of the Detroit House of Correction, 1974, p. 28, Box 9A: Annual Reports, 1960–1979, DHC.
59 Glover, "A Woman's Life."
60 "75th Annual Buck Dinner Program," 2004, www.buckdinner.org.
61 "Ernest Goodman, 90, Civil Rights Lawyer," *New York Times*, April 2, 1997; Carrie Sharlow, "Michigan Lawyers in History: Ernest Goodman," *Michigan Bar Journal*, May 2013, 48–49, www.michbar.org.
62 Rudolph Stahlberg, Regional Administrator, Monthly Report to the Director and Corrections Commission, Southeastern Regional Report, December 20, 1979, Folder 4: Burr. Correctional Facilities, 1980, Box 2: Executive Division, Minutes of Meetings, 1980 T–Z, MDC.
63 *Michigan Department of Corrections 1980 Annual Statistic Report* (Fall 1981), 43, www.ncjrs.gov.
64 Michael Ver Meulen, "Huron Facility Isn't Dehoco, but Women's Prison Is Still Overcrowded," *Detroit Free Press*, August 13, 1978. The Detroit House of Correction was commonly referred to as "dehoco."
65 Interview of Charlene Snow by the author, March 23, 2016.
66 Interview of Mary Heinen by the author, April 30, 2016.
67 (Amicus Curiae) Affidavit of Georgia Deloris Manzie, September 13, 1977, Glover v. Johnson, 478 F. Supp. 1075, 1085 (E.D. Mich. 1979), Box 8, Folder 1, FRC.
68 Interview of Charlene Snow by the author, March 23, 2016.
69 Reed v. Reed, 404 U.S. 71 (1971). The case examined whether a gender preference in a statute violated the Equal Protection Clause of the Fourteenth Amendment. The court held that this was a violation because it was arbitrary. In this case, an Idaho statute gave preference to the father over the mother to administer the estate of a minor who died intestate.
70 See Frontiero v. Richardson, 411 U.S. 677 (1973), holding that different dependency policies based on sex violated the Fourteenth Amendment; Mayeri, *Reasoning from Race.*
71 Craig v. Boren, 429 U.S. 190 (1976).
72 Trial Brief, 30, Box 8, Folder 1, FRC.
73 Affidavit in Support of Jane Doe Request, May 19, 1977, Glover v. Johnson, 478 F. Supp. 1075, 1085 (E.D. Mich. 1979), Box 8, Folder 1, FRC.
74 Charlene Snow, "Women in Prison," 1065.
75 Interview of Mary Heinen by the author, July 14, 2016.
76 In the spring of 1977, Charmaine Cornish and Georgia Manzie, two women serving life sentences, filed a civil lawsuit *pro se* alleging that the MDOC violated their Fourteenth Amendment rights to due process and equal protection. They could not adequately access the courts because of the outdated law library. The case alleged that the MDOC denied women equal protection and equal access to job training that was available in men's prisons. Charmaine Cornish, et al. v. Perry Johnson, et al., Civil Action No. 77–72557.

77 Complaint 771229, filed May 19, 1977, Folder 1, Box 1, FRC; interview of Charlene Snow by the author, March 23, 2016.

78 Deborah LaBelle, "Bringing Human Rights Home to the World of Detention," *Columbia Human Rights Law Review* 40 (2008): 79–105, 99.

79 For more on prison reform and the courts, see Malcolm M. Feeley and Edward L. Rubin, *Judicial Policy Making and the Modern State: How the Courts Reformed America's Prisons* (Cambridge: Cambridge University Press, 1998). Major prison conditions cases included Talley v. Stephens, 247 F. Supp. 683 (E.D. Ark. 1965), Holt v. Sarver, 300 F. Supp. 825 (E.D. Ark. 1969), Holt v. Sarver II, 309 F. Supp. 362 (E.D. Ark. 1970), Ruiz v. Estelle, 503 F. Supp. 1265 (S.D. Texas 1980).

80 See Alexander Reinert, "Eighth Amendment Gaps: Can Conditions of Confinement Litigation Benefit from Proportionality Theory?" *Fordham Urban Law Journal* 36, no. 2 (January 2009): 53–87; Schoenfeld, *Building the Prison State*. Interpretations of Section 1983, from the 1871 Civil Rights Act, allowed citizens to sue state actors in federal courts. This became a popular method for incarcerated people to petition for better prison conditions in the 1970s.

81 The First and Eighth Amendment violations alleged by the incarcerated women applied to the Kalamazoo County Jail, which the MDOC had been using as an overflow facility. Glover v. Johnson, 478 F. Supp. 1075 (E.D. Mich. 1979).

82 Interview of Charlene Snow by the author, March 23, 2016.

83 Glover v. Johnson, 478 F. Supp. 1075 (1979).

84 Glover v. Johnson, 478 F. Supp. 1075 (1979).

85 For more on the political and social implications of the prisoners' rights movement, see Jacobs, "The Prisoners' Rights Movement."

86 William Hart, "Judge Rules State's Prisons Violate Female Inmate's Rights," *Detroit Free Press*, October 18, 1979.

87 Memorandum to the Women Prisoners at Huron Valley Women's Facility and Kalamazoo County Jail from Judith Magid and Charlene Snow, Re: The Federal Court Decision in Glover v. Johnson, December 19, 1979. Charlene Snow Personal Collection, Detroit, MI.

88 Their equal protection claim was based on the Fourteenth Amendment, which represented a compelling legal approach in prison reform cases. Most prison reform cases in federal courts based their complaints on violations of the Eighth Amendment and sought judicial oversight of state prison systems. See Feeley and Rubin, *Judicial Policy Making and the Modern State*, 42–43.

89 See Canterino v. Wilson, 546 F. Supp. 174 (W.D. Ky. 1982) and Klinger v. Nebraska, 824 F. Supp. 1374 (D. Neb. 1993).

90 Hart, "Judge Rules State's Prisons Violate Female Inmate's Rights."

91 Snow, "Women in Prison," 1067.

92 Hart, "Judge Rules State's Prisons Violate Female Inmate's Rights."

93 Memorandum to the Women Prisoners at Huron Valley Women's Facility and Kalamazoo County Jail from Judith Magid and Charlene Snow.

94 Interview of Charlene Snow by the author, March 23, 2016.

95 Snow, "Women in Prison," 1065–68.
96 Feeley and Rubin, *Judicial Policy Making and the Modern State*, 111–12.
97 Glover v. Johnson, 478 F. Supp. 1075 (D. Mich. 1979).
98 See Jacobs, "The Prisoners' Rights Movement," 436.
99 Glover v. Johnson, 478 F. Supp. 1075 (D. Mich. 1979).
100 Glover v. Johnson, 478 F. Supp. 1075 (D. Mich. 1979).
101 See Canterino v. Wilson, 546 F. Supp. 174 (W.D. Ky. 1982) and Klinger v. Nebraska, 824 F. Supp. 1374 (D. Neb. 1993)
102 Memorandum to the Women Prisoners at Huron Valley Women's Facility and Kalamazoo County Jail from Judith Magid and Charlene Snow.
103 Interview of Mary Heinen by the author, April 30, 2016.
104 Snow, "Women in Prison," 1068.
105 Mary Heinen in conversation with the author, April 2017, Ypsilanti, MI.
106 Spelling in original image. Program from the Detroit Chapter National Lawyers Guild 45th Anniversary Annual Dinner Celebrating the Struggle Against Women's Oppression, May 22, 1982. Mary Heinen Personal Collection.
107 Program from the Detroit Chapter National Lawyers Guild 45th Anniversary Annual Dinner.
108 Affidavit of Mary Glover, May 27, 1980, in Glover v. Johnson, Civil Action 77–1229, Judge Feikens Motion for Temporary Restraining Order and Preliminary Injunction, Appendices A–C, Charlene Snow Personal Collection, Detroit, MI.
109 Affidavit of Mary Glover.
110 Stephen Franklin, "Woman Inmates Charge Harassment after Lawsuit," *Detroit Free Press*, June 13, 1980.
111 Patricia Hill Collins, *Black Sexual Politics: African Americans, Gender, and the New Racism* (New York: Routledge, 2004), 193–94.
112 Davis, *Are Prisons Obsolete?* 75.
113 Tekla Miller, *The Warden Wore Pink* (Brunswick, ME: Biddle Publishing, 1996), 100.
114 Miller, *The Warden Wore Pink*.
115 Interview of Mary Heinen by the author, April 30, 2016.
116 "Prison Officials Deny Harassment," *Detroit Free Press*, June 17, 1980.
117 Franklin, "Woman Inmates Charge Harassment after Lawsuit."
118 Rafter, *Partial Justice*, 189.
119 Violent Crime Control and Law Enforcement Act 1994, H.R. 3355, Pub.L. 103–322.
120 Glover v. Johnson, 198 F.3d 557 (6th Cir. 1999).
121 Glover v. Johnson, 198 F.3d 557 (6th Cir. 1999).
122 Mary Heinen, "Untapped Freedom: Mary Heinen at TEDxUofM," *TEDx Talks*, May 5, 2013, www.youtube.com/watch?v=CTqiIuh9_Zo.

CHAPTER 3. CONTESTING FEMINISM

1 People of the State of Michigan v. Juanita Thomas, 126 Mich. App. 611 (1983); Brief in Opposition to Defendant's Motion to Remain on the Basis of Newly Discovered

Evidence, Juanita Thomas Case File, Circuit Court No. 79-29986-FY, 1-3, Ingham County Courts, Lansing, MI (hereafter ICC); People of the State of Michigan v. Juanita Thomas, Circuit Court No. 79-29986-FY, Trial Transcript, May 29 to June 23, 1980, 1270-1273, ICC.

2 Keith Gave, "Woman Details Life with Murdered Lover," *Lansing State Journal*, June 13, 1980.

3 Jacquelynn Boyle, "Wives Who Killed Seek Clemency," *Detroit Free Press*, March 6, 1995.

4 Gave, "Woman Details Life with Murdered Lover."

5 "MSU Employee Accused of Murder," *State News* 74, no. 87 (May 20, 1980): 5. Brief in Opposition to Defendant's Motion, 7-8.

6 McGuire, *At the Dark End of the Street*.

7 See Angela Davis, *Freedom Is a Constant Struggle: Ferguson, Palestine, and the Foundations of a Movement* (Chicago: Haymarket Books, 2016), 138-40; Victoria Law, "Against Carceral Feminism," *Jacobin*, October, 17, 2014, www.jacobinmag.com; Thuma, *All Our Trials*, 7.

8 Beth Richie, *Compelled to Crime: The Gender Entrapment of Battered Black Women* (New York: Routledge, 1996), 12-13.

9 Beth Richie, *Arrested Justice: Black Women, Violence, and America's Prison Nation* (New York: NYU Press, 2012), 68-69, 79-80.

10 Lenore Walker, *The Battered Woman Syndrome* (New York: Springer, 1984); Keith Gave, "Group Defends Ms. Thomas," *Lansing State Journal*, June 12, 1980.

11 Richie, *Arrested Justice*, 80.

12 Christina Greene, "'She Ain't No Rosa Parks': The Joan Little Rape-Murder Case and Jim Crow Justice in the Post-Civil Rights South," *Journal of African American History* 100, no. 3 (Summer 2015): 428-568, doi: 10.5323/jafriamerhist.100.3.0428; James Reston Jr., "The Joan Little Case," *New York Times*, April 6, 1975, www.nytimes.com.

13 Michael Coakley, "Little Trial Is Over but the Issues Remain," *Chicago Tribune*, August 24, 1975; McGuire, *At the Dark End of the Street*, 246-78.

14 Catherine O. Jacquet, *The Injustices of Rape: How Activists Responded to Sexual Violence, 1950-1980* (Chapel Hill: University of North Carolina Press, 2019), 109-39; McGuire, *At the Dark End of the Street*, 246-78.

15 Mike Hughes and Sue Nichols, "Francine Hughes: Her Trial by Fire," *Lansing State Journal*, October 7, 1984.

16 It would not be until 1988 that Michigan would pass a law that made marital rape a crime. Hughes described to the press not wanting to restart the fight and obliging to his sexual demands to end the beating. Otis White, "Deputies Cite Hughes' 'Threat,'" *Lansing State Journal*, October 25, 1977; William Grimes, "Francine Hughes Wilson, 69, Domestic Violence Victim Who Took Action, Dies," *New York Times*, March 31, 2017, www.nytimes.com; Mich. Comp. Laws Ann. 750.520l, passed June 1988, www.legislature.mich.gov. For a study on rape, battered women, and self-defense in Michigan, see Carol Jacobsen, Kammy Mizga, Lynn D'Orio,

"Battered Women, Homicide Convictions, and Sentencing: The Case for Clemency," *Hastings Women's Law Journal* 18, no. 1 (Winter 2007): 31–66.

17 Hughes and Nichols, "Francine Hughes"; White, "Deputies Cite Hughes' 'Threat.'"

18 Hughes and Nichols, "Francine Hughes."

19 Hughes and Nichols, "Francine Hughes"; Matthew D. Lassiter, "De Jure/de Facto Segregation: The Long Shadow of a National Myth," in Matthew D. Lassiter and Joseph Crespino (eds.), *The Myth of Southern Exceptionalism* (Oxford: Oxford University Press, 2010), 27.

20 Elizabeth Pleck, *Domestic Tyranny: The Making of Social Policy against Family Violence from Colonial Times to the Present* (Oxford: Oxford University Press, 1987), 7.

21 Hughes and Nichols, "Francine Hughes."

22 White, "Deputies Cite Hughes' 'Threat.'"

23 White, "Deputies Cite Hughes' 'Threat.'"

24 White, "Deputies Cite Hughes' 'Threat'"; Sue Nichols, "Ordeal Changed Their Lives Forever," *Lansing State Journal*, October 7, 1984.

25 Nichols, "Ordeal Changed Their Lives Forever."

26 White, "Deputies Cite Hughes' 'Threat.'"

27 Hughes and Nichols, "Francine Hughes."

28 Hughes and Nichols, "Francine Hughes"; Michigan Penal Code, Act 328 of 1931, 750.316, www.legislature.mi.gov.

29 Hughes and Nichols, "Francine Hughes"; Scott Michels, producer, "The Domestic Violence Case That Turned Outrage into Action," Retro Report, July 9, 2020, digital film, www.retroreport.org.

30 Grimes, "Francine Hughes Wilson"; Nichols, "Ordeal Changed Their Lives Forever."

31 Nichols, "Ordeal Changed Their Lives Forever"; Trudy Westfall, "Shelter Home Drive Begins," *State Journal*, April 23, 1978.

32 "Abusive Husbands Still Terrorize Wives," *State News*, May 20, 1980.

33 Thuma, *All Our Trials*, 107.

34 Gioia Diliberto, "A Violent Death, a Haunted Life," *People*, October 8, 1984, 100.

35 Kimberlé Crenshaw, "Mapping the Margins: Intersectionality, Identity Politics, and Violence against Women of Color," *Stanford Law Review* 43, no. 6 (July 1991): 1241–99, doi: 10.2307/1229039.

36 *1980 Census Population, General Population Characteristics: Michigan*, www2 .census.gov; Walter Leavy, "Battered Women: Why So Many Suffer Abuse for So Long," *Ebony*, February 1981, 100.

37 The court did not permit the attorneys to question potential jurors, and Thomas's trial attorney had objected to the fact that the court conducted *voir dire*. Order Confirming Conviction, People of the State of Michigan v. Juanita Thomas, No. 54103, State of Michigan Court of Appeals, June 22, 1983, Juanita Thomas Case File, Circuit Court No. 79–29986-FY, ICC.

38 Jacobsen, *From One Prison*.

39 "Woman Details Life with Murdered Lover," *Lansing State Journal*, June 13, 1980.

40 Affidavit of Financial Condition Form; Pretrial Release Information Form; Order Appointing Attorney for Preliminary Examination, Juanita Thomas Case File, Circuit Court No. 79–29986-FY, ICC.

41 Memorandum of Law in Support of Accompanying Motion to Set Aside or Modify Judgment, Juanita Thomas Case File, Circuit Court No. 79–29986-FY, ICC.

42 Jacobsen, *From One Prison*.

43 "MSU Employee Accused of Murder," *State News*, May 20, 1980, 5.

44 Sentence structure errors in the original source. Andrea D. Lyon, Emily Hughes, and Juanita Thomas, "The People v. Juanita Thomas: A Battered Woman's Journey to Freedom," *Women and Criminal Justice* 13, no. 1 (2001): 40.

45 Lyon, Hughes, and Thomas, "The People v. Juanita Thomas," 40–41.

46 Statement of Juanita Thomas, Exhibit II, July 30, 1979, Juanita Thomas Case File, Circuit Court No. 79–29986-FY, ICC.

47 Motion for Discovery, Attachment G, Portions of Closing Arguments, January 15, 1997, 1252, Juanita Thomas Case File, Circuit Court No. 79–29986-FY, ICC.

48 Leavy, "Battered Women," 96.

49 Lyon, Hughes, and Thomas, "The People v. Juanita Thomas," 42.

50 Lyon, Hughes, and Thomas, "The People v. Juanita Thomas," 52–54.

51 For more on the harmful aspects of a color-blind legal system, see Alexander, *The New Jim Crow*.

52 Lyon, Hughes, and Thomas, "The People v. Juanita Thomas," 45.

53 Nicole Gonzalez Van Cleve, *Crook County: Racism and Injustice in America's Largest Criminal Court* (Stanford, CA: Stanford Law Books, 2016), 53.

54 Manning Marable, *Malcolm X: A Life of Reinvention* (New York: Viking, 2011), 25–38. For more on Malcolm X and his childhood in Michigan see Alex Haley and Malcolm X, *The Autobiography of Malcolm X: As Told to Alex Haley*, reissue ed. (New York: Ballantine Books, 1999).

55 Maryanne Conheim, "Ex-Klan Chief Backs Wallace and McGovern," *Detroit Free Press*, June 26, 1972; Buddy Moorehouse, "Bob Miles Would Be Loving This," *Livingston County Daily Press*, January 30, 2005.

56 Lyon, Hughes, and Thomas, "The People v. Juanita Thomas," 45.

57 Lyon, Hughes, and Thomas, "The People v. Juanita Thomas," 54.

58 Michael G. Wagner, "Men Adapt as Guards at Prisons for Women," *Detroit Free Press*, July 9, 1987, 6A.

59 Leavy, "Battered Women," 96.

60 Leavy, "Battered Women," 100.

61 Thuma, *All Our Trials*, 7. Scholars of the carceral state have been critical of VAWA and its role in expanding the reach of the carceral state. Kimberlé Crenshaw, "From Private Violence to Mass Incarceration: Thinking Intersectionally about Women, Race, and Social Control," *UCLA Law Review* 59, no. 6 (August 2012): 1418–72, 1426; Gottschalk, *The Prison and the Gallows*; Mimi Kim, "Dancing the

Carceral Creep: The Anti–Domestic Violence Movement and the Paradoxical Pursuit of Criminalization, 1973–1986," UC Berkeley: Institute for the Study of Societal Issues, October 14, 2015, https://escholarship.org; Deborah M. Weissman, "The Community Politics of Domestic Violence," *Brooklyn Law Review* 82, no. 4 (2017): 1479–1538, https://brooklynworks.brooklaw.edu; Nancy Whittier, "Carceral and Intersectional Feminism in Congress: The Violence Against Women Act, Discourse, and Policy," *Gender and Society* 30, no. 5 (2016): 791–818.

62 Jacquelynn Boyle, "Wives Who Killed Seek Clemency," *Detroit Free Press*, March 6, 1995.

63 Boyle, "Wives Who Killed Seek Clemency"; Jacobsen, *From One Prison.*

64 Boyle, "Wives Who Killed Seek Clemency."

65 Pleck, *Domestic Tyranny*, 182.

66 Boyle, "Wives Who Killed Seek Clemency."

67 Most clemency cases had been decided between 1990 and 1995. Jacquelynn Boyle, "Killer of Husband Is Denied Clemency," *Detroit Free Press*, May 4, 1995, 4B.

68 Boyle, "Wives Who Killed Seek Clemency."

69 Perry Johnson, "Reflections on Times Past," *Corrections* 59, no. 3 (June 1997): 119.

70 Human Rights Watch Women's Rights Project, *All Too Familiar: Sexual Abuse of Women in US State Prisons* (New York: Human Rights Watch, 1996), 225.

71 Human Rights Watch Women's Rights Project, *All Too Familiar*, 224.

72 Jack Kresnak and Dawson Bell, "Prison Report Hailed, Jeered: State Officials, Women's Advocates at Odds," *Detroit Free Press*, March 31, 1995.

73 Kresnak and Bell, "Prison Report Hailed."

74 Thuma, *All Our Trials*, 107.

75 Thuma, *All Our Trials*, 107.

76 "Clemency for Battered Women in Michigan: A Manual for Attorneys, Law Students, and Social Workers," Michigan Women's Justice and Clemency Project at the University of Michigan, http://umich.edu/~clemency/.

77 Boyle, "Killer of Husband Is Denied Clemency."

78 "Clemency for Battered Women in Michigan."

79 Carol Jacobsen, "Creative Politics and Women's Criminalization in the United States," *Signs* 33, no. 2 (Winter 2008): 468.

80 Jacobsen, "Creative Politics and Women's Criminalization," 468–69.

81 Juanita Díaz-Cotto, *Gender, Ethnicity, and the State: Latina and Latino Prison Politics* (New York: State University of New York Press, 1996), 324–25.

82 Thuma, *All Our Trials*, 95–96.

83 Díaz-Cotto, *Gender, Ethnicity, and the State*, 324–25.

84 Thuma, *All Our Trials*, 96–97.

85 "Statement of Purpose," *No More Cages* 3, no. 1 (November/December 1981). The Women Free Women in Prison Collective. No more cages: A Bi-monthly women's prison newsletter, 1981. Cynthia Miller Papers (MS 869). Special Collections and University Archives, University of Massachusetts–Amherst Libraries, https://credo.library.umass.edu.

86 Thuma, *All Our Trials*, 95–96.

87 Lyon, Hughes, and Thomas, "The People v. Juanita Thomas," 33.

88 Lyon, Hughes, and Thomas, "The People v. Juanita Thomas," 43.

89 Lyon, Hughes, and Thomas, "The People v. Juanita Thomas," 33.

90 Lyon, Hughes, and Thomas, "The People v. Juanita Thomas," 55.

91 Lyon, Hughes, and Thomas, "The People v. Juanita Thomas," 56.

92 Lyon, Hughes, and Thomas, "The People v. Juanita Thomas," 56–57.

93 Carol Jacobsen and Lynn D'Orio, "Defending Survivors: Case Studies of the Michigan Women's Justice and Clemency Project," *University of Pennsylvania Journal of Law and Social Change* 18, no. 1 (2015): 20.

94 Lyon, Hughes, and Thomas, "The People v. Juanita Thomas," 57–59.

95 Jacobsen, "Creative Politics and Women's Criminalization," 462–70.

96 Jacobsen, "Creative Politics and Women's Criminalization," 468.

CHAPTER 4. ESCAPING DEATH AND SERVING LIFE

1 Marcus Amick, "Freedom Reunites a Detroit Family: Woman, Now Free, Lost 20 Years in Prison," *Michigan Chronicle*, February 24, 1999.

2 Marian Wilkinson, "War without End," *Sydney Morning Herald*, May 8, 1999.

3 Michigan Public Act 368 of 1978.

4 Monica Pratt, "Drug Lifers: Michigan's Law Doesn't Give Addicts a Second Chance," *Detroit Free Press*, February 3, 1997.

5 For more on this national trend, see *A Living Death: Life without Parole for Nonviolent Offenses* (New York: American Civil Liberties Union, 2013), 20.

6 See Beckett, *Making Crime Pay*; Hinton, *From the War on Poverty to the War on Crime*; Simon, *Governing through Crime*; Wacquant, *Punishing the Poor*.

7 Julilly Kohler-Hausmann, *Getting Tough: Welfare and Imprisonment in 1970s America* (Princeton, NJ: Princeton University Press, 2017).

8 Many books on Detroit have identified its so-called golden years as spanning from the decade following World War II to the 1967 riot, which is seen as the beginning of the city's decline. This timeline largely upholds and engages with a racialized narrative that argues that the city's growing Black population and shrinking white population were causal factors contributing to urban decline in Detroit. Journalist Ze'ev Chafets offered one of the first book-length treatments that supported this narrative. Ze'ev Chafets, *Devil's Night and Other True Tales of Detroit* (New York: Vintage Books, 1990). Recent books about Detroit have affirmed a similar timeline, dating the zenith of Detroit's cultural, economic, and political influence to the 1950s and early 1960s, followed by decades of decline—although these books engage more thoroughly with the history of Black residents. See Mark Binelli, *Detroit City Is the Place to Be: The Afterlife of an American Metropolis* (New York: Picador, 2013); David Maraniss, *Once in a Great City: A Detroit Story* (New York: Simon and Schuster, 2015). Historian Kevin Boyle has criticized this storied twentieth-century timeline for Detroit by unpacking some of the racial implications and longer historical factors that have contributed to

inequity and racial tension. Kevin Boyle, "The Ruins of Detroit," *Michigan Historical Review* 27, no. 1 (Spring 2001): 111.

9 For more on race and mid-twentieth century politics in Detroit, see Sugrue, *The Origins of the Urban Crisis*.

10 "Fatal Shooting of Cynthia Scott Broady, 34/N of [redacted] I.B. #215218, Homicide File #6360," Inter-Office Memorandum to Commanding Office, Homicide Bureau, July 10, 1963, Detroit Police Department, Cynthia Scott, DPD Homicide File, A20-02255 (FOIA File), Combined Records Redacted, available online at Matthew D. Lassiter and the Policing and Social Justice History Lab, *Detroit under Fire: Police Violence, Crime Politics, and the Struggle for Racial Justice in the Civil Rights Era* (University of Michigan Carceral State Project, 2021), "DPD Homicide Investigation of Cynthia Scott Murder," https://policing.umhistorylabs.lsa.umich.edu.

11 Newspaper and police records prefaced reference to Scott's death with her criminal record and sex work before offering details of the fatal police encounter, which was also included in the police reports. For example, a police memorandum that detailed the DPD's version of events stated that two officers had watched Scott and stated early in the memorandum that she was a "known prostitute." "Fatal Shooting of Cynthia Scott Broady," Inter-Office Memorandum to Commanding Office, Homicide Bureau, July 10, 1963, Detroit Police Department, Cynthia Scott, DPD Homicide File, A20-02255 (FOIA File), Combined Records Redacted, available online at Lassiter and the Policing and Social Justice History Lab, *Detroit under Fire*, "DPD Homicide Investigation of Cynthia Scott Murder," https://policing.umhistorylabs.lsa.umich.edu. Newspaper coverage highlighted Scott's body in ways that emphasized stereotypically masculine features. For example, a *Detroit Free Press* article about the discrepancies between police reports and eyewitness accounts of the fatal police encounter included the following introduction: "Cynthia Scott, 24, of 83 Edmund, was a big, tough woman—she stood six feet tall, weighed 193 pounds—and she pursued the world's oldest profession." Don Beck and Hal Cohen, "Cynthia Scott: 9 Versions of How She Died; Eyewitnesses Describe Disputed Police Shooting," *Detroit Free Press*, July 21, 1963.

12 "Edwards Erred, Scott Critics Say," *Detroit Free Press*, August 10, 1963.

13 Fischer, *The Streets Belong to Us*.

14 Beck and Cohen, "Cynthia Scott"; "Edwards Erred"; "CORE Denied Board to Air Police Acts," *Detroit Free Press*, August 1, 1963; Lassiter and the Policing and Social Justice History Lab, *Detroit under Fire*, "The Brutal Murder of Cynthia Scott," https://policing.umhistorylabs.lsa.umich.edu.

15 Approximately 2,509 buildings were burned or damaged, which created significant financial hurdles to restoring property, homes, and communities. Sugrue, *The Origins of the Urban Crisis*, 259–60; "Uprising of 1967," Encyclopedia of Detroit, July 15, 2021, Detroit Historical Society, https://detroithistorical.org.

16 Berger, *Captive Nation*, 60–62.

17 Radley Balko, *Rise of the Warrior Cop: The Militarization of America's Police Forces* (New York: Public Affairs, 2014); Max Felker-Kantor, *Policing Los Angeles: Race,*

Resistance, and the Rise of the LAPD (Chapel Hill: University of North Carolina Press, 2018).

18 STRESS was established in 1971 and abolished in 1973 because of widescale protests against police brutality. During its three years of operation, Detroit police officers in STRESS units killed an estimated twenty-two people, and most of the victims were Black. STRESS received a thirty-five-thousand-dollar grant from the Law Enforcement Assistance Administration and focused its resources on Black neighborhoods. Elizabeth Hinton found that STRESS officers "killed a young, black male roughly once a month" during its first fifteen months, beginning in January 1971. Hinton, *From the War on Poverty to the War on Crime*, 191–92; Lassiter and the Policing and Social Justice HistoryLab, *Detroit under Fire*, "Remembering STRESS Victims." https://policing.umhistorylabs.lsa.umich.edu.

19 Hinton, *From the War on Poverty to the War on Crime*, 191–209; Matt Lassiter, "Fatal 1971 Shooting Galvanized Detroit against STRESS," *Detroit Free Press*, September 5, 2021; Lassiter and the Policing and Social Justice HistoryLab, *Detroit under Fire*, "V. STRESS and Radical Response, 1971–1973," https://policing .umhistorylabs.lsa.umich.edu.

20 Dee Siegelbaum, "Detroit's Crime Down but Still Leads Big Cities," *Detroit Free Press*, April 7, 1977, 3A. In 1976 there were 153,488 serious crimes reported, a decrease from the 155,701 crimes reported in 1975.

21 The researchers received thirteen thousand responses from a survey conducted in all counties in Michigan. "Seventy-three percent of the respondents said more money should be spent to fight crime." Hugh McDiarmid, "MSU Poll Rates State's Concerns," *Detroit Free Press*, May 6, 1977, 3A, 10A.

22 Boyle, "The Ruins of Detroit," 110.

23 Milliken v. Bradley, 418 US 717 (1974).

24 Alexander, *The New Jim Crow*.

25 Michael Maidenberg, "Restoration Attempt Fails: Death Penalty Is Still Strong Issue in State," *Detroit Free Press*, March 19, 1973.

26 Furman v. Georgia, 408 U.S. 238 (1972).

27 Maidenberg, "Restoration Attempt Fails."

28 Maidenberg, "Restoration Attempt Fails."

29 Hugo Adam Bedau, "An Abolitionist Survey of the Death Penalty in America Today," in Hugo Bedau and Paul Cassell (eds.), *Debating the Death Penalty: Should America Have Capital Punishment? The Experts on Both Sides Make Their Case* (Oxford: Oxford University Press, 2004), 40–42.

30 "Canada Outlaws Death Penalty," *Detroit Free Press*, June 23, 1976.

31 "As We See It: Capital Punishment Is Not Way to Deal with Violence," *Detroit Free Press*, December 10, 1976.

32 Johnson was the MDOC director from 1972 to 1984. Perry M. Johnson, *Jackson: The Rise and Fall of the World's Largest Walled Prison; A History and a Memoir* (Lexington, KY: Amazon, 2014).

33 Memorandum, Michigan Committee Against Capital Punishment, July 2, 1976, Folder: Capital Punishment, Box 667: Budget Corrections 1978–1979, William Milliken Papers, 1961–1982, Bentley Historical Library, University of Michigan, Ann Arbor, MI (hereafter BL).

34 Perry Johnson, "Response by Corrections Director Perry M. Johnson to U.S. Supreme Court Decision on Capital Punishment," attached to Memorandum, Michigan Committee Against Capital Punishment, July 2, 1976, Folder: Capital Punishment, Box 667: Budget Corrections 1978–1979, William Milliken Papers, 1961–1982, BL.

35 Johnson, "Response by Corrections Director Perry M. Johnson."

36 Memorandum, "Capital Punishment, Michigan Committee Against Capital Punishment," undated, Folder: Capital Punishment, Box 667: Budget Corrections 1978–1979, William Milliken Papers, 1961–1982, BL.

37 McCleskey v. Kemp, 481 U.S. 279 (1987). See also Adam Liptak, "David C. Baldus, 75, Dies—Studied Race and the Law," *New York Times*, June 14, 2011, www.nytimes.com. Stephen Bright, interviewed by Myron Farber, The Rule of Law Oral History Project, Columbia Center for Oral History, Columbia University, May 25, 2009, p. 90; William Stuntz, *The Collapse of the Criminal Justice System* (Cambridge, MA: Harvard University Press, 2011), 119.

38 The justices arrived at the majority opinion because the legal remedy for racial bias would have upended the criminal legal system. McCleskey's lawyers argued that the uneven administration of the death penalty violated the Eighth Amendment's protection against cruel and unusual punishment. Furthermore, racial bias violated the Fourteenth Amendment's guarantee of the right to equal protection. If the justices acknowledged racial discrimination in *McCleskey*, they also would have had to confront the possibility that judges, jurors, law enforcement officers, and attorneys were vulnerable to prejudice in the justice system. Faced with this possibility, the justices upheld the status quo. Stuntz, *The Collapse of the Criminal Justice System*, 120.

39 President Reagan's and Nancy Reagan's Address to the Nation on Drug Abuse from the Residence, September 14, 1986, Ronald Reagan Presidential Library and Museum, www.reaganlibrary.gov/.

40 Hinton, *From the War on Poverty to the War on Crime*, 307–10.

41 Schoenfeld, *Building the Prison State*, 93–95; Sherry, *The Punitive Turn in American Life*.

42 "Aid Urged for Junkies—and Jail for Dealers," *Detroit Free Press*, March 31, 1977. Geralds was expelled from the state legislature in 1978 when he refused to resign from his position after he was convicted of embezzling twenty-four thousand dollars from a client in his private practice. Paul Egan, "In History, 3 Michigan Lawmakers Expelled," *Detroit Free Press*, September 10, 2015.

43 "Aid Urged for Junkies."

44 "Aid Urged for Junkies."

45 "House Rejects Wiretaps to Catch Drug Kingpins," *Detroit Free Press*, April 6, 1977, 11B.

46 All of the bills focused on heroin and cocaine and did not target marijuana use or possession. "Michigan House Oks Wiretaps in Drug Cases," *Detroit Free Press*, April 7, 1977.

47 Tom Morrissey, "Catching Up with Paul Rosenbaum," *Michigan Historical Society News*, Spring 2010, 5–6, http://mipoliticalhistory.com.

48 "Life Terms Voted for Drug Czars," *Detroit Free Press*, February 22, 1978.

49 "Crackdown on Pushers Finally OKd in House," *Detroit Free Press*, May 5, 1978.

50 "Crackdown on Pushers Finally OKd in House."

51 "Milliken Signs Anti-Drug Law," *Detroit Free Press*, May 13, 1978.

52 "Appeals Court Stays Tough Coke Penalty," *Detroit Free Press*, February 20, 1982.

53 Lassiter and the Policing and Social Justice HistoryLab, *Detroit under Fire*, "DPD Report on Crime, 1981–1986," Uniform Crime Reports, 1981–1986, https://policing.umhistorylabs.lsa.umich.edu; Lassiter and the Policing and Social Justice HistoryLab, *Detroit under Fire*, "Drug Policies in Michigan," https://policing.umhistorylabs.lsa.umich.edu.

54 Alexander, *The New Jim Crow*; Schoenfeld, *Building the Prison State*, 94–95; "Briefing Paper: Federal Crack Cocaine Sentencing" (Washington, DC: The Sentencing Project, October 20, 2010), www.sentencingproject.org.

55 Rudolph H. Stahlberg, Regional Administrator, Bureau of Correctional Facilities, Monthly Report to the Director and Corrections Commission Southeastern Regional Report August 20, 1980, Folder 4: Monthly Reports, Box 2, RG84-3, MDC.

56 Stahlberg stated, "The population at Huron Valley can best be described as being in a militant, authority-challenging mood." Rudolph H. Stahlberg, Regional Administrator, Bureau of Correctional Facilities, Monthly Report to the Director.

57 By 1999, penal policies pushed the inmate population to 1.273 million men and 90,428 women. Carson E. Ann and Joseph Mulako-Wangota, Bureau of Justice Statistics (Count of total jurisdiction population), Generated using the Corrections Statistical Analysis Tool (CSAT), Prisoners, www.bjs.gov.

58 The facility had also been a mental hospital in the mid-twentieth century. Ron Dzwonkowski, "State Scrambles to Build Prisons," *Detroit Free Press*, March 17, 1985. Rudolph Stahlberg, Monthly Report to the Director and Corrections Commission, Southeastern Regional Report, January 20, 1980, Folder 4: Monthly Reports, Bur. Correctional Facilities, 1980, Box 2, RG84-3, MDC.

59 Oral History Transcript, Interview of Mary Heinen by Noor Mooghni and Nora Krinitsky, Ann Arbor, MI, May 15, 2020, 12, https://sites.lsa.umich.edu.

60 John Eason, *Big House on the Prairie: Rise of the Rural Ghetto and Prison Proliferation* (Chicago: University of Chicago Press, 2017).

61 Gilmore, *Golden Gulag*; Gottschalk, *Caught*; Schoenfeld, *Building the Prison State*.

62 Generally, states have welcomed federal funding and resources for prison construction, which is discussed in the following texts: Alexander, *The New Jim Crow*;

Hinton, *From the War on Poverty to the War on Crime*; Gottschalk, *Caught*; and Schoenfeld, *Building the Prison State.*

63 James N. Crutchfield, "Cauldron of Convicts: What Will Michigan Do about Its Prisons?" *Detroit Free Press*, June 16, 1981.

64 Crutchfield, "Cauldron of Convicts." For more on Jackson's prison and its history, see Charles Bright, *The Powers That Punish: Prison and Politics in the Era of the "Big House," 1920–1955* (Ann Arbor: University of Michigan Press, 1996).

65 Perry Johnson, "The Case for Regional Prisons," Internal Memorandum, Michigan Department of Corrections, November 27, 1978, page 3, Folder: 1978 Executive Correspondence: Perry Johnson, Box 607: Milliken Papers, BL.

66 Johnson, "The Case for Regional Prisons."

67 Johnson, "The Case for Regional Prisons."

68 Holland was a city of 26,281 in 1980, when many residents voted Republican and attended the Dutch Christian Reformed Church. Fewer than 1 percent of its population was Black and 11 percent of its population was "Spanish origin," according to 1980 Census data. Table 14, Holland, MI, Summary of General Statistics, 1980, www2.census.gov.

69 George and Lora Mauphens to Perry Johnson, March 18, 1977, Folder 9: Opposition to Minimum Security Construction, 1977, Box 4: Correspondence, RG 84-30, MDC.

70 Mrs. Vernon Lohman to Perry Johnson, January 19, 1977, Folder 9: Opposition to Minimum Security Construction, 1977, Box 4: Correspondence, RG 84-30, MDC.

71 Dekuim and Mary Riddis to Governor William Milliken, January 10, 1977, Folder 9: Opposition to Minimum Security Construction, 1977, Box 4, RG 84-30, Correspondence, MDC.

72 Dekuim and Mary Riddis to Governor William Milliken.

73 Emils A. Avots to Perry Johnson, January 10, 1977, Folder 9: Opposition to Minimum Security Construction, 1977, Box 4, RG 84-30, Correspondence, MDC.

74 Wayne Dykhuis to Perry Johnson, January 10, 1977, Folder 9: Opposition to Minimum Security Construction, 1977, Box 4, RG 84-30, Correspondence, MDC.

75 Wayne Dykhuis to Perry Johnson.

76 Fennville City Commission to Perry Johnson, March 24, 1977, Folder 9: Opposition to Minimum Security Construction, 1977, Box 4, RG 84-30, Correspondence, MDC.

77 Eason, *Big House on the Prairie.*

78 Businessmen in Allegan County to Governor William Milliken, January 21, 1977, Folder 9: Opposition to Minimum Security Construction, 1977, Box 4, RG 84-30, Correspondence, MDC.

79 Herb Eldean to Perry Johnson, March 19, 1977, Folder 9: Opposition to Minimum Security Construction, 1977, Box 4, RG 84-30, Correspondence, MDC.

80 Mr. and Mrs. Charles A. Lethen to Representative D. J. Jacobette, Chairman Appropriations Committee, April 8, 1977, Folder 9: Opposition to Minimum Security Construction, 1977, Box 4, RG 84-30, Correspondence, MDC.

81 Mr. and Mrs. Charles A. Lethen to Representative D. J. Jacobette.
82 Perry Johnson, "The Case for Regional Prisons," 6.
83 Perry Johnson, "The Case for Regional Prisons," 6.
84 Perry Johnson, "The Case for Regional Prisons," 6.
85 "Revolving Door Prisons: Where Prison Beds Will Be Added," *Detroit Free Press*, September 27, 1985, 11A.
86 Ruiz v. Estelle, 503 F. Supp. 1265 (S.D. Texas 1980), was a major prisoners' rights case filed in federal court in Texas that dismantled the corruption and violence in the model of incarceration that dominated in the state for most of the twentieth century. Florida officials responded to Costello v. Wainwright, 430 U.S. 325 (1977), a decision that ordered the state to reduce severe overcrowding in prisons, and state officials decided to comply by building more prisons.
87 Schoenfeld, *Building the Prison State*, 4–5.
88 Díaz-Cotto, *Gender, Ethnicity, and the State*.
89 Mary Heinen in conversation with the author, April 2016, Ypsilanti, MI.
90 Ryan S. King, "Governance," in Mary Bosworth (ed.), *Encyclopedia of Prisons and Correctional Facilities* (Los Angeles: Sage Publications, 2005), 379–81; John DiIulio, *Governing Prisons: A Comparative Study of Correctional Management* (New York: Free Press, 1987).
91 "Corrections Director Stresses 'Responsibility,'" *The Report*, p. 12, Folder 20, Administrative Subject Files, Correspondence, 1975–1980, Box 3, RG 84-3, MDC.
92 "Corrections Director Stresses 'Responsibility.'"
93 The most influential example of the control model was implemented in the Texas Department of Corrections, a prison system that had modeled itself after chattel slavery, under the leadership of George Beto in the mid-twentieth century. Perkins, *Texas Tough*, 257. For more on the prisoners' rights movement and the control model in Texas and other southern prisons, see Robert Chase, *We Are Not Slaves: State Violence, Coerced Labor, and Prisoners' Rights in Postwar America* (Chapel Hill: University of North Carolina Press, 2019).
94 Chase, *We Are Not Slaves*, 393.
95 California and Arkansas implemented Michigan's participatory model. In Arkansas, prison staff resisted participation from prisoners because they felt it threatened the established power structure. In California, the participation of prisoners began in fits and starts and was never a stable, uniform model across California's expansive prison network. Gilmore, *Golden Gulag*; King, "Governance," 380.
96 "Standard Punishment Sentencing," Michigan Department of Corrections, April 29, 1983, Folder 2: Director's Files, American Correctional Association, 1983–1984, Box 1, RG 88-1, MDC.
97 "Standard Punishment Sentencing."
98 "Standard Punishment Sentencing."
99 Perry M. Johnson, "A Selective Incapacitation Approach to Corrections," June 22, 1984, Folder 2: Director's Files, American Correctional Association, 1983–1984, page 3, Box 1, RG 88-1, MDC.

100 Johnson, "A Selective Incapacitation Approach to Corrections."
101 Hal Farrier to Perry Johnson, January 3, 1984, Folder 2: Director's Files, American Correctional Association, 1983–1984, page 3, Box 1, RG 88-1, MDC.
102 Memorandum, Robert Brown Jr., Director, to Alvin Whitfield, Deputy Director, Bureau of Administrative Services, October 20, 1984, Subject: Monthly Report—Bureau of Administrative Services, September 21, 1984–October 20, 1984, Folder 7: Director's Files, Admin. Services—Monthly Report, 1984, Box 1, RG 88-1, MDC.
103 Harmelin v. Michigan, 501 U.S. 957 (1991).
104 Harmelin v. Michigan, 501 U.S. 957 (1991).
105 Denis Cauchon, "Mich. Revisits Tough Drug Law Critics: Too Many 1st-Time Offenders Imprisoned for Life," USA Today, September 2, 1997. Eighty-six percent of those sentenced under the law had no prior convictions.
106 Young v. Miller, 883 F.2d 1276 (6th Cir. 1989).
107 Michigan Public Act 314 of 1998: www.legislature.mi.gov.
108 Amick, "Freedom Reunites a Detroit Family."
109 Amick, "Freedom Reunites a Detroit Family."

CHAPTER 5. FROM CIVIL RIGHTS TO HUMAN RIGHTS

1 Stacy Barker in conversation with the author, October 25, 2022. L. L. Braiser, "Prison Hero Gets a New Day in Court," Detroit Free Press, August 9, 2001; Barker v. Yukins, 199 F.3d 867 (6th Cir. 1999).
2 Stacy Barker in conversation with the author, September 23, 2022; People v. Barker, 468 N.W.2d. 492, 493 (Mich. 1991); Barker v. Yukins, 199 F.3d 867 (6th Cir. 1999); Carol Jacobsen, Kammy Mizga, Lynn D'Orio, "Battered Women, Homicide Convictions, and Sentencing: The Case for Clemency," Hastings Women's Law Journal 18, no. 1 (Winter 2007): 36.
3 L. L. Brasier, "Slaying Trial Uncovers Old Wounds," Detroit Free Press, November 5, 2001; L. L. Brasier, "Woman Gets 21–70 Years in New Murder Sentence," Detroit Free Press, December 6, 2001; interview of Stacy Barker with author, September 23, 2022.
4 Under the PLRA, incarcerated people had to exhaust the prison's internal administrative processes before bringing complaints before the courts. Prison Litigation Reform Act, Pub. L. (104-134 at 42 U.S.C. 1997e et seq.)
5 Felber, Those Who Know Don't Say, 186.
6 Jack Kresnak and Dawson Bell, "Prison Report Hailed, Jeered," Detroit Free Press, March 31, 1995.
7 Jacobsen (dir.), From One Prison; Mary Heinen, interview by Tirtza Even, digital audio file in the author's possession, Ann Arbor, MI, 2012.
8 Mary Heinen, interview by Tirtza Even.
9 Mary Heinen, interview by Tirtza Even.
10 Edward A. Trudeau to Warden Tekla Miller, August 11, 1988, Charlene Snow Personal Collection, Detroit, MI.
11 Edward A. Trudeau to Warden Tekla Miller.

12 Charlene Snow to Clark Cunningham, Re: Medical Conditions at Florence Crane Correctional Facility, August 5, 1988. Charlene Snow Personal Collection, Detroit, MI.

13 Estelle v. Gamble, 439 U.S. 97 (1976).

14 Kresnak and Bell, "Prison Report Hailed, Jeered."

15 Jack Lessenberry, "A Crusade to Help Battered Women," *Livingston County Daily Press and Argus*, August 8, 2004; Albert Hazan and Danielle Trief, "The Patient with Systemic Disease," and Frank Cao, Nataliya Pokeza, Allison Rizzuti, and Stephen C. Kaufman, "The Patient with Other Ocular Disease," in Francis Mah and Michelle Rhee (eds.), *Dry Eye Disease: A Practical Guide* (Thorofare, NJ: SLACK, 2019), 117–18, 124–26.

16 Jacobsen and D'Orio, "Defending Survivors," 13; "Linda Hamilton," Michigan Women's Justice and Clemency Project, http://websites.umich.edu.

17 Kresnak and Bell, "Prison Report Hailed, Jeered."

18 Keith Barber to Anita Alcorta, Re: Response to September 24, 1991, September 27, 1991, page 1, Folder 12: MDOC Subject Files, Central Office, 1999, Box 1, RG 93–115, Corrections, Florence Crane, Warden's Subject File, A-C, 1982–1990, MDC.

19 Keith Barber to Anita Alcorta.

20 Former MDOC director Perry Johnson described his interpretation that racial integration of prison staff and the prison population "began to change fitfully and grudgingly during the 1960s, but only for inmates and minority male workers. Female workers would be forgotten until well into the 1970s." Perry M. Johnson, "Reflections on Times Past," *Corrections Today* 59, no. 3 (June 1997): 119.

21 Johnson, *Jackson*, 216.

22 Griffin v. Michigan Department of Corrections, 654 F. Supp. 690 (E.D. Mich. 1982).

23 Under Title VII of the Civil Rights Act of 1964, employers could not prohibit employment on the basis of gender unless the potential employee's gender was necessary to do the job, and the MDOC permitted male guards to work in women's prisons. Michael G. Wagner, "Men Adapt as Guards at Prisons for Women," *Detroit Free Press*, July 9, 1987.

24 Wagner, "Men Adapt as Guards at Prisons for Women."

25 Sequita Eaves, interview with the author, April 16, 2013.

26 Wagner, "Men Adapt as Guards at Prisons for Women."

27 Fischer, *The Streets Belong to Us*; Gross, *Colored Amazons*; Haley, *No Mercy Here*; Jacquet, *The Injustices of Rape*.

28 Memorandum to Acting Warden Foltz, From Pat Balasco, Director of Prison Services, Subject: Sexual Harassment Allegations/Barto, October 6, 1986, Folder 13: Dept. Corrections—Warden's Subject File, Chaplain, 1987–1989, Box 1, RG 93–115, MDC. Emphasis in the original document.

29 Sequita Eaves, interview with the author, April 16, 2013.

30 Wagner, "Men Adapt as Guards at Prisons for Women."

31 Wagner, "Men Adapt as Guards at Prisons for Women."

32 "Corrections Pioneer Tekla Dennison Miller," WHYY Fresh Air with Terry Gross, July 17, 1997, www.freshairarchive.org; 750.520b, "Criminal Sexual Conduct in the First Degree; Circumstances, Felony; Consecutive Terms," Michigan Penal Code, www.legislature.mi.gov; A. Widney Brown, *Nowhere to Hide: Retaliation against Women in Michigan State Prisons Legacy Reports* (New York: Human Rights Watch, 1998).

33 Keith Barber to Anita Alcorta, Re: Response to 9/24/91, September 27, 1991, page 3, Folder 12, MDOC, Subject Files, Central Office, 1991, Box 1, RG 93–115, Corrections, Florence Crane, Warden's Subject File, A-C, 1982–1991, MDC.

34 Keith Barber to Anita Alcorta.

35 Edward A. Trudeau to Warden Tekla Miller.

36 Ashley Nellis, *Still Life: America's Increasing Use of Life and Long-Term Sentences* (Washington, DC: The Sentencing Project, May 3, 2017), www.sentencingproject .org.

37 Farmer had attempted sex reassignment surgery and estrogen therapy, and had breast implants when she was sent to prison. Brennan v. Farmer, 511 U.S. 825 (1994).

38 Clarence Thomas wrote a concurring opinion and clarified that he did not believe the Eighth Amendment applied to conditions of confinement. Brennan v. Farmer, 511 U.S. 825 (1994); Wilson v. Seiter, 501 U.S. 294 (1991) also held that in order for officials to be held liable for physical harms prisoners endured in prison, a prisoner would have to demonstrate that officials exhibited "deliberate indifference," a standard set in Estelle v. Gamble, 429 U.S. 97 (1976), in their refusal to act to protect the prisoner in question; Linda Greenhouse, "Supreme Court Roundup; Prison Officials Can Be Found Liable for Inmate-against-Inmate Violence, Court Rules," *New York Times*, June 7, 1994, www.nytimes.com.

39 Margo Schlanger, "Inmate Litigation," *Harvard Law Review* 116, no. 6 (April 2003): 1557–1706. For more on the PLRA, see Dorothy Schrader, *Prison Litigation Reform Act: An Overview, Congressional Research Survey* (Washington, DC: Congressional Research Service at the Library of Congress, 1996).

40 Chase, *We Are Not Slaves*, 394.

41 Ross Sandler and David Schoenbrod, "Prison Reform Act Helps Michigan, Puts Local Officials Back in Control," *Detroit Free Press*, December 5, 1996.

42 Neal v. MDOC, Civil Action File No. 96–6986-CZ, Washtenaw County Circuit Court Case, 1996.

43 Nunn v. Michigan Department of Corrections, No. 96–71416, DT (E.D. Mich. 1997), https://clearinghouse.net; "Wayne Law Alumna Deborah LaBelle Reflects on 13-year Lawsuit, $100 Million Settlement," *Wayne State University Law School News*, August 18, 2009, https://law.wayne.edu.

44 Baer, *Beyond the Usual Beating*.

45 For the language of the Convention Against Torture, see Convention Against Torture and Other Cruel, Inhuman, or Degrading Treatment or Punishment, General Assembly of the United Nations, December 10, 1984, https://treaties.un

.org. For discussion of feedback loops of American torture abroad and practices in the criminal legal system at home see Sherry, *The Punitive Turn in American Life*, 190–204.

46 *"Not Part of My Sentence": Violations of the Human Rights of Women in Custody*, Amnesty International, March 1999, 3, www.amnesty.org.

47 Brown, *Nowhere to Hide*, 2–8.

48 Brown, *Nowhere to Hide*, 19.

49 Historian Julilly Kohler-Hausmann's work demonstrates how the degrading moniker positioned Black women receiving welfare benefits as suspects of fraud. Journalists, politicians, and the media deployed the pejorative term to describe women who sometimes committed fraud, although in many instances simply struggled to make ends meet, which also made them potential targets for punitive policing and incarceration. Kohler-Hausmann, *Getting Tough*.

50 Brown, *Nowhere to Hide*, 20–21; Nunn v. Michigan Department of Corrections, No. 96–71416, DT (E.D. Mich. 1997), https://clearinghouse.net/.

51 Brown, *Nowhere to Hide*, 20–22.

52 Letter from Deval Patrick, assistant attorney general, Civil Rights Division, US Department of Justice, to John Engler, Governor, Michigan, March 27, 1995 as quoted in Dorothy Thomas, *All Too Familiar: Sexual Abuse of Women in US Prisons* (New York: Women's Rights Project at Human Rights Watch, 1996), 35.

53 "State Lawmakers Doubt Prison Abuse," *Battle Creek Enquirer*, March 31, 1995.

54 "Retaliation against Women in Michigan State Prisons," in Brown, *Nowhere to Hide*, 23–24.

55 "Retaliation against Women in Michigan State Prisons," 24–25.

56 Settlement Agreement Regarding Injunctive and Declaratory Relief, Nunn v. Michigan Department of Corrections, No. 96-CV-71416-DT (July 31, 2000), https://clearinghouse.net.

57 Stipulation and Order of Dismissal, Nunn v. Michigan Department of Corrections, Case No. 96-CV-71416-DT, April 25, 2007, https://clearinghouse.net.

58 Neal v. Michigan Department of Corrections, Civil Case File, 96–06986, Michigan state trial court, https://clearinghouse.net.

59 Elliott-Larsen Civil Rights Act ("ELCRA" or the "Civil Rights Act"), M.C.L. § 37.2101 et seq.; M.S.A. § 3.548(101) et seq.; Michigan Public Act 202 of 1999.

60 Michigan Public Act 220 of 1976.

61 Deborah LaBelle, "Local Comment: Bills Strip Power from Jailed Victims," *Detroit Free Press*, December 8, 1999.

62 "In Our Opinion: Rights Stripped; Lansing Rushes to Keep Prisoners in Their Place," *Detroit Free Press*, December 8, 1999.

63 LaBelle, "Bringing Human Rights Home," 83.

64 LaBelle, "Local Comment."

65 Jeff Seidel, "A Prisoner Tells Her Terrible Story," *Detroit Free Press*, January 6, 2009.

66 Seidel, "A Prisoner Tells Her Terrible Story."

67 Neal v. Michigan Department of Corrections, No. 285232, Washtenaw Circuit Court, LC No. 96–006986-CZ, January 27, 2009. A divided court affirmed the lower court's ruling that the 1999 amendment was unconstitutional.

68 Seidel, "A Prisoner Tells Her Terrible Story."

69 "Michigan: Prisoners Lawsuit," *New York Times*, August 20, 2009, www.nytimes .com; Neal v. Michigan Department of Corrections, 96–06986, Michigan State Court, https://clearinghouse.net.

70 Sue Pleming, "Abuse of Women Inmates Seen Rampant," *Boston Globe*, March 7, 2001; *"Not Part of My Sentence."*

71 Seymour Hersh, "Torture at Abu Ghraib," *New Yorker*, April 30, 2004, newyorker .com; Sherry, *The Punitive Turn in American Life*, 190–204; *Getting Away with Torture? Command Responsibility for the U.S. Abuse of Detainees* (New York: Human Rights Watch, April 23, 2005), hrw.org. Bryan Stevenson has spoken about the amnesia of many Americans who first encountered terrorism within the United States after September 11, 2001, neglecting collective memories of the history of lynching and other forms of racial terrorism that targeted Black people and people of color in the late nineteenth and early twentieth centuries. Bryan Stevenson, *Just Mercy: A Story of Justice and Redemption* (New York: Spiegal and Grau, 2014), 299.

72 "Prison Rape Elimination Act, 2003," National PREA Resource Center, www .prearesourcecenter.org.

73 David Kaiser and Lovisa Stannow, "The Shame of Our Prisons: New Evidence," *New York Review of Books*, October 24, 2013, www.nybooks.com.

74 Kunzel, *Criminal Intimacy*.

75 Kaiser and Stannow, "The Shame of Our Prisons."

76 Barker was a named plaintiff in Glover v. Johnson, 9 F. Supp. 2d 799 (E.D. Mich. 1998), Nunn v. Michigan Department of Corrections, No. 96–71416, DT (E.D. Mich. Feb. 4, 1997), Neal v. Michigan Department of Corrections, 454 Mich. 886; 562 NW2d 201 (1997), Bazzetta v. McGinnis, 148 F. Supp. 2d 813 (E.D. Mich. 2001), and Cain v. Michigan Department of Corrections, 451 Mich. 470, 548 N.W.2d 210 (1996), https://clearinghouse.net.

77 Interview of Stacy Barker with the author, September 23, 2022; Carol Jacobsen, *For Dear Life: Women's Decriminalization and Human Rights in Focus* (Ann Arbor: University of Michigan Press, 2018), 167.

78 Wendy Sawyer, *The Gender Divide: Tracking Women's State Prison Growth* (Northampton, MA: Prison Policy Initiative, 2018), www.prisonpolicy.org.

EPILOGUE

1 Little River Band of Ottawa Indians Tribal Directory, August 2022, https://lrboi -nsn.gov.

2 State Response to Clemency Petition, 2007, Supplemental Police Report Muskegon Police Department, 1977, Wabindato Case files, Muskegon Criminal Court, Muskegon, MI; Antoinette Martin, "Dear Governor Engler," *Detroit Free Press*, July 26, 1992.

3   Kelly Lytle Hernández draws connections across mass imprisonment, racial oppression, and white settler colonialism and argues that prisons are a tool of erasure and elimination in her book, *City of Inmates*. Luana Ross has also studied the criminalization of indigenous people in the United States. Luana Ross, *Inventing the Savage: The Social Construction of Native American Criminality* (Austin: University of Texas Press, 1998).

4   For more on women serving life sentences in Michigan, see Lora Bex Lampert, *Women Doing Life: Gender, Punishment, and the Struggle for Identity* (New York: NYU Press, 2016).

5   Martin, "Dear Governor Engler"; Nellis, *Still Life*.

6   Rafter, *Partial Justice*, 189.

7   Crenshaw, "From Private Violence to Mass Incarceration"; Gottschalk, *The Prison and the Gallows*; Kim, "Dancing the Carceral Creep"; Perkinson, *Texas Tough*; Keramet Reiter, *23/7: Pelican Bay Prison and the Rise of Long-Term Solitary Confinement* (New Haven, CT: Yale University Press, 2016).

8   For more information on the prison movement in the final decades of the twentieth century, which has been described by some scholars as a "bleak period," see Berger and Losier, "Chapter 5: Retrenchment; Mass Incarceration and the Remaking of the Prison Movement, 1980–1998," in *Rethinking the American Prison Movement*, 143–74.

9   Davis, *Are Prisons Obsolete?* 105–7.

10 Buzz Alexander, *Is William Martinez Not Our Brother? Twenty Years of the Prison Creative Arts Project* (Ann Arbor: University of Michigan Press, 2010), 80, 102; *Prison Creative Arts Project Newsletter*, November 2016 (Ann Arbor: University of Michigan College of Literature, Science), https://lsa.umich.edu.

11 Lyon, Hughes, and Thomas, "The People v. Juanita Thomas," 59.

12 Lyon, Hughes, and Thomas, "The People v. Juanita Thomas." For more on Thomas and her work with the Clemency Project, see Jacobsen, *For Dear Life*.

13 Oral history interview of Mary Heinen by Parter Kehrig, University of Michigan LGBTQ Oral History Project, November 20, 2020, Bentley Historical Library, University of Michigan, Ann Arbor, MI, https://bentley.mivideo.it.umich.edu; "What Is Understood Need Not Be Explained," While We Were Away Podcast, season 1, Summer 2018, https://lsa.umich.edu.

14 "About Us," Nation Outside, nationoutside.org; Stacy Barker in conversation with the author, September 23 and October 25, 2022.

INDEX

650 Lifer Law, 89, 98–100, 112; "lifers" prison atmosphere and, 101, 172n56; mass incarceration resulting from, 90, 101

abuse, 101; MDOC investigations of sexual, 82–83; prison staff downplaying women's, 133; sexual violence and torture, 123–31, 177n38; women prisoner openness about, 80–81. *See also* violence, intimate partner; violence against women

ACLU Michigan Battered Women's Clemency Project, 3, 41, 84, 91

activism: of formerly incarcerated women, 9, 139–40; from prison, 9, 37, 138; race v. gender, 82. *See also* prisoners' rights movement; women's movement

Alexander, Buzz, 138

Allen, Tim, 89–90

Allen, Violet, 80–81, 84, 88

American Association of University Women, 46–47

American Correctional Association, 33, 111

Amnesty International, 123, 131–32

Angel of Death Row, 86

anti-death penalty activists, 67; attorneys, 7, 9, 63, 85–86

Anti-Drug Abuse Act, 101

antiviolence movements, 71, 131; carceral feminism and 1990s, 79–83

Attica prison uprising of 1971, 36, 41–42

attorneys: anti-death penalty, 7, 9, 63, 85–86; clemency, 84; gender of prosecuting, 79; juror questioning by, 165n37; prosecuting, 69, 73, 75, 79, 87; state-appointed, 78; volunteer, 47. *See also* trials; *specific cases*

Barker, Stacy, 3, 9, 134, 140, 179n76; rape of, 113–14, 127–28

battered women's defense, 65–66, 65–72, 70, 84, 164n16; Thomas trial, race and, 73–79

Battered Women's Defense Committee (BWDC), 65, 76

battered women's syndrome, 65, 69

Bazzetta v. McGinnis, 134

Black women: all-white juries and, 7, 73, 77; convict leasing as obstacle for, 20; Detroit clubs of, 19; education level of incarcerated, 156n73; first to work in Women's Division, 15; incarceration rates, 28; as racialized policing targets, 12–13, 17, 153n26; solitary confinement of, 25, 85; stereotypes, 75

Black women, incarcerated: disproportionate representation of indigenous and, 28; Smith, Belle, transfer incident and, 25–26, 155n67. *See also* prison population; *specific names*

Brownlee, Richard Wiley, 77–78

Brown v. Board of Education, 4, 94

Buck Dinner, 47–48

The Burning Bed (McNulty), 71–72

burning-bed syndrome, 72

Bush, George H. W., 79

and penal power for women in, 14–19; state legislators ignoring problems of, 33; vice districts and, 17–18, 153n26; women's prison campaign and construction, 14–15, 24, 154n55. *See also* Women's Division, MDOC

Detroit House of Correction, 1970s and 1980s: (nine)1977 lawsuit and, 1–2; discipline through gendered programs in, 38–41, 158n13; Engle at IBM punch card job in, 40, *40*; food in, 41; Glover arrival to, 36, 157n1. *See also* lawsuits

Detroit Police Department (DPD), 26; 1920s, 12; first woman in, 15; policing of black women and, 17–19; riot of 1967 response of, 92, 94, 169n15; STRESS unit of, 93, 94, 170n18

DFWC. *See* Detroit Federation of Women's Clubs

Dick, Timothy Alan. *See* Allen, Tim

DOJ. *See* Department of Justice

DPD. *See* Detroit Police Department

drug laws, 171n42; war on drugs and, 99–101, 103, 172n46. *See also* 650 Lifer Law

education, incarcerated women's prior, 46. *See also* vocational training

Education Amendments, of 1972, 52

Eighth Amendment, 52, 95, 118, 162n80; proportionality and, 112; sexual violence and, 124, 126, 177n38; 650 Lifer Law as violation of, 100

Elliot-Larsen Civil Rights Act, 130

Engle, Kathy, 40, *40*, 42, 159n19

Engler, John (Governor), 81, 83, 128, 136; Glover sentence commuted by, 60, 139; 650 Lifer Law revisions approved by, 112

equality born of retrenchment, 8, 115

Equal Protection Clause, 50, 161n69, 161n76, 171n38

Equal Rights Amendment, 56

eugenics, sterilization and, 23–24

evidence, destruction of, 76

factories, prison, 26–28

Fair, Susan, 84, *87*

Fair Sentencing Act, 101

Families Against Mandatory Minimums, 112

"family ideal," 69

Farmer, Dee, 123–24, 177n37

Fawcett, Farrah, 71–72

FBI, 47–48

Feikens, John (federal judge), 52–54, 52–55, 57, 59

female guards, 120

femininity, hegemonic, 57–58

feminism: anticarceral, 6; carceral, 64, 73, 79–83; Eighth Amendment and, 52, 162n80; intimate partner violence focus of, 76; MDOC interpretation of, 58; 1970s and 1980s, 3, 7, 63, 76; prisoners' rights movement and, 38, 158n11; self-defense focus of 1980s, 3, 63; Thomas support groups in, 63, 78

First Amendment, 52

Florence Crane Correctional Facility, 79, 82, 102, 111, 125–26, 172n58; Glover transfer to, 103; "medieval dungeon" description of, 115; Wabindato in, *136*

Fourteenth Amendment: Equal Protection Clause, 50, 161n69, 161n76, 171n38; *Glover* precedent for using, 52, 162n88

Francine Hughes Defense committee, 69, 72

Franklin, Clarence LaVaughn (C. L.), 91

Furman v. Georgia, 7, 95, 112

gender: discipline and, 38–41, 158n13; labor strikes and, 32; parity, 57–59, 120, 137, 176n23. *See also* vocational training

gender discrimination: activism success against, 82; Allen, T., v. Young, J., cases example of, 89–90; gender stereotypes and, 45–46; prosecuting attorneys and, 79; solitary confinement and, 25, 85; Thomas trial and, 79

Joan Little Defense Fund, 66
Johnson, Lyndon, 98
Johnson, Perry M. (MDOC director), 48,
    50, 58, 82, 176n20; career and educa-
    tion of, 96–97; day fines proposed
    by, 110–11; death penalty opposed by,
    97; MDOC directorship dates, 111,
    170n32; participatory model embraced
    by, 109–10; regional prisons proposal
    of, 103–5, 108, 109, 110; rehabilitation
    championed by, 96, 110
juries: all-white, 7, 73, 77; court law on
    potential jurors, 165n37
juvenile detention facilities, 133

Kalamazoo County Jail, 48–49; Glover
    and, 52, 54–55, 162n81
King, Martin Luther, Jr., 91
Kingsley, W. Charles (attorney), 74, 86
Ku Klux Klan (KKK), 12, 15, 66, 77–78

LaBelle, Deborah (attorney), 130
labor: black male factory workers, 11,
    151n1; unions, 32–33, 156n88
labor strikes: General Motors 1936–1937,
    33, 156n88; public attention captured
    by, 35; Women's Division 1957, 29–35,
    30, 32
law library, 39, 47
lawsuits: civil rights/human rights and,
    126–27; Eighth Amendment and, 52;
    equal protection civil, 161n76; filed
    by male and female prisoners, 134;
    first class-action, 7, 49–57, 51; Neal
    settlement for sexual violence, 131;
    need for medical care, 118; 1977 class
    action, 1–2; PLRA obstacle to filing,
    124; from within prison, 3; retaliation
    for, 114; security, solitary confinement,
    134; sexual violence and harassment,
    125–26; on visitation privileges, 134.
    See also specific cases
League of Catholic Women, 44

Lee, Lareta Coleman, death of, 21–23, 34
liberal feminism, 37, 58
lice, 117
Lifeliners, 46–47
Little, Joan, 66–67
Little River Band of Ottawa Indians, 135
Lyon, Andrea (attorney), 9, 63, 85–87

Magid, Judith (attorney), 49, 50, 54–57
Malcolm X, 77
male guards, in women's prisons, 82–83,
    119–23; agreement barring supervision
    by, 129; Civil Rights Act and, 176n23;
    privacy and, 49; rape by, 127–29, 131
mandatory minimum sentences, 89–90,
    98–101, 172n46
marital rape, Hughes case and, 67–72, 70,
    164n16
Martha Cook Building, 25
mass incarceration: gender inequalities of,
    37–38, 89–90; Midwestern politics of,
    91–94; prison reform blunted by, 110–
    12; punitive politics and, 44; retrench-
    ment politics as sustaining, 114; 650
    Lifer Law leading to, 90, 101. See also
    prison population
mass incarceration, of women, 3; penal
    policies of 1999 and, 149n12; VAWA
    contribution to, 80; visibility of, 4. See
    also prison population
maternal justice, 14, 21–23, 34
maximum-security prisons, 38, 97, 104–5,
    124
McCleskey v. Kemp, 98, 171n38
McEvoy, Mrs. James P., 29, 32
McNulty, Faith, 71–72
MDOC. See Michigan Department of
    Correction
medical care, 117–19, 130
Michigan: death penalty in, 7–8; number
    of life-without parole prisoners in, 137;
    as representative site for US, 4; single
    prison of, 3. See also specific topics

privacy, male guards and, 8, 28, 49, 83, 115, 125–27

prostitution (sex workers), 12, 17, 40, 91–92, 169n11

punishment: clubwomen impact on, 15; MDOC governance models and, 109–10, 174n93; punitive, 42–43, 48–49; selective incapacitation alternative to, 111

punitive turn, 5, 44, 79–80

racial integration, 119–20, 176n20

racial segregation, 19, 82, 94; prison staff, 119–20, 176n20; Southern de jure, 68; Sweet family case and, 16–17, 152n17

racism: 1960s, 16–17, 91–94; male factory workers, 11, 151n1. *See also* police brutality, toward Black people; racism and racial inequality

racism and racial inequality, 36; all-white juries in black women trials, 7, 73, 77; battered women's self-defense and, 79; toward Black Detroiters, 16, 91–94; colonialism, oppression and, 180n3; death penalty case demonstrating, 98, 171n38; Detroit riot of 1967 and, 92–93, 94, 168n8, 169n15; in drug-crime convictions, 89–90; gender discrimination activism v., 82; incarceration rates of 1970s, 3; justice system widespread, 98, 171n38; PREA and, 133; press on Fulghan case, 160n47; racialized policing of black women, 12–13, 17, 153n26; 650 Lifer Law, 100–101; social class and, 31–32; stereotypes of Black women, 75; Thomas trial infused with, 77; war on drugs, 100–101, 103. *See also* police brutality, toward Black people

radical feminism, 37

rape, 118; of Barker, 113–14, 127–28; fear of reporting, 129; by male guards, 127–29, 131; marital, 67–72, 70, 164n16

rats, 115–16

Reagan, Nancy, 99

Reagan, Ronald, 56, 98–99

Reception and Guidance Center (RGC), 117

Reed v. Reed, 50, 161n69

reentry, 9, 60, 139–40; regional prison proposal on, 104, 108; vocational training and, 54

reflection (punishment practice), 42–43

rehabilitation: clubwomen ideal of, 28; *Glover* judge on, 53–54; labor exploitation and, 34; labor strikes resulting in narrative of, 35; MDOC director support of, 96, 110; Michigan state goal of, 159n29; model v. reality, 46; special committee and, 41, 44, 159n29, 159n31

Republican National Convention, 56

retaliation, 1, 50, 132; deterrent against reporting, 121, 129; gender parity and, 57–59; after lawsuits, 114

retrenchment politics, 129–30, 133–34; civil rights cases decline and, 114; equality born of retrenchment, 8, 115

RGC. *See* Reception and Guidance Center

Richardson, Gloria (warden), 49, 57, 58, 102

Robert Scott Correctional Facility, 80–82, 125–26, 129

Rockefeller Drug Laws, 100

Rozycki, Stanley, 94–95

Russian, Gertrude, police killing of, 11, 12–13, 34

sanitation, 115–17

scholarship, 4–6

Scott, Cynthia, 91–92, 94, 169n11

self-defense: conviction in spite of, 7; legal definition of, 66; 1970s and 1980s convictions for crimes of, 83; 1977 case of, 67–72, 70, 164n16; 1980s feminism focus on, 3, 63; theories of, 86. *See also* battered women's defense

ABOUT THE AUTHOR

BONNIE L. ERNST is Assistant Professor in the Department of Criminal Justice at Indiana University–Bloomington.